AF365330

THE ARK WITHIN
One and Diverse

Volume I

Adelheid Oesch

The Ark Within
One and Diverse
Volume I

An Initiatory Journey from Inner Conflict to Inner Peace
'Voice Dialogue' and the 'Aware Self'
A Harbor for the Child Within and the Suffering Selves

TO BE USED IN CONJUNCTION WITH:

The Ark Within, VOLUME II
EXERCISE MANUAL

A Key to Unified Consciousness
'Voice Dialogue' and the 'Aware Self Process'
A Harbor for the Child Within and the Suffering Selves

BY THE SAME AUTHOR

Rêver Dieu
Au 1er & Au 21e siècle

Éditions Persée 2020

The Ark Within
One and Diverse

An Initiatory Journey
From Inner Conflict to Inner Peace
'Voice Dialogue' and the 'Aware Self'
A Harbor for the Child Within
And the Suffering Selves

Volume I

Adelheid Oesch

Second Miracle, The I that is a We, Words that Shine both Ways, The Mandala of Being, Inside-out Healing.

◆ ◆ ◆

"Thank you for *The Ark Within*. It is a superb and far going work. I savor it step by step and will speak about it!"
Late Father Humbert Biondi. Lecturer of the philosophy of Pierre Teilhard de Chardin, Université Populaire, Paris.

◆ ◆ ◆

"*The Ark Within* is nourishment for the Soul. As a powerful and wise midwife for the birth of a new era of sacred consciousness, Adelheid Oesch guides us inward, into "our true homeland" to build our relationships on 'inner abundance.'

She inspires us to live vibrant, conscious, and reconciled lives. She writes with candor, and uncompromising tenderness, about the fulfillment of an essential paradigm shift: Outer wisdom must become inner wisdom.

Read *The Ark Within,* and receive a practical and 'magical first aid kit to unveil a world within the worlds,' and to consistently find the extraordinary within the ordinary."
Hedy Schleifer, Master Relationship Builder, guides couples and trains mental health professionals, coaches and executives. *Washington DC.* https://hedyschleifer.com/

◆ ◆ ◆

"With *The Ark Within* Adelheid Oesch has opened a secret door onto the soul. By mystically weaving together ancient tales, spiritual teachings, philosophy, psychology, poetry and heart-bearing confessions, she has taken the art of storytelling to a new level. If ever the story of the universe has found a Vessel for its telling, it is in this book. May millions read *The Ark Within*: As those who will, will not only lose themselves within its pages, but will also find themselves, over and over again, within its magic mirrors, and will be blessed by what they discover."

Richard M. McErlean, Jr. Switzerland. Writer, editor, poet, and author of two collections of poems: *Recital,* and *Memento Mori.* Member of the Academy of American Poets, and the Poetry Society of America.

❖ ❖ ❖

To the Reader

I am forever grateful to Hal and Sidra Stone for having transformed my personal and professional life and vision, and for having so generously given freedom to their students to work in their own ways. Day after day, 'Voice Dialogue' has been for me, and for all those who have worked with me, for now thirty years, a constant blessing, joy and enrichment.

I hope to have been faithful to the spirit of *'Voice Dialogue and the Psychology of selves and of the aware ego,'* as developed by Hal and Sidra Stone. Yet, I hereby take full responsibility for whatever understandings and views may be strictly my own, and therefore differ from their original teachings. A.O.

Caveat Lector

Any resemblance to people known or unknown by the author is a coincidence. If you think you resemble one of the characters mentioned in the events described in this book, know that you have recognized nothing more than what you share with the human person, with all of us.

The Ark Within: Table of Contents

Volume I ✦ An Initiatory Journey
From Inner Conflict to Inner Peace
'Voice Dialogue' and the 'Aware Self'
A Harbor for the Child Within and the Suffering Selves

📖 TO BE USED IN CONJUNCTION WITH VOLUME II:
The Ark Within. *Exercise Manual*

A Key to Unified Consciousness
'Voice Dialogue' and the 'Aware Self Process'
A Harbor for the Child Within and the Suffering Selves

PART ONE: The Body is a Person

PART FOUR: 'Voice Dialogue'
From Sensitive Body-Self to Universal Self

PART FIVE: The Gift of Sorrow. The Unveiling
The Epiphany of Love

Preface by Marie de Hennezel

We have been journeying, without a doubt, upon sister paths for a long time. One day we met in a little group that came together around Richard Moss to explore the field of relationship; relationship to oneself, to the other, to the divine. It was there where I had the chance to approach Adelheid and discover a little of her interior world, so rich, so sensitive.

In her book, *The Ark Within* Adelheid invites us on an inner Journey, a voyage where we meet ourselves. Who are we? Do we know it? Will we ever know it? Complex beings made of *'subpersonalities'* unrecognized, rejected, waiting for love. The voyage begins and ends with the meeting of a child. And behold, this is the vulnerable *'Inner Child'* that each one of us carries deep within the citadel we have built to defend it. It is the child that plays such a primordial role in our problems, our reactions, our conflicts, and because it is so often isolated and deprived of love and attention, it is at the origin of most of our difficulties.

In her unique way, Adelheid takes us by the hand like an older sister who has already traveled the path, and helps us to listen and dialogue with this child who waits to rediscover its *joie de vivre*, its creativity, its loving spontaneity. "This is how, little by little, our fortress transforms into a garden!"

With Adelheid, you will feel safe because the sensitivity, the delicateness of the heart, is solidly anchored in common sense. This is not a journey one engages only with one's imagination. It means going into it with all the senses, with the heart, with the entire body—a body that isn't an "object" but a "person"—a sensitive body, a body of presence.

The "Exercises" (Volume II)—that emanate intelligently from the text—help us along the way. Yet this requires that you accept to enter into the experience. It requires that you take the risk to try it with a new spirit, calling on other tools than your intellect or your rationality, drawing from these so often unemployed resources: the attention, the breath, the warmth of the heart.

This is how we learn "... to take care of ourselves, to provide ourselves with what we so painfully miss—without vainly expecting and relentlessly demanding it from others! In becoming our own Friend and neighbor, we will heal our capacity to relate and create bonds that are not those of neediness and dependency, but those of mutual sharing and generosity."

May this beautiful book show a light to each one of its readers!

Marie de Hennezel[1]

Paris, January 11th, 1998

---

[1] **Marie de Hennezel** is a specialist in the psychological and spiritual tending to the dying and terminally ill. Author of *Intimate Death: How the Dying Teach us How to Live*, A. A. Knopf Publ. 1998. A major best seller in France, translated into fifteen languages.

Author's Introduction
The Story of our Courage:
Everyone is a Universe

The Story that you are about to read, is one of a Quest; one of a Prayer that we share with all Creation. It is about recognizing ourselves, one and multiple, in the image of the Universe! It begins and it ends close to a child; a Core-child who carries our treasure, who hides and reveals itself in each of us; to meet it is to be surprised, touched, moved. This child will give air to your soul, to your joy, to your body; it will imbue you with spirit and fantasy.

Poetic and yet pragmatic, Volume I & II disclose a Journey that invites you to take flight as much as to land, that leads you to build a loving relationship with yourself that becomes a relationship with the whole world. Wingspan of the Heart!

In rediscovering the intense *beingness* that links you to your physical, emotional, mental and spiritual dimensions, it will lead you to unfold into a conscious Vessel, a tender Womb, a sheltering Ark, stable and vast enough to welcome inside you the totality of who you are. Your body, the Body of the Earth, every facet of yourself, every life form then will become your Ally, a sacred Person, a loved person, a person you bond with, a person who responds to you!

'**The Ark Within. An Initiatory Journey**' Vol. I and in its re-lated *'Exercise Manual,'* Vol. II - has been deeply inspired by my life experience and by the discovery of the "*Psychology of Selves and of the Aware ego,*" developed by Hal and Sidra

Stone, Ph.D., creators of a groundbreaking consciousness tool called **'Voice Dialogue.'**

The Exercises are for the most part the result of my practice and teaching in the field of "Voice Dialogue." They were born from years of work as a facilitator. Volume I and Volume II, shed light on each other, mirror and enrich each other. The story will invite you into your human venture, a cosmic venture. May you decipher it upon your own interior pages; may you put the Exercises to the test in the crucible of your own awareness.

The Tale of *Aurora's*, *Friday's* and *Robinson's* Quest for 'The Ark Within' and the Exercises in Volume II, can be read for the sole pleasure of imagination. Yet - being intimately and step by step interwoven and related to each other - you are invited to use them jointly. Tuning into the magic of the Tale will help you! Creative imagination, light and shadow, joy and pain of the human soul, will become your guides and allies and support you in your intuitive understanding of the Exercises. It will be your thread in the labyrinth; it will point toward the Center, toward your treasure chest.

The Exercises will be valuable tools for those who wish to take full responsibility for themselves. They are for the Curious Explorer, the Consciousness Wanderer, who wishes to put himself to the test in the crucible of his heart and body. They progress in successive stages, each facilitating the next.

About 'Voice Dialogue'[2]

'Voice Dialogue' is an individuation process. This process guides us in the discovery of the energies that animate us. At the same time it furthers the enfoldment of an Aware Self, of an Inner Witness. Developing such a 'witnessing, and aware space" inside us will help us to exercise free choice, enable us to build a loving relationship with who we are, and to hold the 'tension of opposites" in our psychic structure.

Voice Dialogue is based on the 'The Psychology of Selves and of the Aware Ego" as created and developed by Hal and Sidra Stone, PhD. USA. It conceives our psyche as a Family of *subpersonalities*, or Inner selves, and teaches us to relate in a conscious and loving way to who we are and how we feel.

Voice Dialogue is a powerful device for self-growth, a wonderful complement to any other technique or therapeutic endeavor. It invites us to a concrete and judgment-free experience of our psychological processes and of our dynamics in relationships. However, it is not a therapy; it is a consciousness tool; it should not be used as a substitute for psychiatric treatment.

It really teaches us an Art of living, an Art of loving, of understanding oneself and the other; a way of entering the Mystery of Self. We will experience ourselves as a 'three dimensional Mandala,' a volume of Conscious Presence, where our sensations, emotions, images and thoughts, become Inner persons.

---

[2] **See also Volume II: "The Ark Within. Exercise Manual."** See Appendixes I, II, III at the end of the present Volume. See the *"Voice Dialogue,* the *Psychology of Selves* and of the *Aware ego,"* developed by Hal and Sidra Stone, Ph.D. USA. See Bibliography.

Inner persons, who respond, relate and find their place and peace in our welcoming Awareness.

To love is to know. It is to embrace our light as well as of our shadow. As the moon wanes and waxes and back again, we too will travel from strength to frailty, from joy to pain, from turmoil to silence. Each of these 'forms of self' weaves the Body of our life and challenges us to honor it as it is!

Love requires a body, demands an incarnation, a quality of substance, an intensity of being. We can awaken this by a sensitive, feeling relationship with ourselves, with the other, with Nature, with Life itself. We can further it through an ongoing encounter and sharing process that unites heart, spirit and matter; that builds on our five senses, on our creative imagination, on the power of our love. This can be seen as a spiritual service, a spiritual discipline, leading us to an intimate linkage and acceptance of our present moment experiencing.

'Voice Dialogue' practice is full of spontaneity; it stages a lively face-to-face between facilitator and client. It sends us on a Journey where we explore, discover, and nourish all our energies. It is a dance of selves, full of humor, of surprises, serious and yet tender, where we grow rich, not only with what we have mastered or acquired, but also with what we ignore or reject in ourselves!

What can we gain? To be true; to find a lost quality of being, the bubbling aliveness that we knew as small children— close to tears, close to laughter and sheer joy, close to the heart. Don't we yearn, deep down, to turn to our feelings, to our needs, to a meaningful life; to see the world afresh, to recapture this early enchantment, when we were still curious about everything?

Our work begins when we consciously experience our personality, as it manifests itself in our everyday life. We will access what stimulates, enraptures, discourages, hurts or frightens us. We will learn to live with our contradictions, to recognize the value of our resources, to balance our strengths and weaknesses, to renew our capacity for joy and our sensitiveness. We will translate our life situations into the physical experience of emotions, images and thoughts. We will meet the Inner Selves who rule over us, move us or block us, and realize why we act and react in certain ways.

As we start to draw from our inner well of Love and Wisdom, as we relate with stability and kindness to our various Selves … we will become our own guide, our own Spiritual Friend. These Selves will speak to us, quiver in us, cry and become angry, impart their knowledge, share their experience, and finally come together inside us like an Inner Tribe, an Inner Family. As a Witness, we will step back; stand upright in the Center of who we are, of what we go through. We will enfold a Holding, conscious Presence, harmonizing the infinite variety of life's expressions inside us.

We will learn to respond to our vulnerability, to what we lack, to the small helpless child we become when we are hurt. We will gain maturity, autonomy; support ourselves in difficulty; create peace where division reigned.

We hold in our hands the key to our universe. When we take responsibility for ourselves, we acquire the capacity to choose our own direction; we actively partake in our own evolution. We reduce compulsive dependence; we stop accusing others, and start relating more consciously instead.

You and I can open ourselves to the most radiant adventure of love; the inner and outer adventure of relationship, born between yourself and yourself, between one and the other, between the Cosmic Source and our human Heart, at the core of our Being.

Part One

The Body is a Person

"He, who stops in something, ceases to throw himself into Totality."
—St. John of the Cross

Letter to Aurora

'You are called Aurora. Very few people in this world hold such a place in my life, you are everywhere, inscribed in my body, in my soul, in my heart.

And truly in my heart, shines and pulsates the childhood of your gaze. I dive into it with ease; there in the cavern of the heart, the time—your time, wholly blossoms and completes itself. I catch a glimmer deep in your eyes, it goes, comes, shines, hides; it is a flash of moon passing behind the big trees of the forest. I breathe in the fragrance of the humus, the trees are immense; they have consumed the sky. I hear the raindrops that fall, one by one, slow, precious, a rustling, a beating!

And you, you sleep in the woven hammock, your skin is soft and smooth and glows sometimes under the fleeting course of the moon. I love your breathing that I can dimly hear. A canopy of leaves protects your face. You are four years old, you have no fear; the entire earth is like a mother to you.

At sunrise you stretch like a young lynx and you run toward the fire, starved and joyous. You are the most agile climber of trees.

I notice also that you don't easily surrender your secrets; that I don't really know you. There are big expanses of shade, like landmarks in space, like mysterious rooms: At times it is a forest, where you leap like a gazelle. At times it is a temple, where you remain silent.

Sometimes also, I hear the clash of swords and see the flicker of moonbeams ricochet off your armor. In the distance the castle has closed its doors, hoisted the drawbridge. Behind the high walls, you shelter your tenderness, your weakness, the woman, the child. I saw you fight for life and death on the desert sands to protect those entrusted to you. It seems your armor always has a rift, and I love how you know to die.

And the landscape changes, grows softer, we are in a different land, I see you in love with a young laughing blue eyed warrior; you cradle babies of every color, some of which resemble you. Later, you teach them how to build a dam in the stream, carve little wooden sailboats and deliver them to the current.

You know how to surprise yourself, and it's maybe what I like best in you: The bag of mischievous tricks that contains everything, the infinitely small, the infinitely large. There is a shaman in there; a little girl in tears; a *passionaria* on the barricades; a young man dressed in white cotton, who walks without baggage toward the mountains; a bow and arrows; a feathered headdress. There is a woman who has more to say. A tamed rat and its provision of cheese; an oasis, camels, and tents, round like the horizon; a Saracen in his shroud...this bag is bottomless; it is a cosmic mammal, a bagpipe!

Ah! I forgot, there is even more to you: A woman of the 20th century, a businesswoman, sitting in a Louis XIV armchair; she writes this letter. And in her heart, in the cavern of her heart, there is a laugh that rings: Tomorrow, soon, in a Boeing 747 over the Atlantic, she will fly off to meet her prodigal son and the New World.

And farther, in the penumbra of the great forest, sits a very old bush woman; her skin is wrinkled like the bark of a majestic tree, but her eyes are those of a child. With an attentive hand, she rocks a woven hammock; one barely distinguishes a little shape in it that sleeps. A shining warrior stands guard.

Time and time again, you leap out of my heart; you are reborn from my spirit! You are called Aurora, and I love you.'

Gstaad, February 16th, 1991

I

A Return to the Origins

My name is Aurora.

Know that I am a Magical Inner Spring Child; that I can whisper into your ear. If you choose to listen, together with the scribe of this tale—you will hear my song inside you!

Don't be surprised if I shape-shift as children so easily do; if you have to follow me through heaven and hell and from tears to delight. Don't be taken aback, if most of the time I am a little girl and then a boy; if without any warning I turn into an adolescent or into a grown up; if I age without aging and sometimes transform into a nomadic truth-seeker, a spiritual midwife or a tribal shaman!

Even though I now live in the 21st century, I have traveled down the ages. My memory spans the millennia. I've lived through every phase of evolution, from the age of the amoeba until…

I am the 'flesh and bone' of every life ever lived and the narrator of every story ever told…and so are you. And as we journey together through this Tale, I will show you how this is true.

So don't be afraid when sometimes you must leave the comfort of what you know and cross over into the discomfort of the Unknown: There, waits a secret passage—in between conflicting realities—that opens the very space where all things reconcile! A space you will have to navigate time and time again throughout your entire life.

If you let me be your guide, I will lead you through metamorphoses. I will show you that Teddy bears and Trees are persons; that Robinson Crusoe, Friday, and even the cannibals, exist in us—and we in them!—that we can learn to listen when the Grasshopper speaks.

And don't be disconcerted if we return to the Garden of Eden and become Adam and Eve, expelled. If we are swept away by the Flood, but survive by transforming ourselves into our own *Ark*. This journey, our story, is Universal; we have written it together on the same page, with the same hand. It springs from the recesses of the Self as we struggle through our lives. It grows in our heart's chambers, in the slow assimilation of our viscera, in the caverns of our wombs. It gushes forth in us, between pain and joy, fragility and strength. It waits for us in the trunks of fallen majestic trees, between the bark and the wood, between two rings of time…

If you let me, I will show you that we are all One, that the Universe is simultaneous! And as we travel together, you will grow closer to yourself, you will learn to befriend all that inhabits you, learn how to lend a *Voice* to your own energies, and how to be the co-creator of a vibrant, conscious, reconciled life!

Then you will understand why being the adult and the child, the tree and the pages, the paper and the wood—isn't strange after all! Or how, from one second to the next, one can change from a baby into a youth, from a Red Indian into a white mother, or from a raven into a dove. Or how I can, at any moment, feel like a young man, a warrior, or even an old woman. Or that suddenly, my body becomes a boat, a bird, or Noah's Ark…

Because we are as old as the Earth itself, we harbor in us all that was, is and that will be. There is no limit to the realm of our Awareness!

In the 20th century, I was sent to school against my will and trapped in the classroom like a prisoner. What I really learned, I learned elsewhere, during long escapades, while skipping class, exploring…or sometimes when—bound to my desk—I disappeared through the window, carried off on the wings of a seagull, on a leaf caressed by the wind, in the hull of a cloud, or on the lake, alight with the blue hues of the horizon.

The day I turned fourteen—and I remember this well—I was on the train with my schoolmates, on our way to visit the Swiss town of St. Gallen, which happened to be the birthplace of my forefathers, my canton of origin!

For me, the train embodied a locus of transition and nostalgia; a rite of passage between one time and another. I can still see the compartment window and the countryside rolling past: The exterior world blending with the interior world in a marriage of reflections. I felt dragged into the future and yet immobile and withdrawn from the scenery in motion.

I remember passing through a tunnel, then a forest. In the reflections I could see my face, and my companions' faces, superimposed on the rocks and sometimes on the trees. Suddenly, sadness overwhelmed me and I heard a little phrase. It trembled somewhere between the window and the fresh air, between inside and outside: 'Fourteen years old…life is over. Fourteen years old, life stops.' I found nothing appealing in my future, in the place of 'adult women and men' that waited for me. I was quite sure that there everything that was precious to me would be lost! Already the changes in my body had turned me into an exile—banishing me from the Kingdom of Wonder and Innocence all children share.

As far back as I can remember, I had felt like Robinson Crusoe, called to an 'elsewhere,' to far-off lands; lands of the soul…I longed for my independence: To be self-sufficient, protected and invisible— high in the hidden branches; deep in the impenetrable forest. I yearned to nourish myself on berries, to savor their bitterness while they were still green. It was the taste of my freedom!

But freedom has a price. Like Robinson, I was destined to remain at grips with my solitude, while building a personal world on an island surrounded by the great waters, where only the trees, the parakeets, and the goats kept me company. And, also like Robinson, I scanned the horizon looking for a friend, the one who would be closer to me than a sister or a brother. Today still, I admit, my throat tightens, my heartbeat quickens, when I recall meeting 'Friday.'

Although I eventually left my island to rejoin the adult continent, I felt for a long time as if I had no country of my own. Be it the realm of childhood or the world of grownups, one or the other was always just out of reach! The resulting state of constant dissatisfaction did have its benefits: I traveled widely...I ceaselessly challenged the detours along my route, without doubting for a moment, that every landscape, that each fellow traveler, each trial upon my path, would finally take on the Face of the Friend. I didn't doubt that our Universe is a giant Mirror, in which Life—upon seeing itself, achieves Consciousness.

Like the ancient alchemists, I searched. However I did not seek ways to change lead into gold, but rather how to turn the Universe—others, and my body itself—into my true homeland, into a place where I intimately belonged.

Even though I had excellent parents, whose care and affection had never failed me, I felt orphaned. Like Adam and Eve, and all the people who came after them, I carried the pain of a Lost Paradise. But knowing that I'd lost it also meant I was certain it existed! This is why I never abandoned the Quest: To find the fatherland within myself. But to do this, I first needed to learn how to balance and reconcile opposites. In this case, it meant blending—in a conscious meeting of love—the 'Old magical land' of childhood, with the 'Land of bitter waters' of adulthood. It meant leaving what I knew and crossing over into the Unknown.

II

The Wisdom of Children-Number One: Miracles are Completely Ordinary Events

Everything seemed possible when I was little. Around the age of five, during my bedtime prayers I used to ask God to turn me overnight into a boy. And in the morning, when I awoke, for one fleeting moment, I would thrill in the possibility that maybe He had answered my prayer. God, far wiser than me, decided otherwise.

I must admit, I hadn't realized yet that climbing trees, exploring the forest and taking pleasure in my own strength—all those things I feared were masculine privileges—were in fact, everyone's birthright.

However, I had been perfectly correct to believe that miracles can happen at any time, and that they aren't only reserved for extraordinary people or extraordinary circumstances. In later years, I never doubted that all things originate from the Spirit, that all forms of life are wholly contained within an unlimited potential on the verge of blossoming, a hitherto unexplained Spiritual Source of Matter. I also believe that for miracles to happen we must call upon them with Intent and Love and that the moment we do they will leap out of their hidden mold—in the same way that human life springs forth from shared love and great trees are invisibly contained in tiny seeds.

Just after I turned six I could have used a miracle of my own. My world faltered and I lost some of my faith. Not in the God of my heart, so obvious, so close to me, but in these admired adults who represented Him on earth. I lost trust. And from that moment onward, I decided to keep my secrets and my love, and to only share them with my Teddy bear, the Maple tree in my garden, or the true Friend I was to find one day.

Already a few years before, when I was barely four, I had started to notice that the 'God of grown-ups' and his Saints sometimes appeared in strange, punishing and unpredictable disguises that rendered them foreign to me. Like the one, for example, of a hooded Saint Nicholas who only promised presents to the 'good' children and either handed out candy or gave them a switching with a birch branch...A capricious Santa Claus whose plans were never clear! It was at that point that I suddenly realized he was just wearing a mask and a fake cotton beard! Fortunately the Bearded figure and other saintly adults I had trusted were not sent on earth by the real God.

By the grace of candor and hope all children share, little Aurora didn't grow up inside me as fast or doubt as much, as I—the scribe of this Tale, did. On the contrary, she waited and waited, not to become a little boy any more, but for the miracle of feeling free, happy in her body and sure to be loved. More than seventy years later—it's amazing how *Inner children* can be patient—she is still here, looking over my shoulder, listening to my thoughts, guiding my hand as I write our story!

As long as we keep in touch with the innocence and the trust within us, we won't need proof to believe in miracles. And to this little girl, who lives deep inside me, just as the sun simply resurrects every morning, so does God. He is as real and natural to her as her Teddy bear or the giant Maple tree in the garden—just because she loves Him! And that's why she never tires of hearing once again the Story of Ezekiel...

And so I take her small hand into mine, gravely and yet smiling, because I feel so moved by this story myself, and I begin:

'Once upon a time, some two thousand five hundred years ago, in Israel, lived a Prophet named Ezekiel. And back then the world wasn't too different from what it is today! War, famine, hate and injustice were just as prevalent as they are now. And so it came that through a vision God instructed Ezekiel to deliver His people from violence and captivity and to return them to their homeland: The land of their joy, the land of their freedom.

'And Ezekiel tells us: "The hand of the Lord was upon me, and carried me out in the Spirit of the Lord and let me down in the midst of the valley which was full of bones … and behold, there were very many in the open valley, and lo, they were very dry. And He said unto me, 'Son of man, can these bones live?' And I answered, 'O Lord God, thou know it.' Again He said unto me, 'Prophesy upon these bones, and say unto them, O ye dry bones, hear the word of the Lord … Behold, I will cause the breath of Spirit to enter into you, and ye shall live.' … So I prophesied as I was commanded … and behold there was a shaking; and the bones came together bone to his bone … the sinews and the flesh came upon them, and the skin covered them above; but there was no breath in them. Then said He unto me, 'Prophesy unto the Spirit … and say: Come from the four winds … and breathe upon these slain, that they may live.' So I prophesied as he commanded me, and the breath of Spirit came into them, and they lived, and stood up upon their feet …"'[3]

Now that is amazing! Aurora and I hold our breath … Awe and silence descend into our heart. Does this mean that to re-assemble the scattered parts of you and me, heal them, bring them back to relationship and to life, all you need is Faith; all you need is to call on the Spirit of the Lord, and then to let it blow upon that which has gone dead inside us?

This seemed impossible! Nevertheless this wondrous tale encouraged me to experiment—not how to resurrect those

---

[3] The Bible, Old Testament, Ezekiel, Chapter XXXVII, Verses 1–10

who have passed … but how to generate life's intensity, life's circulation within us, within our own bodies and our own Hearts.

I call this the 'Ezekiel Experience.'

It's up to us to make Ezekiel's story true in our everyday life. Haven't we misplaced the 'land of milk and honey, of immortality and of love,' over which all children struggle so hard to keep watch? For, even though this land doesn't exist on any map, it is perfectly real, intimately ours, deeply interwoven with who we are, in body, heart and soul.

This is an Abode we can resolve to find … because it is our heritage, our very nature. Anyone who chooses to, can set out on an Inner Journey to his Original Source, where 'lead does indeed turn to gold,' where matter becomes Spirit, and Spirit imbues matter; where what is dead returns to life.

It is our free option in faith to change the Written Word into the Living Word, the ordinary breath into the Breath of Life. In time, we will all recognize that the Breath of the Spirit — and its life-giving power — exists in each of us as an Untapped Source ready for us to call upon it. So don't be afraid, don't hesitate when you face pain, fear and sorrow. Call upon The Source and it will manifest in you by the Grace of God, through the radiance of your smile, the love of your gaze, the healing warmth of your hands, the liberating wind carried by your breath, the truth ringing in your words. You too can make miracles happen.

📖 ***You are now invited to go to Volume II, Exercise 1***
The Ezekiel Experience: The Breath of Life

III
The Wisdom of Children-Number Two:
All is Sacred Presence

To be acknowledged and feel related to as a 'person' outgrows our preset boundaries. And as you read this book you will understand better how 'objects can become persons' and how 'persons can become objects!'

From the wisdom of children we can learn so much. They find it quite natural that the '*invisible,*' that the '*inanimate,*' responds to them the moment they address it with faith and affection. When I was a little girl my Teddy Bear was *alive.* I loved it with all my heart. It reassured me when I was scared; it consoled me when I was sad. To me that Teddy Bear was a Person—not a thing. It still is!

Love and relatedness do reveal to us 'the person inside the object' and 'the being inside of matter.' When we reflect on the resurrecting wonder of Love, we understand that whatever and whomever we treat without love becomes *thing* to us.

How does nature, how does a woman, a man, an unborn child, an 'Inner self,' cease to be persons to us? Isn't it the moment their sacredness is negated? Have we forgotten that it is 'kindhearted mutual connection' that founds our true happiness, relieves our suffering, bonds us to existence? In truth, 'to be a person or not' depends on the presence or the absence of a *current of love and awe* that renders us precious to ourselves and to each other.

Have we forgotten that trees, rocks, animals, water, fire and stars used to be 'Sacred Persons to mankind?' Since Creation is no longer seen as a 'Living Presence,' we have become blind to its needs and have lost our respect and gratitude for its gifts. It seems almost standard to abuse and deface it; to commit mass destruction and genocide, to manipulate matter, to treat people as a mere 'device' that one can dispose of at will!

Isn't this just as dramatically true of self-relating? When our souls and bodies aren't '*persons*' to us any more, we lose all reason to cherish them.

It is up to us to decipher every sign, to initiate a reciprocal connection, a sensitive dialogue. Little by little, such a listening will make us the Partner and Caretaker of an entire human Tribe: It awaits us and whispers to us in your innermost recesses. Loneliness, exclusion, separateness, will melt in the warmth of our attention for all what lives and quivers in and around us. We will discover that everything is part of us.

By gaining this kind of awareness, we unveil a 'world within the world,' the extraordinary within the ordinary. We realize that even the stillness of inanimate objects, embodies meaning, gives direction; generates energy, love, inspiration.

The sculptor's heart soars when he takes up his chisel and hammer, when his eyes penetrate the uncut marble, when he envisions the dormant life, the captive spirit… and frees it from its stone prison. In truth, it was Michelangelo's Heart that guided his hand to awaken and quicken petrified souls. And, in turn, those souls he called out and liberated from the rock filled and expanded Michelangelo's Heart—through the silent language of matter and shapes! And for centuries to come, these works of art continue to set afire—with ache and surging freedom—the hearts of thousands of men, women and children who meet with them.

The first time I stood before Michelangelo's 'slaves' in Florence, strong and beautiful—but forever half imprisoned by rough and unpolished stone—was also the first time I became aware of the depth of my own feelings of confinement. And this was long before the disasters to come. The contrast between their powerful shining muscles, their aliveness, and their everlasting powerlessness, expressed exactly how I felt! It was as if they were me, the flesh of my flesh.

Everything in the universe whispers or cries out to us not to forget our link to seemingly inanimate matter; a link that is not so different from the one we create with a person we love. Aurora inside me instinctively knows the language of nature, of 'living objects.' In fact, every child knows it, as do the so-called primitive people. To the aboriginal, to the Pygmy, everything has a soul, everything participates—the mineral and the plant, the animal, the human, each and every tool of our daily lives. The earthen jugs, the bow, the arrow, are not fundamentally different from the tree, the waterfall, the stars, or the spirits of the men who gave them their names.

Since consciousness dawned on humankind we have all questioned our origin and meaning. And so did I.

The hunter's heart skips a beat when he picks up the trail of the animal he's tracking. With the patience of a hunter, I pursued my answers to life's riddles, tirelessly stalking them in my dreams and in the dreams and ventures of others— picking up their leads in the kinship I felt with Robinson Crusoe; in the ancient wisdom of the American Indians,[4] in Milarepa's[5] Quest for enlightenment; in Christ's teachings about our divine Father and Love.

The answers, however, never sprang from ready-made solutions, not even from alleviating suffering, but came in finding my way to an Inner Homeland, where all my contradictions can co-exist and find peace in my own compassionate awareness of all that inhabits me.

And this proved particularly true, and a burning issue, when at thirty five, I was unexpectedly launched into

---

[4] 'Moeurs et histoire des Peaux-Rouges' by Paul Coze & R. Thévenin. Payot, Paris 1928

[5] 'The Life of Milarepa,' translated by Heruka Tsangnyon, Penguin USA 2010

abandonment and divorce and the solitary raising of my four still very young kids. I urgently needed in my everyday life to turn despair into hope; doubt into trust. I needed to re-align my now disoriented self; to uncover in my own depth an unimpaired wholeness. Could it be that mankind, that our entire Universe is the physical expression of a higher Consciousness? A Consciousness beyond separation, that links everything with everything else; in which every single element holds information about every other element in infinite realms? In the past, this origin, this essence of all being, was called God, while today certain physicists propose that the universe is maintained by an 'Implicate order.'[6]

When our life goes asunder, we need the whole of Creation to become our Ally. I had to find back to the innocent faith of my childhood, to pick up the thread where it still was unbroken, to reconnect with the so vivid spiritual Quest of my youth. This sudden chaos required me to restore balance to my now shattered world. It had become mandatory to transmute matter into Spirit, and Spirit into matter; to understand, how heavy becomes light, the unknown familiar, the enemy a brother.

I also recalled that in the traditional sense, there cannot be alchemic transformation without the crucible, the flames, and the ingredients. To find my inner truth, I had to put myself to the test! We can only begin to discover ourselves when we experiment. To unravel my inner turmoil, I had to

---

[6] *See Bohm's quantum theory.* His basic assumption is that "elementary particles are actually systems of extremely complicated internal structure, acting essentially as amplifiers of 'information' contained in a quantum wave." As a consequence, he has evolved a new and controversial theory of the universe–a new model of reality that Bohm calls the "Implicate Order." The theory of the Implicate Order contains an ultra holistic cosmic view; it connects everything with everything else. In principle, any individual element could reveal "detailed information about every other element in the universe." The central underlying theme of Bohm's theory is the "unbroken wholeness of the totality of existence as an undivided flowing movement without borders." *See*: bizint.com/stoa del sol. The cosmic Plenum. Bohm's Gnosis: The Implicate Order.

gain knowledge of my own nature and to consciously feel and observe how and why I perceive and react in certain ways. Every upheaval in my life has helped me to understand myself; to embrace what moves me, what unites me and divides me; what elates and what contracts inside me. To create this lucid relationship to myself and to my circumstances, I had to travel the currents that set my body, my mind, my heart, aflame and aquiver. To know, to befriend, all this in myself, I had to explore it with all my senses.

Be daring, be not fainthearted; be curious, not skeptical. Test your Faith, check your assumptions and question your beliefs. After all, science itself is built on two challenging steps: A hypothesis and its experimentation! So let us ride our imagination, envision the possible; heighten our awareness. As we penetrate the intimacy of things, we deepen our insight. We break new ground. We open ourselves to change.

My life experience was to be my alchemic laboratory! In it I ignite, cool and separate the energies that trigger my reactions. In it I seek out the 'Thousand Faces' that reflect how I feel; I probe into what is volatile, fixed or shifting inside me; I *differentiate* and *reunite* my physical and emotional sensations, my thoughts, images and memories—all the way down to my innermost Core.

The magic formula is already contained in the title of this chapter: 'All is Sacred Presence.' In fact, the key to '*who* I really am,' I found inscribed in an infinite number of signals in my own flesh, in my life situations, in each and every element of the world I live in.

Everything can be related to and relates to us! This is the wisdom that helped me not to drown.

IV

The Wisdom of Children-Number Three:
The World, the Body, is a Person

'What is a person?'

Because we instinctively resist to being nullified, the meaning of the word *person* tends to breaks free from our conventional views. The French dictionary[7] says: '*human being*' and adds '*individual, considered in himself and judged morally responsible.*' But when a baby, a child, an adult, is partly or wholly deprived of moral responsibility—by simple virtue of sleep, youth, old age, coma, sickness of mind or body—aren't they still persons? Aren't they still filled with needs and feelings and capable of awakening feelings in others?

I would like to ask: 'How does one cease to be a person?'

In English as in French, the word *person*—as an 'indefinite pronoun in its negative form,' means '*none, no one, nobody.*' Doesn't this shake us awake? Is it acceptable to randomly validate or invalidate one's right to personal uniqueness, to unchallenged 'beingness'?

I would like to ask: 'How do we become a *thing* for ourselves?

I remember that as a teenager, I let myself be persuaded by social pressure and inner fears and wants, to adjust my face and curl my hair... to live up to the image dictated by fashion. The result proved treacherous: I no longer recognized

---

[7] Petit Larousse illustré, Ed. Larousse, Paris 1985

myself! And this threw me into a strange despair. In town, I kept as close as possible to the walls of the buildings, but each time I unexpectedly came upon my reflection in a store-front window, I had to gasp: It wasn't me! I concluded that it doesn't take much to betray oneself. All it took was conforming to a trendy stereotype and I vanished into nothing more than a plaything! It's exactly this: When we deny our true Self, we are transformed into 'lead soldiers in someone else's battle,' into fake heroes, into dominating or submissive seducers. It reminds me of the old slave markets: 'Open your mouth, show your teeth, show your curves...' In order to fit in, we hide, we disfigure, we pretend to... We clothe into advertisements to sell ourselves, or to sell underwear, vacuum cleaners, perfect women or strong men.

Taken in by the rush and the complexity of public adaptation, my body became a stranger to me. At times, I even felt contempt and indifference for it, viewing it as little more than a commodity. As long as it wasn't sick or worn-out, as long as it was a 'good beast of burden,' I didn't think to speak to it, to place my hand affectionately upon the scrapes on its knees or over its aching heart. Still to this day, I'm surprised when during a morning shower I realize I'm washing myself without tenderness, as if were only cleaning an object!

It was soon after my 50th birthday that the first signs of frailty, the first physical tears and wears began to appear. My body, after a long silence, was telling me: 'I've had enough; your 'beast of burden' is tired, hurt, defeated from the heart to the hip.' But even then, it didn't really complain; instead it just laid down... And still, it uttered not a single reproach, not one word of bitterness. If only I had paid the slightest attention to it, understood its pain, it would have looked up at me with its big soft eyes, surprised, and I would have led it to a lush green field, caressed it, and given it the time and the space it needed to rest and heal.

Was it my body that was mute, or was I blind and deaf to it? One day, I realized that I'd never thanked it; never asked its advice; never expressed through loving gestures my concern for its well being. How many years had it been since I looked at it for any other reason than to scrutinize its imperfections or its capacity to please or be accepted?

Despite all this, my wondrous body has never lost its generosity. Accomplice of heaven and earth, of animals and humans, it continuously gifts me with the entire world: I can nest beach stones in my hands—soft and smooth like the lustrous skin of babies; I can capture in flight the shared smile of lovers, the spark in the eyes of my friends, the affectionate and joyous welcome in my mother's voice. It carries me through the elation of movement and the serenity of rest; it sings and dances in the moonlight; it fills with the intoxicating fragrance of shrubs and bushes, with the sound of ocean waves. It supports me, it works diligently; it loves with faithful passion. It safely carried and nourished my children.

It has also borne my suffering. Each separation, each descent into the Maelstrom, has used it and polished it like a beautiful wood weathered by the torrents, and I began to look differently at the bodies of others! And often, as I did so, mine tightened with sadness: I was moved by the sight of vacant bodies; by those who are 'nobody' to the person who inhabits them, and 'nobody' to those who disrespect them… Starved bodies, bodies stuffed with food, pawed at, abused, raped, polluted and endangered in innumerable ways. And this, not only in the extremes of racism, torture, war, misery or hunger, somewhere very far away, but right here in my own hometown, my own homeland, in my own psyche… all this because we have forgotten, or never wanted to know, that every part of matter is woven of spirit, soul and feeling; that bodies aren't 'things!'

Although I had always recognized that the body of my

beloved, the bodies of my children, were real persons, I had ignored that my own was a person too! To 'touch' is not only to 'place a hand on…' it is to bond.

It was now up to me to decide to be my body's best friend until death does us part. Never again will we travel along like two strangers.

◆

Once we realize that we have flawed our most faithful ally, the time comes to put some changes into practice.

Why not begin to relate consciously to one's *own* 'shoulder, knee, foot, circulation, organs' …and so prove—down to every one of our billions of cells—that indeed they do reply to a tender gesture, to an affectionate word, in the same way a *person* would! It is our privilege to make this happen: Everything—including our bodies and all of their parts—will magically transform into responding beings the moment we express our love for them, speak to them, listen to them and look at them.

If we pay attention, we will experience that they love us and speak to us in return: We have restored the gift of relatedness! And every time we put this into action, we heal, we evolve.

To befriend all we 'sense,' invites us to a further step: Let us consider every feeling, emotion, image and thought, and whatever we enact—as an *Inner person*! We will, for instance, be surprised to discover that our 'Inner Child of the past' is fully here, alive and active in our *now…* waiting to be recognized, mirrored, freed from isolation and constraint, by our love and attention; ready to inspire us. And more: Though most of our 'feeling states' originate in this child, this is not, and by far, the only *Inner self* competing for our understanding! Indeed, since the moment we were conceived, a *Host* of vulnerable or protecting and reacting *Inner selves*—that we don't even suspect!—exists inside us; has developed around our sensitive kid.

◆

Let me give you a simple example. Imagine that you just banged your elbow against the doorway. The pain shoots through you like a lightning bolt. Blood rushes to your head. Shock and hurt trigger a chain of emotions and self-shielding answers. Tears fill your eyes. You feel betrayed by the doorway. Anger surges at having been taken by surprise; a sudden impulse to avenge yourself… You might punch the doorframe that 'did that to you,' before you finally 'get hold of yourself to regain your composure.'

This shows how fast our 'survival personality' moves from one 'state of being' into another… from one *person* into another! And this happens constantly to every one of us in all of life's situations. Like recurring dreams, these conflicting interactions of our *Inner selves* re-emerge on the screen of our minds. They may last but fleeting moments, yet they rule us…

The point is that they will only evolve towards consciousness and appeasement, if we take the time to be aware of them, to listen to them. Shouldn't we consider—as a priority—to address and embrace 'all of humanity' inside ourselves?

◆

Let's imagine a 'remake' of the standard 'banged elbow incident;' something more in tune with the 'wisdom of children *number one-two-three* and the healing power of love;' something that brings a different response than only 'betrayed victim, blind avenger, and mere regaining of one's composure!'

The next time you bang yourself or feel hurt in your feelings, why not try this:

- First, repeat several times exactly, but very softly, the cycle of the hurting gesture or incident; this amounts to listening to the story.
- Second, put a tender hand on your chest. Inhale a gentle breath from the midst of your heart. Imbue it with the Love that houses there.
- And then… blow softly on your wounded me or elbow, as you would on a crying child. This amounts to relating to your vulnerability.

Immediately, your bruised body—together with the hurt child deep within you—will relax; will welcome the cool wind, the caring breath. Each of your cells will open, expand instead of contracting; will become aware of your 'Loving Presence.'

- Now, listen to the feeling of trust that responds from inside you. Your body, your *Inner family of selves* and you, have become intimate.

You reconcile with the doorframe! Now all is calm and alleviated. Your emotions have ceased to make waves. You feel supported and secure; protected by the certainty that you are close to yourself.

Spontaneously, you reconnect with Life; you sense its flow, you touch its vibration.

◆

Aliveness rises from this heightened Presence to our joys, pains, impulses and needs.

A compassionate *Aware Self* develops inside us.

You can exercise with this any time. Whenever you feel distressed or neglected or fearful, simply play this fabulous game: Start to 'live in your own skin;' dialogue with yourself!

Recognize and meet whoever is calling out from within. Use your perceptions and your imagination in the service of shared affection. [8]

As you proceed in this apprenticeship, you will see that 'Inner and outer world' reflect each other like two giant mirrors. To 'Love your neighbor as yourself,' as Jesus bids us, we must first learn to take *all* that inhabits us into our care… and this will enable us to gain understanding for those around us.

We so undo our Fall from Paradise! And with it, the hell that springs from abandonment and loss; from shame, fear, defiance and rejection. Isn't this the aim of our evolution: To reclaim our birth from the Loving Breath of God and to extend His gift of Hope Love and Faith to all and everyone!

You are now invited to go to Volume II, Exercise 2
I. The Presence that Heals
II. The Presence that Praises

---

[8] **See also Volume II: "The Ark Within. Exercise Manual."** See Appendixes I, II, III at the end of the present Volume. See the "*Voice Dialogue,* the *Psychology of Selves* and of the *Aware ego,*" developed by Hal and Sidra Stone, Ph.D. USA. See Bibliography.

V

The Seven Antennas of the Senses

I wanted—or was it the 'Inner Child' in me?—to explore the Self on the wings of the Breath. I wanted to have faith in this divine Spirit that God insufflates into Adam's shape of clay. I wanted to experience Love's healing force as it journeys through us; to share miracles, to make them part of my everyday life. I had arrived at a point where I understood that we are a mysterious living pulsing textbook, but nobody had ever taught me how to decipher it.

I wanted to express and understand what I really felt; to find out how to respond rather than react! And my first steps toward opening and decoding this textbook were to seek a dialogue with all of my senses.

One summer afternoon, while sitting in the garden, feeling from tip to toe as if I were a fiery question mark, all antennas alert, I asked myself: 'How many senses do people really have?' Simultaneously, as if by magic, a bright green Grasshopper jumped into my lap. And there, reaching toward the heavens, erect and vibrant, tenuous yet hard and brilliant like coarse golden wires, were *seven* antennas. The answer leapt at me: *Seven antennas for seven senses*! The afternoon filled with the sound and the movement of wings. The Grasshopper and I have remained friends ever since.

In school I learned that we have five senses and that grasshoppers have two antennas; but that hadn't quite convinced me. I had always been sure that there is a reality behind the reality.

I know the taste of a lemon, the sound of a crying baby,

the soft touch of my cat's fur to my fingertips; I know the smell of the ocean's salt air and the splendor of a sunrise to my eyes… all those things are familiar to my five senses. But our insights, our callings, the capacity to be one's own witness, to tap into other realms, how can they be explained, unless we have two additional senses: The 'Sense of Love' and the 'Sense of Creative Imagination!'

Was it my surge of desire that called this Grasshopper into existence? Or has the insect awakened me by claiming my love? This is the mystery of relationships, of births, of synchronicities: The Grasshopper now bounds in and out of my heart; makes it impossible for me to forget the Seven Antennas of the Seven Senses! They live and flash inside me.

When fully served by touch, sight, hearing, taste and smell—Love and Creative Imagination are my most precious Guides. They bring meaning, beauty and the sparkle of the unexpected to my life. Together we ride the seven horses of their energies; we lower the seven drawbridges to the 'body-castle;' we unlock the seven doors of the 'walled city of me,' and we cease to be strangers to Heaven and earth and to ourselves.

Whenever you feel trapped, lost or uncertain about your next step, ask each of your seven senses for advice. Their answers are already written deep inside you! What does your heart yearn for? What does your mind envision? What do your hands reach out to? What words do you long to hear or speak? Listen to your body-heart-and-soul's responses… let them become your faithful Allies.

When I try to imagine where the antennas of my senses originate, when I intimately listen to my perceptions… everything begins to delicately undulate inside me: Each of my cells has been waiting for this! My understanding multiplies by billions of eyes, ears, arms, mouths, noses and intelligences. The Universe shares its living conscious Body with me. Together we fully inhale, hear, see, touch, taste… create and love!

Yet I try in vain to trace my antennas all the way... because they emerge from a cosmic blueprint; because they are rooted in the infinitely minute; because they reach into the infinitely distant— so far and so deep that I cannot fathom where they begin or end. What I do know is that they lead me as far as my Heart can go, as deep as my Love can embrace: Closer than microscopes can see, beyond what telescopes can reach.

But do they even have a beginning? Will they meet with an end?

If each cell carries in its DNA 'the totality of the program and functioning of our fully developed brain and body,' then why shouldn't each cell contain also the Galaxies? Why shouldn't each cell contain our future as well as our past; hold in itself 'millions of years' of evolving consciousness, unbounded *Spheres* yet unknown to us? All this in less than one thousandth of a millimeter! Maybe there is even more to this, something indefinable that mankind used to call God, that our science hasn't proved yet, that the dictionaries will make clear in the future.

To this day, I wonder why the Grasshopper happened to be a messenger in my life. It certainly wasn't just any Grasshopper, but one of indescribable radiance, one from another dimension. Perhaps it fell from the green planet that shocks us into transformation—Uranus.

I no longer consider my senses as restricted, but trust them to be part of a *Holographic[9] Awareness* in which 'I am.' My Grasshopper whispers to me—yes, it speaks!—that my body is as vast, as weightless, as space itself; never isolated, yet differentiated, yet always related to the wholeness of an ever living, ever loving Universe.

------

[9] *The hologram,* or three dimensional photograph, was first discovered in 1947 by the mathematician Dennis Gabor. In 1971 he was the single recipient of the Nobel Prize in Physics for his invention and development of the holographic method. See also under 'The Hologram as Consciousness Model.'

And I remain amazed; I marvel at the most surprising of kingdoms: A body like this, one that contains the totality of what is, can I really make a Friend of it? Can I really travel on the wings of Breath and Love? Can I descend to the Core of Being by a simple touch, a simple word… a subtle listening to so many realms embedded into mine?

Be vigilant! Miracles, conjunctions, the unexpected… are the Magical Grasshoppers that can change your life, that blow apart your limited frameworks; creating space for what is new.

Don't discard fantasy. Don't reject the irrational. Life springs from what we cannot understand. And it is our 'Seven senses' that enable us to enjoy the earth, as children do, in faith and in wonder.

VI

The Alchemy of Love
Touch the Body, Touch the Person
Touch the World

Isn't true relating '*to be aware of me* and—at the same time—*to be aware of you?*'

Not fusing, but weaving a bridge of mindfulness and love in-between us; in-between two pillars. For it is the wholeness of me and the wholeness of you, that sustains the balance of dedicated love and hallowed freedom; of self-care and mutual care. You and me: Two Hearts holding their Inner child; two Pillars that anchor what joins us. Together they carry the union of opposites, the alchemy of love, its maturation—where deep in our roots, an accretion, the blooming of our souls, the emergence of our deeper Self, is nourished to be shared.

I remember certain early moments when, to me, to touch was a 'holy gesture,' a silent incantation. Long ago, when I was still a little girl, a Maple tree lived in my garden. And from this old solitary giant, a stately branch extended itself, just at the height, where, one day, I was able to jump up and seize it.

Until I'd grown tall enough we'd had to wait, like two betrothed of ancient times. This waiting heightened our longing for each other. The tree dreamed of telling me its secrets; I dreamed of climbing high into its branches. I remember a wondrous moment when, leaning against it, I let my eyes follow the lines from where it originated in the earth... up along its sinewy roots to its thick trunk wrapped in a robe of bark, almost black; creased and cracked with long crevasses; grooved and engraved. Seeing such nobility, such strength, filled me with a respect and a fascination I had never felt before. Almost as if in a trance, I reached out with my hand toward its elephant-like skin. Imagine, one timid minute hand, reaching... The words from the story of Snow White came back to me: "Red like blood, white like snow, black like ebony." I can still see my hand so pale against the dark wood. I can still hear my heart beating; feel the blood rush into my cheeks!

And then, we touched…

From these caresses of a child, a long intimacy was born. But it wasn't until much later that a jump enabled me to seize the huge branch, hoist myself up into the fork of the tree and straddle the powerful bough—taking refuge within its rough sides and blending with its rustling leaves.

Fortunately, each Love still springs from the Source, guiltless and unsuspicious. In coming together, the heart of the Child, the heart of the Maple tree, have shown me the way. This is the journey that matters: *Simply to touch what touches me.* To go forward—fresh tender and daring—like a new born infant, like a virgin lover, who for the first time reaches out! And feels.

◆

For a long time, to walk my life meant taking risks! The risk of being hurt or ridiculous or an *alien* or proven wrong; and this did require my courage; the courage to embrace what scares me; to challenge my capacity to jump into the chasm when it opened under my feet.

But now, in my later years—and ever since I realized that Aurora, my *Inner Child,* journeys at my side—I do not test my fate so recklessly anymore, as if I were a 'lord less samurai!'

I just hold her little hand tightly in mine, so that she isn't afraid when it gets dark. Together we trust the unfamiliar to be our Friend.

The Alchemy of Love is not only a 'Magnum Opus' for dreamers! This is why Aurora and I ceaselessly probe into the mystery of relatedness in which sharing love with '*what is,*' the union of matter and spirit, eventually will spawn a new Man, a new Earth.

Our bodies physically age, but in our souls nothing grows old. In our psyches nothing dies. All we've ever gone through and enacted endures in form of *Inner persons,* leading an autonomous, hidden and often insulated life in our inner realm! And as long as we ignore them, as long as we give them away to be carried by others, or reduce them to *things;* things we would correct, get rid of or deny… these *selves* will remain unchanged and unhappy inside us. If we do not relate to them as 'alive and sentient' in our flesh and blood, they stay trapped in some blind spot of ours: 'Complexes and defense mechanisms' as they are called! But, whether they are dormant, condemned—frozen in our past or in a stillborn future—they do hope for deliverance and love. And if we reach out to them with an understanding heart, with our caring gestures, with our gentle words, they do transmute.

Our egos are redeemed by Love!

Even to this day, I trek paths previously concealed to me; saving paths in the wilds and the jungles of this earth, where I struggle to 'be.' Each of us embodies and discloses *who* suffers, defends, rejoices, needs space. Let us unfold a *Womb of Kindness* in our Heart; shelter in it our *Inner Family of selves* and why not—once we have commended our roots to the earth and our branches to the sky—the suffering of so many people near and far. Our Heart is fathomless; it can speak with simple words of utter tenderness: 'I am here. We are together, I love you! I will not judge you.' Let us pray with each other for forgiveness; for 'faith, love and hope;' pray to expand God's gift of primal innocence and love to inner and outer world.'

Watch and behold! When we do so, our 'reactive sentinels, 'our suffering selves,' start to relax and heal. All we need to soothe 'pain and anger,' to give birth to peace, is to step inwards and, from there, to pick up the severed thread of lost relatedness and reconnect with whoever is distressed or trying to save our day by fight or flight. Neediness then turns into abundance, shame into innocence, blame into gratitude and suspicion into trust.

Maybe you never imagined that a 'relating to yourself' in the same tangible manner you relate to a 'loved other' is possible! Yet we humans are the only creatures conscious and differentiated enough to be 'witnesses to who we are and partners to what we feel:' To be both the one who sees and the one who is seen; the one who calls and the one who answers; the one who searches and the one who is found.

Paradoxically, it is our excruciating exile, the memory of our mislaid love and liberty that kindles—at the very marrow of our bones—the blazing nostalgia, the burning certainty, of our Oneness. In spite of this, as long as our *Free will* doesn't reclaim it, we remain oblivious of the 'cosmic hologram we partake in;' blind to our own soul.

It was not discernment that condemned us in the Garden, splitting us apart, but our judgments exempt of love. Yet this isn't without remedy.

Our egos, mine and yours, are redeemed by Love.

We don't have the power to destroy the 'Pristine Self' in us. It dawns and murmurs in the lap of God. It reveals itself at the favor of growing awareness; of a going beyond our little patch of safety; beyond our 'walled city of me!' Once our hard shell cracks open, allowing us to share from inborn entirety and caring—instead of alleged lack—our separateness drops away like an optical illusion. We start to be in awe and wonder at the magnificence of our 'Primal Source.' It radiates from every spark of love; it glows at the core of every single atom in the world.

My loves for Aurora, her love for me, have led me to become my own closest friend; maybe this is so, because she never gave up tugging at my sleeve, insisting, as children know how to do, and because I could never resist her candid and uncompromising affection. In time, this led me step by step, closer to *loving my neighbor as my Self.*

📖 ***You are now invited to go to Volume II, Exercise 3***
The Experience of Touch: I. The Relational Gesture
II. Touch the Surrounding World

Part Two

'Love Your Neighbor as Thy Self'

VII
What I Learned from Robinson Crusoe

As a child, I read Daniel Defoe's book, Robinson Crusoe, passionately a great number of times and absorbed its smallest details! Had this been a premonition, or had my rebellious solitary nature confined me to a personal island long before the shipwreck to come?

Whatever the case, it was already in my early years that I ventured to make of Nature my Kingdom… that I decided to defeat solitude and the cannibals; and to make trees, rain, wind and wild children my trusted companions!

I might not have questioned later the importance of relationships so deeply, had I not—at the age of thirty-five—found myself in the same situation as Robinson Crusoe when the boat of my life sunk unexpectedly, leaving me stranded on a foreign shore. A shore called 'abandonment and divorce, collapse of our love, of our dream; of the family we had formed.'

Bewildered, scared, my four young children—though seemingly still cheerful and carefree—fell silent inside themselves. And unfortunately—in my desperate efforts to salvage our daily lives, to survive the loss of the man I cherished—I didn't realize the extent of their disarray, of their fear and pain. In my inexperience and panic, I didn't take the full measure of their own loss. And—much too early in their years—they also were left on isolated islets.

My heart had run aground on a hidden reef, been washed up on a desert island. Like Robinson Crusoe, I now had to learn to walk barefoot and empty handed; to carry on while no longer protected by what once made me feel happy and safe. Spellbound, unable to integrate what had happened and to foresee its consequences, I felt powerless, numb with hurt, and most importantly—alone.

Petrified, Aurora stayed mute. The Grasshopper had disappeared into the virgin forest without even giving a sign.

This forced me to reach out. And when I did, I realized I wasn't the only *person* who had to endure despair. And this is what taught me my first steps in compassion. It became clear to me that if I didn't want to die, or lose my mind, I would have to learn how to love myself and find new ways to love the world around me.

Like Robinson, I pondered the ruin of my venture with bitterness! I felt cheated by my own destiny. With revolt, I considered the forsaken patch of earth that was now to be my home. All I had left to rely on was my bare body and the grace of God. My only tools were my industry, determination, and resourcefulness. My only provisions were those I salvaged from the ruptured belly of the ship.

Yet, much to my surprise, along with loads of memories—both good and bad—I was to rediscover, in this unwanted enterprise, some of my old dreams, my youthful independence and many a long-forgotten treasure chest floating about the wreckage of my past.

With each new day I had to come to terms with my confusion, with my ignorance, with my paralyzed heart. I often felt condemned to a never ending prison sentence on my solitary inner island… But, little by little, as I worked hard to decipher and tame my enforced environment, I reconnected with the wisdom and enchantment that as a child I had gathered from the tale of Robinson. My unshakable perseverance proved stronger than my deprivation. Eventually, the measure of my hardships became that of my breakthroughs and of my joys! Each time I faced the unexplored or developed a new skill, hope and strength surged within me like the sap in springtime!

One morning, while bending over to pick up a gleaming shell from the lagoon, I discovered the reflection of a radiant woman smiling at me! Suddenly, Aurora and the Grasshopper were looking over my shoulder! Aurora's love and faith, the Grasshopper's daring leaps into the realms of imagination, have never failed me; have always reminded me, to come back to myself with candid simplicity.

Standing in the shallow lagoon, I felt the reassuring happiness of a companionship I had missed for so long. I felt like a young tree sprouting in maternal waters, rooted in sacred soil, rising toward the light, dancing upon the soft sea winds.

It was in this time of utter solitude that I realized how important it is to simply hold hands with myself. My body, my senses, my feelings, became my true neighbors, became these *Inner friends* I dialogue with and relate to, still to this day. They sing and dance in each of my hopes and joys. They tremble and cry in each of my fears and pains. I am their companion who doesn't leave, doesn't betray; who will die at their side, breathe their last breath within mine. They share with me this simple need—as does everyone else in the outer world—to hear someone say: '*I love you. You are precious to me as you are. Nothing will ever destroy my love for you.* And this also helped me to bond with others—and I hope with my own children, in a way hitherto unknown to me.

Say it to yourself; say it to your Inner Tribe; say it to one another; whisper it in your heart to the lonely... They will respond and smile and return your love.

Storms will go on blowing and some of your crafts will sink, but if you can learn to relate with love and safe boundaries to yourself and to the world around you, no matter what shore you find yourself cast upon, it will always be your Homeland.

❑ ***You are now invited to go to Volume II, Exercise 4***
To Dance like a Leaf in the Wind

VIII

The Encounter with Friday
Listen, Place your Ear
On the Cave of the Heart

Standing alone at the cliff's edge, I accompany the evening. I watch the sun wane, swallowed back into the belly of the sea. Night oozes from in between the stones, ascends from the jagged crevices of the boulders; spreads in between the trunks of the dense forest. Darkness rises from the dells, licks up the mountain slopes. The coming night sinks all the way into my entrails and unfolds within me like a giant corolla. I close my eyes; I let myself fall into this peaceful chasm.

This is the hour of the waiting; the hour of transition, when day blends into night. The silence is heart gripping. This is the hour when there is nothing left to hold on to, nothing to fill the emptiness, nothing to distract me. Obscurity closes over me like the skin of a giant drum, stretched over the vault of a somber sky.

I become aware of a faint beating: Deep, rhythmic, almost painful. It throbs in the intensity of my seclusion, precise like the Star of Hope in the cave of my body. It pulses under my ribs, under the membrane of my Heart. I hear it murmuring there like an incantation: "*Where are you, my brother, my friend, my betrothed, my child?*"

I don't know if I'm dreaming, but now I sense—like an echo of my throbbing heart—a distant call that circles in space, fringes the shores of my island. The soil resonates from its rhythm, the air fills with its ring; it swells in jolts. A strange anguish takes hold of me, fear rushes in.

Almost without knowing why, I begin to run toward this beating. Breathless, almost blind, I fight my way through the jungle. I speed down to the sea. I can hear someone gasping for breath. Footsteps run up in wild flight. There is a sudden leap out of the darkness: A child collides with me.

And as I seize it tightly in my arms, the Love that bursts forth within me triggers the contractions of a surprising birth: Another child, a yet unknown child, caught in strenuous inner bonds, readies itself for delivery and pulses inside me with all its might. I realize that the child pushing from within, the child that fled the shore and every child of mankind are one and the same. But who is this child? Is it the eternal child? Am I then the eternal birth-giving womb? Is this the birth of a new, of a deeper, a more universal love?

I hold the little stranger in my arms with a strength that I didn't know I had. He panics and trembles like a bird caught in a net. He freezes still or tries to flee; emits inarticulate sounds. At times his voice becomes beseeching, tenuous like a young animal's cry. I see his dark skin, wet and glistening. I don't know what else I can do, except to keep him pressed tightly to my chest. I wonder: Is he born from my heart, from my belly, from my loneliness?

It seems to me now that there is only one pulsing heart beating in the night. Our intertwined bodies root themselves into the soil like a powerful tree.

I don't know how long we stay like this—motionless, timeless. Little by little the child's vigorous body, slender like a vine, begins to relax, its breathing grows calm. I carefully ease my hold, attentive to its life, both fragile and wild.

An imperceptible whiteness heralds the dawn. At last the child has fallen asleep. I carry it off to safety, cradled in my arms, light as a wing.

Deep in my breast there is an unknown softness, a quivering, a forgotten shiver of tenderness. These feelings swell within me like windblown sails.

The sun envelops us; it filters through my walls of dried grass and bamboo. Ever so gently, I lay Friday—my *Inner child,* my *Outer child*—down on a bed of leaves, in the shelter of our home.

IX

Finding *Friday* and Never Losing Him Again Even if You Have Never Been *Robinson*

My encounter with *Friday* unlocked an inner closure, liberated in me a fountain of Love.

I had always imagined that Love would come from outside. I hadn't suspected that the moment I ceased to hold it back, it would so freely flow from my own Heart.

With the return of its flow, I also awoke to my four children's concealed suffering… Although I cherished them deeply, although they were my only treasure—adrift and forlorn as I was—I had not been fully conscious of their needs and qualms. Somehow, in the shipwreck of our family, we had gone under as *one*—as if my children had returned into my womb. I remember that in the first months of their father's absence, we used to draw close at night, like frightened animals in their den! The youngest ones, Basile, not yet two and Aloyse, five, in my bed; Eléonore, slightly over seven, on a mattress carried near; Grégoire, the oldest, who was ten, on the sofa in the adjoining living room.

The recognition of Aurora, the running into Friday, the progressive dismantling of the building blocks that obstructed in me the river of love, awoke me to a feeling of kinship with all I am, with all there is… And this has proved enough to survive every trial; enough to sustain a flicker of light in the darkest of circumstances, along a tireless journey through the years toward reconnection, forgiveness and hope, finding the way back to my wounded offspring and to my own Inner child.

Only Love bridges; speaks all languages, crosses the abyss of our separateness and of our dying.

◆

In my exile on the island, I had etched every passing day into the bark of a huge tree, now all scarred and wrinkled like the face of an old shaman. Was it only to keep track of time, or was it a ritual of deliverance, a monk's prayer mill endlessly spinning in my hands? Was it a service to the Gods, to the stars and planets, to the laws of constraint I had so defiantly ignored in my schooldays, regardless of my father's foresight? From the firmament they now imposed on me their decrees and their cycles: Mondays for childhood and dreams, Tuesdays for battle, Wednesdays for thought, Thursdays for guidance, Fridays for love, Saturdays for wisdom and Sundays for the Divine, for gratitude and rest, for crossing into the beyond, into a new life or another week!

'Fridays for love' is an understanding that comes after we have tried most other avenues; after we have lost our track in illusions and conflicts, in mind and power games. I found— as in time we probably all do—that except for unconditional cherishment nothing ever suffices. From the moment we are conceived to our last breath, we yearn for the Father, the Mother, the Friend, the Sister, the Brother, the Lover.

We do dream of '*The Master of all Arts,*' embedded in the heart of man. Yes—dream of an 'inner widening' that would host and reveal the entire spectrum of our skills, colors, and deeper melodies: the bard, the shaman, the knight, the Red Indian, the grandmother, the divine child… a mountain deer, a ferocious yet tender feline, a strong-limbed tree, a reflecting pool, a sleeping beauty, an orange robed monk, a magical child, an outstretched hand.

We thirst for the One who will redeem us from our

narrowness, from the mediocre, from the meaningless, from what we have left undone; the One who trusts our wildest dreams, our finest accomplishments; who stands by us in our most cruel and shameful falls. Save this total non judging Love, nothing else, none of our greatest achievements, none of our innumerable substitutes, will ever put our heart at peace.

Do we fail to realize that our desperate quest for human acceptance stems from our inbuilt memory of God's Love; expresses the yearning for our oneness in Him, for our oneness with Creation, that we deem lost? Is this arrogance or is this the buried Source of Aliveness itself: The Voice of our native Truth in our own Core?

Each of us, roots in an *Ancient universal Mother*! Within *Her*—all we ever were, are, or will be, all our 'Inner selves,' all fellow beings, can feel contained—are held dear. She is full of the sun of laughter; full of the rain of tears… She is as old as the Earth; a sunken vessel, a primordial amphora, lying in the recesses of the sea. She keeps millenniums in her flanks. Time and the currents have clothed her into softness; shaped her into a giant shell caressed by seaweed. In her Heart, in her Womb, nothing goes astray. Everything is there, waiting to be reborn from her Bounty.

◆

While growing up, I had lost my *oneness.* To protect myself from suffering, I kept falling into rounds of wants and qualms; I kept shutting out Aurora and Friday, my *Inner children*—the very font of my Love. I looked for better, for more, for different, completely unaware that I already had it all in me! That's how I lost contact with my Amphora-self. That's how I became numbed and amnesic. The energy necessary to fight, to survive, the havoc of grief, of doubt and reason, had covered the *feeling voices* inside me like rolling thunder and flooding waters. Aurora, the Teddy bear, the Maple tree, the Grasshopper, Friday and the Universe itself had simply vanished into hiding.

Again and again I felt washed up on a lonely shore; this obliged me to pay attention to my body, to the tightening in my chest, in my throat; to my contracted stomach and knotted shoulders… these were the 'Forgotten Allies' calling from within! But instead of listening to them, I unconsciously adjusted my armor, thickened my skin, hardened my shell.

We are in constant danger of traveling through existence like prehistoric creatures, almost petrified—so well protected, but forever insulated! And this will last until some ordeal breaks us open, delivers us to overwhelming sorrow—and with it to a possible resurrection. When death, heartbreak, a night of immemorial solitude, leave us naked and mute, we can again detect—in a faint beating, in the palpitation of our anguish, in a shiver of despair—an improbable love: It trembles and amplifies in the cavern of the body, upon the drum of the heart, dismantling our carapace.

This is the time! The time to listen, to stay near, to stay unprotected! Replace your brazen metal gauntlets with your living hands and arms. Find your way back to 'the touch, the smile, the look, the first words, the first gestures,' you needed at birth—so similar, so close, to those we always need, and will still need at Death's door. Murmur, sing softly to the 'Inner Child' that wants to be born out of your tenderness! Uncovered by your fractures, your innermost core will show itself—wild and new, like a chestnut gleaming through its cracked open husk.

The moment I embraced Friday he reciprocated my love with the ardent simplicity of a child. The caverns of fear became treasure chests. Bonding replaced estrangement. Joy welled, soon shared by the trees, birds, beasts—tamed and untamed—of our island. Aurora and the grasshopper radiated happiness.

◆

Sabotaging what is dear, true and sacred to us is a repetitive, though absurd, human proviso. Time and again, my instinct toward hardcore survival and identity-preservation—insidious negative judgments!—still overrun my loyalty to my Deeper Self and to my Inner Child.

No sooner had I regained Friday's and Aurora's trust, than I slipped back into the old snare. One day, Friday and I were racing each other along the white sandy beach, happy like two carefree greyhounds, when suddenly I spotted a sail in the distance. Wild desire stirred; I madly waved my arms, hoisted animal skins, lit an enormous fire!

When the ship's silhouette faded from the horizon, I collapsed. The island turned grey, my body indifferent, my spirit numb; Friday was again a stranger, the living proof of my misfortune. In a flash, we lose it all again! In a flash, I had imagined a different life and this threw me out of balance, uprooted and disoriented me. I felt abruptly launched into an '*other self*,' a totally alien Robinson!

Gone was what I treasured; sold out to the 'image' of this *White Champion* gliding on the wave! All it took was to spot—on the screen of my desires and fears—this Seafaring Knight in shining array, sailing in from outside, from elsewhere—and to see him go; to see him leave me! How cruel to picture oneself abandoned and unseen, blotted out from the surface of the earth, expelled from hope, love and rescue! I felt devastated by the loss—not of my reality, but of my illusion: A *fata morgana* before the eyes of the strayed traveler.

Beware of self defiling beliefs, of deeming yourself a miser: You will be an easy prey to delusion. Don't make the other responsible for your emotional safety. Quench your thirst for attention; appease your hunger for tenderness, by taking a leap into solidarity: Close your arms around yourself and be your own Trusting Friend.

Unless we plug into our Divine Source—the Loving Breath of God that endlessly births us in Him—we feel poorer and poorer; we go on pursuing and imploring love from absent hands, from averted eyes and missing words. We mourn lost treasures, unaware that they abide inside us. The Sufi mystic and poet, Djalâl-ud-Dîn Rûmî, says: "You beg for a crust of bread while a full basket rests on your head; you thirst for a mouthful of water while your feet bathe in a river of milk."[10]

◆

Now, whenever I feel insufficient or unhappy, I ask myself: To what, to whom, do I assign the responsibility to restore my joy, to appraise my value, to confirm my identity? And in answer to this question, I hand myself over to God's and Life's wisdom; I take up my rudder, I redress my course; I listen to the natural warmth of my Heart who is the Friend. I embrace Friday and Aurora, my *Wild child,* my *Sun child.* I acknowledge my 'Inner Tribe' without judgment. I hold close whoever feels distressed inside me.

The fulfilment we reap, the bliss of reuniting—be it with our own contradictions and sorrows—naturally leads to a further step: We can now send out our Love, share our smiles and our words, stretch out our hand, to our fellow men, to the stranger, to the passer-by. Life becomes a Celebration, a

---

[10] From the Masnawi, by the Persian Sufi mystic and poet, Djalāl ad-Dīn Rûmî, Balkh 1207 - 1273 Konya.

return to the world, not as a shipwrecked survivor, but sailing our *Ark*; rich of what we have to share!

📖 ***You are now invited to go to Volume II, Exercise 5***
How to Find your Way Back to Your Inner Child;
Respond with Love to its Needs.
The Ten Essential Affectionate Gestures
The Ten Essential Affirmations of Love

X

Noah's Ark
The Womb-Body, the Boat-Body

As far as I can remember, I felt drawn to men and women who dare to venture beyond their little garden-fence, beyond their secure and familiar world; those who follow their heart to a new level of reality—like children whose spirit soars as their kite takes flight. In sailors and glider pilots, poets and physicists, medicine-men and eremites, I recognized a will to see through appearances, to penetrate the mysterious essence of things.

To reach for such achievements, I pursued my first Journeys in the realms of my fantasy; I rode my thoughts like power-horses. Freed from all weight, I felt enflamed by such magisterial leaps. They carried me effortlessly to the summit of the magic mountain, without having to toil or lose my footing or scrape myself at the cutting edges of their mirrors.

Yet Life itself soon skinned my knees and often left me stranded and bare on its slopes! Had I gone adrift? Was I nothing more than an empty boat tugging at its mooring?

In spite of all straying and hardships, I remain eternally grateful to Aurora's visionary spirit and faith that enabled me to see the Promised Land from the heights of my early dreams!

I believe that we need to serve a paradoxical double errand: One is to remain true to the *Dream of the Child* in us—for it is close to the Star that guides our Way and if we forsake it, we lose it and with it our stamina; the other is the necessity to embody our *Dream* into everyday and down to earth reality, for if we merely keep fantasizing, we will only build castles in the sky.

Did I, at eight years old, have a sense of future fates, as the seed obscurely knows about the tree; about spring and frosty seasons? No, I did not imagine myself losing what was to be the dearest to me; bound to explore wondrous, but also cruel and uncharted lands. I did not imagine myself watching a beloved son go under in darkness beyond my help.

In my youth, I was impatient, proud and obstinate. I wanted to play it my way, save and conquer the world, and it took nothing less than the stripping of all my reference for me to discover, in the depth of despair, the meaning of love, the rising of light. I learned that love can grow in solitude, power in powerlessness and inner abundance in depletion. All treasures are indeed guarded by dragons! My head had to bow to the higher, my feet to submit to the path. And in truth, every time I was delivered to helplessness, I could also measure the extent of my own resources and the fathomless generosity of Life. I learned to trust the blows of the 'unexpected' and to meet them as signposts and Allies. It also meant that on our Journey, we simply cannot leave our own *Self* behind, or forget God and our Planet, or desert our fellow men.

◆

We cannot divorce ourselves.

It would have been pointless to leave my island and forsake Friday; pointless to silence my 'Inner voices;' pointless to imagine that 'another companion, another horizon,' might…

What we avoid inside catches up with us outside; for within and without are mirrors to one another. No matter how fast we run from it, *it* will be there. Sooner or later, we must embrace, we must unite. Better we marry ourselves straightaway, stay close and bear in the Womb of our Heart our easily broken and unpredictable *me* and all our circumstances!

Biologically, we naturally evolve from being *a child* to our parents to being *a parent* to our children. Likewise, once we are grown up, it becomes our own task to meet our *Inner child* with the 'unconditional love' it hoped for from its biological parents. As long as we are unaware of this possibility as adults… we will keep on transferring on our loved ones the responsibility of sustaining our self-worth and of answering our hunger for emotional reassurance! This leads to burdensome and dysfunctional relationships.

The importance of a 'holding environment' for the infant's development in Donald Winnicott's work,[11] has inspired me to apply his concept to 'relationship processes' between adults and their vulnerable *Inner Child*—in exactly the same manner than with the biological infant. Experiencing this principle within the framework of 'Voice Dialogue' practice has corroborated that 'what is true of adequate holding with the biological baby, proves true when self-applied in adulthood.

It's up to us to address what our care-takers or others may have impaired or missed, rather than stay distressed or blaming them for it! It is our responsibility to individuate beyond mere social adaptation; to assuage who is wounded in us; to probe into what keeps us prisoners of unmet emotions and associated memories.

And we can do so from scratch! Our psyche transcends time and space. If we work at it, we can respond to our *Inner selves* all the way from our intra-uterine stages to our present day; and from the present day to our last breath. And even beyond: What we amend and unravel inside us also liberates our biological children; frees previous and oncoming generations from problems we carry, perpetuate and transmit.

---

[11] *See:* D.W. Winnicott's (1890-1971) "The Maturational Process and the Facilitating Environment." Ed. Karnac, London 1990. *See* his pediatric work with children and mothers, and his ground breaking concept of the 'holding environment.' A concept we can and should extend to lifelong aware self-relating.

Creative imagination and the capacity of our brain to reflect itself, give us the means to *re-parent* our 'Inner Child. To do so, we can learn to structure and unfold a 'self-holding environment.'[12] We can learn to acknowledge and mirror our own suffering, shame, and fear of abandonment. We can establish ourselves as a *Womb*—in body, heart and mind. We can weave an *envelope* around whoever feels destabilized inside us—with the *sound* of our affectionate words, with the *feel* of our tender gestures.

How could we otherwise give birth to our faith, enclose in our love our 'Inner family of selves,' cross the Ocean of Life?

◆

Sailing a boat for years in all weathers—often with my four children throughout the summer holidays of their youth— has taught me many a skill and indeed an Art of navigating my own destiny.

Our boat was called *Leto,* after a Greek Nymph with a significant story: 'Seduced by Zeus, heavy with child, chased by jealous Hera over the seas, and about to enter labor... Leto sent down two strong pillars through the waters and so found refuge by giving rise to a well rooted Island named Delos where she safely gave birth to her divine twins: Apollo and Artemis.' Menace

Was this one of these winks that heralds insights to come? To sail a boat teaches us to sail our lives. Our 'Aware Self,' our aware flesh and our senses, make up a high-performance vessel. Whenever we readjust our position between earth and

---

[12] *See:* 'The Alchemy of Freedom.' A.H. Almaas: *"A good 'holding environment... provides a sense of safety and security, the sense that you are, and can count on, being taken care of... the child can develop in the context of a continuity of being which allows and supports the individuation of the soul—one's unique embodiment of Being.*
Because... no holding environment is without failures, we typically develop a real (essential) and a false (egoic) self in varying proportions. Basic trust is usually not totally missing, but it is seldom complete."

sky… straighten our spine, deploy our volume and ground ourselves, we regain our balance. Our body, heart, mind and spirit, do respond to each other like a fine boat responds to perilous weather! When we take shelter in a 'full-fledged body-hull,' when we set our sails, rely on the laws of gravity, espouse our waves and opposing elements… we succeed in riding emotional storms.

Our welfare lies in such 'Conscious sailing,' while resting our hand on a sensitive tiller! So equipped, I can navigate my inner and outer trials… maybe not without work, pain or risk, but without losing myself and without losing you. When Mindfulness and Love set my course, I know how to change heading, how to run before the gale, how to anchor securely in hospitable ports when 'Inner births' are at hand.

I found that a good sailor simply leans on what is given. I found that there is nothing on the high seas of life that we should evaluate as good or bad; as fair or unfair. This helped me feel less and less excluded, fearful, guilty or judgmental; and this may well be the definition of serenity.

So let us cherish the boat, breathe in accord with the wind and the sails… unfurl the being, run with the flow, steady the ship against the sea; embrace our own Mystery. Let us come and go in the arms of Being… anchor in our Center, in the entrails, in the Heart.

There is movement and there is rest, and both are inscribed in the movement and the rest of the Universe.

◆

Each time I am tempted to run from myself, the little inner voices, the little inner hands call me back! 'Not without me! Not without my antennas that capture the invisible,' chirps the Grasshopper. 'Not without my tender paws,' grumbles the Teddy bear. 'Not without my swift legs,' shouts Friday. 'Not without my innocence and joy,' hums little Aurora.

Was I again about to take off, dismissing my crew like outgrown dreams?

I could never do so for very long. Whoever is waiting to be seen, heard and associated, will not let me silence him! I decided to never forget any of my 'Inner Companions' again. Now we are inseparable: Together we inhabit this conscious, loving, sheltering *Boat-body*... a Boat-body that can also include and welcome all those we meet along the way.

And this is nothing less than the modern version of Noah's famous Ark! And our crossing of the Great Waters, is the *remembering* of the initial Covenant between God and the Earth, from stones to plants, to animals, to men and angels—on the way back to their Homeland in Him

When the Grasshopper extends his antennas, when Aurora starts to sing, when Friday jumps on deck, everything quivers and sways: Our craft is full of life! Together we harness Energy, Presence, Winged Imagination... whilst also relying on strong ballast, rounded sides and a clear deck!

To seize the tiller, all I have to do is place my hand softly over my Heart, pace my breath, set my intent and listen... envision the Inner Star guiding our course.

Aren't the most sought for truths right before our eyes? Is this why it is so hard to see them? Is this why, according to the Gospel, we should be 'like small children for whom the Kingdom is always open?'

At each stage of this apprenticeship, sailing my Ark, my Body- Boat, appeared to me more precious: So straightforward and faithful; a strong hull in the storm; a beautiful bird under the heavens. I didn't tire to speak with it, to question its wisdom, to carefully note the observations of its instruments. And as I marveled at its seafaring skills, I felt less alone.

Always eager to learn rather than despair, it has been with the help of many falls—swallowed, expelled, like Jonas from the belly of the whale—that I slowly gained substance. Substance of being, substance of feeling, substance of flesh and spirit! This showed me that the moment my 'body-heart-mind' and my awareness team up, they turn into a Vessel of awakened corporeal Presence.

To understand this more deeply I become a great ear… quiet and open, so that my senses might capture the slightest signal, my sails the slightest shiver of the air, my flanks the slightest pressure from the water.

I take interest and pleasure in following the wave, in beaching at low tide or mooring in restful havens.

When we make this 'Ark' our own, we align the will of man with the Will of God; matter with Spirit. We connect with the Loving Source who births and gathers us in Itself. And this will prove true for you if you initiate a '*self-holding environment*' and put it to the test in your daily practice.

📖 *You are now invited to go to Volume II, Exercise 6*
The Experience of 'The Posture of the Aware Self'
The Womb-Body, the Boat-Body

XI

Everyone is a Universe

*"We become radiant when we stand
in the center place, within the triangle
of me, my neighbor and God"*[13]

Many of my guidelines are rooted in my childhood's affinity for the North American Indians and their teachings. I owe them some of my earliest learnings—something I recognized as part of myself, like an exile who remembers the shores and songs of his fatherland! My true abode, I felt, was in the circular wombs of their tents, in the midst of the rounded horizon of the boundless prairie.

I felt inspired by their heroic bearing, by their intimate connection to the Great Spirit, to beasts and plants; by their trust in a 'cosmic blanket' shedding unfathomable abundance into our minds, hearts, bodies and surroundings.

Of faithful friends, of lovers, they say that their souls unite above them in a rainbow—while they lie with one another, walk side by side or join through space in spirit.

I still have the peace pipe that our secret kinship had inexplicably delivered from America to Europe, and into my young hands. An original Lakota pipe, carved from their sacred red stone,[14] extracted from their holy mountain.

Carried on the wings of breath, its hallowed smoke

---

[13] Richard Moss. 'Words that Shine Both Ways.' Enneas Publ., Oakhurst, CA, 1998

[14] Catlinite, also called Pipestone, is an argillite (metamorphosed mudstone) reputed to carry the energy of connecting the spiritual and the physical. It is used to ground prayer and ritual into the physical, everyday life.

traveled for me *The Seven Directions of Space,* turned my battles to stillness, my isolation into brotherhood; steadied inner and outer Universe.

The *First* breath I blew to the East for life to be reborn; the *Second* to the South for warmth and love to unfold; the *Third* to the West to cradle the dying; the *Fourth* to the North to honor Wisdom; the *Fifth* went down into the belly of the Earth, our nourishing Mother; the *Sixth* ascended to Father-Sky, uniting us to Everlasting life. The *Seventh,* I gathered with awe into my Heart, welcoming in it all creatures. Conscious breath and sacred smoke journeyed through Space, linked its Seven Directions, balanced the tilting World; invited all life forms to be Allies.

◆

Let us see how the wisdom of this cosmic ritual can enhance our body-consciousness in our daily life.

Every one of us is a microcosm in a wider universe. Like small earths in their atmospheres, we have our own gravity and attraction field. We have our nucleus, our Center.

Try a leap into practice:
Choose a moment when something hurts or threatens or destabilizes you.

- Prior to any analysis of your inner turmoil, re-establish your physical posture, gravity and orientation.
- Straighten your spine, your Vertical axis between earth and sky. Ground yourself deep into the soil under you. Reconnect with your sense of Gravity by letting your weight drop below the waist; settle into your base, into your seat, into your feet, into your roots.
- Now, establish yourself in the midst of the Six Directions of space. Link with the four cardinal directions: In front, on

the left, on the right and behind you. Include the above and the below.

- Now unfurl yourself as a Volume with the help of your breath: Fill your entire body from tip to toe as if it were a giant lung. Sense your physical boundaries at skin level; add 30 cm all around to include your Energy field.

- Settle into your Center—in your chest or belly. Inhabit it by simply placing a loving hand right there.

- Gather all these elements in your Awareness: your Vertical axis, your Grounding, the Six Directions of space, your physical and energetic Volume and your chosen Center in the midst of them.

- Feel! Be aware of a new quality of Oneness, spaciousness, stability and peace in your whole being.[15]

You will discover to your surprise and relief that once you tune into a rooted and oriented perception of *your body-self in space*, you simultaneously begin to recover your psychological balance!

Our physical, emotional, mental and spiritual fields not only overlap, but congruently superimpose! All four are so sensitive, that they expand, shrink, build up or falter in relation to each other with every move. They behave as reciprocally harmonizing systems. By perceiving them and relating to them more consciously, we can learn to pilot them from any starting point in the service of overall stability.

To adjust and poise our physical body first... is much simpler than appeasing and sorting out a commotion in thoughts and feelings! We can efficiently help ourselves by redirecting our focus... away from our rudderless projections and back to a centering in our body.

Throughout the ages, the expressions of language have

---

[15] ***See also:*** Exercise 6, Volume II. The Experience of 'The Ark Within.' Establishing the Posture of the Aware Self. The Womb-Body, the Boat-Body.

shown how the body's attitudes and gestures and our feeling tones intimately interact and reflect each other.

Don't we say, to describe our moods and reactions:

"I'm blown away. I'm walking on clouds. I'm over the moon. My heart soars. I lost track. I feel disoriented. I need to gather my thoughts. My heart tightens. I lose foot. I falter. I stand on firm ground. I fade off to sleep. I am paralyzed with fear, shocked into silence. I regain my senses. He flipped his lid, he blew his top, flew off the handle; he got carried away. This breaks my heart. I follow my heart. She is broad-minded. She is narrow-minded. He is cold hearted, warm-hearted, soft-hearted. She has no heart. I'm depressed. I feel crushed. I feel on top of the world. I have to forge my character. She is upset, she is out of balance; he is out of his mind, beside himself with anger; weighed down by guilt. I pull myself together."

And these aren't only metaphors! They show us the inter-relationship between our bodies and the 'personifications' of various energies inside us; they signal *Inner selves,* who take shape in our billions of cells; who call for recognition via postural, muscular, sensory, nervous and hormonal variations.

When you are distressed, when your spirit abates, if your mind goes blank, if your courage falters, if your anger flares: Remember the laws of Gravity, the 'Seven directions and your Volume in space!' They structure the Cosmos; they structure your body; they regulate your psyche... with four simple words and actions: Gravity, Orientation, Volume, Center.

Set them up consciously; direct your own microcosm. Encompass and welcome inside it whatever arises. Feel how your *Inner selves* now nestle like birds in and around you. Hold them near to your heart. Feel the joy, the energy, the soft wind in your sails.

What shuts can open; what grows tense can relax; what is knotted can untangle. It is possible to free our soul by adjusting and tuning the body; to assuage physical pain, to console grief, by resting our hand upon it. It is such simple relating, such loving interaction with ourselves, that steers our ship and secures our navigation.

We can experience our 'aware body-vessel' as it unfolds into a *sphere* or as it wanes into a *point*. Ultimately, and this isn't the slightest of paradoxes… we can relax into the dissolution of our egotistic contractions—by absorption into the infinitely small or by expansion into the infinitely wide.

◆

From all I learned in my life, nothing was ever really far from the inner vistas that comforted and instructed my youth.

When I turned fifty—long after the lessons of the peace pipe!—the discovery of 'Voice Dialogue,' imported to Europe from the States, gifted me with a Vision and a tool that integrated paradox, married conflicting forces, unified inner and outer world.

The personal Tribe, the realm of nature and the Tribe of humankind; the male and the female, the welcomed and the disowned, past, present and future, could now flow together and head for a shared journeying within Consciousness.

My body itself, my awareness and my days—by becoming the 'Ark where all can abide,' found their transpersonal purpose, their kinship with the Universe.

XII
The Mandala-Self

Consciousness and Creation are two Lovers birthing Uniqueness, Brotherhood and Freedom. We are challenged to become *Noah's Ark in Awareness*; to shelter and redeem in *It* all forms of life, all forms of self, in the Womb of Love.

Once we have learned to redeploy ourselves as a Living Volume—in which our emotions and behaviors can ebb and flow in conflict as well as in peace—we gain Equanimity. But to steer our navigation, we need to reopen this 'Ark of our Heart' on a regular basis, in order to meet and encompass our *Inner selves* as they arise within us—often like an undisciplined crew or worse like a bunch of mutineers on our ship!

Taken in clusters, they form what we call our survival personality, our ego; what we refer to as: *That's me*! As physical and psychological survival devices, they largely function as reactive autonomous systems. When balanced, these serve us, but like all preset structures they do get out of hand, thereby becoming damaging rather than resourceful and protective.

Addressed, perceived and dialogued with separately, our changing energies can be met as *Inner persons*. Each of them clothes into one of our behavioral, emotional, mental and spiritual expressions. They convey our resources, our defense strategies, our contradictory impulses, our denials, our afflictions, our inspirations. They have in common that they all partake in the same sensitive flesh—our own! Each one of them hopes, suffers and waits for love; our aim, in developing a more and more *Aware Self,* is to tune into their particular keynotes; is to listen to them as we would to friends asking us for our understanding and help.

What we show, hide, feel, ignore, favor or criticize, is akin to the *multiple enactment* of a very large *Inner family*. And our task can become that of a Peacemaker, starting with our Inner world! We thereby alleviate stress, take distance, hold the tension of opposites and set a frame of care and security to what inhabits us. The more we probe into such a perspective, the more we will experience ourselves as a 'reciprocal reflection,' a continuous exchange of deepening connection, between inner and outer Universe.

Envisioned in the eyes of Conscious Love, this can be understood as our personal embodiment of a divine 'Field of Loving Intelligence,' in which everything divides and multiplies into an infinite number of *sub-fields* that are perpetually conceived and dissolved. Our consciousness process then becomes an overall *Mandala-Self*, a 'Remembering of divine *Isness*,' a Presence to be sensed and to be met inside us, in every fellow man, in the most infinitesimal particle of energy and matter.

The 'mandala,'[16] basically a circle, is a symbol of the universe and by extension a 'holding environment,' a symmetric space—in which a variety of elements organize around a center and within boundaries. As a guiding image for meditation, 'mandalas' are usually represented in two dimensions, as a world or temple viewed from above, in which the distribution is flattened out. The Swiss psychologist Carl Gustav Jung has used them as powerful creative ventures with his patients to further emotional healing and restore balance in the psyche.

And indeed 'mandalas' manifest in countless modulations of structure and stability in inner and outer realms: Each atom is a dance of electrons around a nucleus; each

---

[16] Sanskrit word, literally 'circle,' is a spiritual symbol in Hinduism and Buddhism, representing the universe.

cell has its membrane, center and contents; most fruits have a core and flesh, surrounded by a skin or husk. Our societies and their architectures reflect them. Cities were traditionally built around their palace or their cathedral and protected by enclosing walls. Countries establish themselves around a capital, a government, a faith; they clearly mark their borders. Our earth has its axis, an incandescent center, a beautiful crust… it is enveloped by an atmosphere that filters out the rays of the sun and insures us a safe breathing space. Our human body organizes around our heart; our skin protects and contains our flesh and organs; we are surrounded by an aura, that radiates our unspoken messages and insures us a personal energetic space.

Why should our psyches, be structured differently? We have access inside us to a 'Transpersonal Heart, a Core Axis,' an original nucleus, around which our varying physical, mental, emotional and spiritual *selves* gravitate in the evolutionary field of our consciousness. A field that connects us to the Deeper, the Higher, the Wider… A field enclosed in a more mysterious one that we used to call God.

Isn't our task the most beautiful: To tune and shape our 'personal microcosm,' like one would a lute or a sail; to sing, dance and reflect the Spirit that imbues us and Creation itself with a Soul.

XIII

The Return to the Civilized World
Everyone Has an Inbuilt North Star
And Can Hold the World in *His Ark Within*

As a child, I wasn't aware of what I knew, yet with the reliability of a migrating bird, I felt drawn toward a Spiritual Pole like the Lover toward the Beloved, the heliotrope toward the sun! I was eager to decipher the clues, winks and synchronicities that lead to it: Inner and outer signs! To this day they easily catch my eye or leap into my hands like magical companions of my Quest. They are the unspoken Language of Matter, of the Unseen; the disguised Messengers of the Self.

What is inbuilt in flowers, in birds and fishes—as they turn or return to their Source, to their Birthplace, to create offspring—is also inbuilt in us humans, in every one of our cells... as our most intimate North Star. Even so early on, most things prompted an unending dance of questions in me. How to free myself while keeping safe? How to protect myself without excluding you? How to shine and share without losing my treasure? Yes surely, Hope and Despair, Life and Death, Joy and Sorrow, circle around us like bewitched Lovers who cannot separate!

I still recall my delight and anticipation as a child, when gathering the first chestnuts blown to earth! Split open, their prickly shell revealed their luster, their smooth inner strength and frailty: Velvet clouded with dew—filling me with wonder and possessiveness. But disappointment soon followed. Stripped of their protection they tarnished quickly and their magic was gone. This often left me with a foreboding of waning youth and fading love. But I also discovered that chestnuts, when caressed in my pocket… miraculously preserved their fragile brilliance! Decades later, I still burn with an intense nostalgia and determination to let go of my prickly thorns, to 'give myself without tarnishing,' to open up without becoming prey to the other, to expose my softness without getting hurt.

◆

I didn't foresee though, that I would need years of pondering in solitude and exile, on islands where my rebellious and despairing adolescence and later shipwrecks left me. It is only after learning to navigate through hope and sorrow without letting go of the tiller, that I could return, by the Grace of God and with the help of my 'Inner Ark,' to the shores inhabited by our society.

Having been away for so long, I discovered the world with greater clarity. Much to my surprise, I realized that on the threshold of the 21st century, the human continent had split into a giant archipelago! Countless *Robinsons* are now living separately on minute private islands.

The circulation is intense and bustling, but the values that have bound us together for millenniums, that used to guide us collectively, no longer weave the strong fabric uniting us for better and for worse. Our rites of passage, our connection with something greater, the commitment to family, homeland and the social group have worn thin.

The more we dwell in huge impersonal cities, the more we migrate far from our home-countries—the more we feel exiled and excluded! A growing number of people divorce, remain childless, single, or long-standing widowers; feel left aside in reason of mutual estrangement, illness, old age or broken family ties. Although wars and forced exodus have always existed, such an overall dismantlement of our closer ties has never happened in the two million years that separate us from the first tribes. Community is no longer our holding environment.

To counterbalance this individualistic isolation, to bridge our scattered islets, we urgently need to respond to the decline of age-old codified relating by a step-up of mindful connection and conscious relationships.

Increasing solitude, the denial of a spiritual foundation, the spurning of sacred relating—suppressed by materialistic views and by cannibalistic consumerism—quickly renders our lives rootless and meaningless. Slowly and painfully, we come to realize that human beings do not bloom, do not find happiness, unless the feeling of belonging and sharing is upheld. Deprival of linkage is the open door to despair, to a 'loss of self' setting us adrift on the sea of all hazards.

Ongoing expectation to be acknowledged is a trying concern: We are in danger of spending our entire lives relentlessly seeking our identity in others or in illusionary self-images! While we go on hoping to be held and reflected... recurring disappointment, evasive arms and flawed mirrors, will ruin our relationships and silence our joys.

What should we do? What can we do, in the face of an environment that leaves us cut off in the midst of a gridlock and will eventually destroy us? Child abuse, conflicts, divorce, displaced populations, poverty, unemployment, involuntary solitude, dormitory towns, concrete walls for the young, dead ends for the old, abound. There has never been a society—from the most barbaric to the most civilized—where we would have lived so alone; without partaking in a community throughout our lives and without referring daily to shared meaning and values. Families, religion, society, have become dysfunctional and torn envelopes.

Overwhelming technological changes outgrow and accelerate our innate rhythms beyond the bearable. The 'biological man' still walks at more or less 4 km per hour, still sleeps and eats as he used to in the Stone Age! Will our bodies and psyches be able to stomach this escalation of the ever new, of an ever increasing social and psychological pressure? Can we, under such conditions, stay healthy, keep in touch with our 'natural self,' while also listening to our Deeper Self?

We stand, I believe, before a total change of paradigm that requires of us to replace or complete our past models of 'assigned relating,' with new and experimental models of 'aware relating.' This is a serious challenge, but also a wonderful opportunity to break fresh ground in a context where a mere return to the old seems way over our heads.

◆

Only since approximately 1950,[17] has 'scientific data' started to corroborate that a baby is not just an alimentary canal, but *a Person*;[18] a person whose sanity depends on 'active reciprocal linking' with a consistent caregiver. Save this, the newborn is in danger to die or to never learn to relate in a healthy balanced way.

The irony is that the so-called primitive man and innumerable animal species have known this instinctively for millenniums!

Further research has highlighted the infant's urgent

---

[17] *See: René Spitz.* He began his research in the area of child development in 1935. He was one of the first to use direct child observation. In 1945, he investigated children in a foundling home, bringing evidence that emotional deprivation (the loss of a loved object) for more than five months in the 1st year, produces irreparable psychosomatic damage to normal infants. He called this 'hospitalism.' His film 'Psychogenic Disease in Infancy' (1952) shows the effects of emotional and maternal deprivation on 'attachment.' The film was the cause of major change, in childcare sections of institutes and hospitals.

[18] *See* : 'Le bébé est une personne' (The baby is a person). A triple video (3 x 1h) French television TF1 1984

need of a *holding environment*[19] and a dependable *mirroring*. Disturbances and traumas in infancy being repeatedly reactivated in adulthood, the above data has then widely inspired 'relational integrative psychotherapy.'

My personal hypothesis has been that what proves fundamental for the biological child and similarly in therapeutic procedures with adults—can also be successfully *self-applied* as a healing device with one's 'Inner child.'

Events, as such, are in the past. But the 'little person' who experienced them is fully alive in our cellular memory and therefore permanently accessible. It abides in us with its unsolved suffering in a timeless dimension of our bodies and psyches.

And the good news, indeed, is that we can alleviate our wounds, let go of our binding expectations—by becoming a '*Loving Other*' to ourselves. The evolution of our cortex and frontal lobes has gifted us with an extraordinary asset: The aptitude to relate intimately to what we feel;' to become one's own Witness and Caretaker; to create a 'self-holding-environment in our awareness' that we uphold in our bodies and plug into our deep-set Love!

Our own 'body-heart-and-mind-continuum' can become a *self-holding environment* for our wounded selves; can respond to them with integrative self-mirroring and self-linkage procedures. And we can learn to meet and heal 'identity construction and attachment deficit.' We can free ourselves from recurring distress, from persistent affective dependency in our couples and partnerships; from therapeutic dependency and high inferring social cost.

I have experienced these premises as a 'Voice Dialogue' facilitator for over twenty years and found them very efficient.

---

[19] D.W. Winnicott: 'The Maturational Process and the Facilitating Environment,' Ed. Karnac, London 1990 'Playing & Reality' Tavistock Publ. 1971 Chap. 9: Mirror-role of Mother and Family in Child Development

Regardless of age and culture, we can create for ourselves a *relational biotope* by means of physical, emotional, mental and spiritual self-connection, self-holding and self-containing. We thereby help ourselves to regain basic security, trust and love and to mature into fully individuated humans.

It's up to us to become the 'selfless mirror' that reflects how we feel and who we are, with kindness and with truth. A mirror that does not confuse the subject and the object; cleared of the fears, desires, judgments and expectations carried by our parents and our egos; cleared of what we project unknowingly on self and others.

What is vital for the developing infant, remains vital throughout life. What we lack ceaselessly strives towards replenishment. Without understanding why, we turn our clothing, our houses, our couples, offspring, professions, power, sex, social status, material possessions, opinions and knowledge, into 'cocoons for our hungry selves!' Our 'insecure child of the past' goes on waiting within us to be understood and embraced. Sooner or later, the adult we become has to face eluded personal truth and wholeness.

Our famished souls and hearts want to partake in their Source; in a quality of relating that founds inner peace. To turn within—instead of mainly without—will help us to reverse our perspective; to support what really fulfills us.

The practice of 'Voice Dialogue,' has provided me with the means to know and to cherish myself. By embodying consciously my *vulnerable selves* as well as my *power selves*, I was surprised and moved by their humaneness. And this is what really motivated me to seize my own hand with tender care; to call to redemption in Awareness and Love 'whoever inhabits me…' all the way—from 'Inner terrorist to Inner innocent!'

The lost thread unravels the knitting. It is our responsibility and our privilege to pick it up and tie it in again; to *re*-member the vagabond soul, to befriend who in us feels prey to pain and disorientation. Self-awareness and self-empathy enable us to reflect *who* suffers inside us; to pronounce affectionate responding words, to embrace ourselves with our own holding arms, and so soothe our wounds, while also supplying us with a *model* for a respectful and healing connection to others.

Whatever your age or your life story, sense and listen to what touches you! Watch for these signs given to you by your 'Inner child.' They signal its questions, its hopes, its fears, its suffering. They are the clues to the awaited *Answers* that will revive Inner Joy. For truly, question and answer are one, like lover and beloved, like head and tail of the same coin.

◆

As soon as I watch and listen… little Aurora's faith, Friday's trust, resurrect in me! Again I head for my North Star… in quest of the Pole ingrained in my Heart. Again I invite and unfold the 'Ark Within;' the Ark we all remember, that awaits us in the Memory of Love, in the vibrant recollection of our cells.

The other day I rediscovered an ancient Friend in my toy chest, in my Treasure Chest. And this is what makes treasures extraordinary: They wait forever to be found. As soon as I had glanced into the old trunk, I saw it. My Matrioshka doll! Smiling at me as if we had never parted!

In case you don't know what a Matrioshka doll is, I'll explain: 'It is a Russian version of Noah's Ark, carved in the likeness of a large wooden doll, shiny, colorful, solid, cheerful, and shaped much like an egg. A kind of Womb-body that looks at you with big eyes, yet without revealing what it hides in its entrails! But it opens, and inside it there is *another* smaller doll that also opens to uncover *another*, even smaller doll. And that's how it goes! Each *houses* the next—down to the *smallest*, minute like a Lilliputian compared to Gulliver."

My special own Matrioshka doll has the face of a clown. Perhaps it is a Father-clown, because inside, guess what… you discover a blond healthy Mother; and inside the mother an elephant; and inside the elephant a lion; and inside the lion a tiny, tiny, baby girl! Together they are my *Inner family of selves,* embedded in my Fun-Womb, in the Divine Trickster that shakes us awake with contrary lessons. Each inner family member is different in age, sex, nature and character. When I assemble them all in my hand or in my heart, we embody the diversity of the world.

I hold these numerous *selves* in my Body, Psyche and Heart. This is very practical for love, for relating, for traveling as one, for never abandoning the tiniest by keeping it safely in my midst! Now that I have taken the 'Matrioshka way' into my everyday life—and with it the Inner family it harbors, we jointly write this book. I invite every self to take shelter in the womb of my awareness; the smallest into the largest so that my little girl isn't afraid, isn't alone. Every morning we wake up together, we renew our dialogues and play. In the evening, we go to sleep, one within the other, cradled in the secure space of our Loving Self.

I believe the whole Universe is magnetically pulled toward a Pole of the Heart, an Orient of all Hearts, called Love, called God. For whenever we lose track of it, we feel deprived and hollow; we yearn to find our way back to the wholeness and the sharing we miss. A universal Matrioshka is present in every one of us! She teaches us that all our *Inner Persons* hope to be rediscovered in their cellars and attics and taken on board. Like forgotten travelers of our past, they wait to be rescued from chaos, exclusion and flood. They wait to be invited at last into 'The Ark Within.'

Robinson, the Cannibals, Aurora and Friday, the Teddy Bear, the Maple tree, the Grasshopper, the Indian Chiefs, the Fair and the Dark Knights, roaming in our souls, lend their voices to all kinds of Selves in me; Selves who feel too fragile or too wild to find their way in this urbane society. Some are jungle selves who could shatter you with one blow of their fist; some are delicate vulnerable selves, like mountain berries, like daisies from the field. Consciously and unconsciously, we house countless 'Inner beings.' Their energies, tears and smiles, reflect the same questioning, the same patient despair, the same aggressiveness... but also the same brightness, the same spontaneous tenderness, which every other creature holds in itself.

Because 'what is outside is like what is inside,' we can recognize—in the children, adolescents, women, men, and elderly, who vibrate in our own interior world, the feelings and contradictory selves that animate our fellow humans in the outer world. And this will really help us to acknowledge their anger and their fears, to embrace their trembling love and their choking sorrow, with lucid empathy. With openness and compassion we rediscover that in our diversity we can be truly One.

I look at the world. I feel this incredible multitude quivering within me. I feel my kinship with a Universal Ark! Laughter explodes and joy carries me off... How could I fear abandonment when the Universe is my tribe! Wonder takes hold of me. I have the Body of a giant like Gulliver! In me I have water, fire, stars... the Lover and the Beloved, people that turn into boats, branches that become arms, leaves that flutter like sails... Floods can come and set us adrift in the void without even a port showing itself on the horizon... we will remain as One. 'Magic is nothing more than a shift in consciousness."[20]

The Grace of God, who for all eternity excludes no one— and our resolve to accept this for ourselves, suffices to enter this greater dimension of Being. For Love is enough to open

---

[20] Jamie Sams, "Sacred Path Cards," Harper S.F. 1990. Seneca quote from the Wolf clan.

the Heart, to probe the Heart, to discover God in it; to offer a haven to the world.

And we take so long to know and remember it!

May we never forget the Divine Child that stands guard in our depth over our Source and our Completion. It is re-born in every child opening for the first time—in wonder and defenselessness, his eyes upon the world. May we remember that Human sciences are meant to be an art in midst of a dehumanized technological society; an art to transmute rea-son into kindness and trust. An art of healing our lacks and failings '*by learning to perceive attack as a call for love*,'[21] by lifting the veil from our inbuilt treasures, buried under so much construction waste.

This vision, this awakening, transforms whatever I ac-knowledge into someone I meet, a double, a Companion. Exile, separation are no more. No longer will we be strangers to each other. Friday, you will never again be this dark fugitive before me!

There in the middle of my own chest—where I so often feel pain, longing, or loss—a serene Void expands, something grows in its Center like a Shining Egg. It radiates an unknown incandescent softness; it burns without burning. Is this the same as the Holy Grail?

Is this the Nameless… the Nameless Love that all crea-tures sing, unfold, whisper? It is the Love we all carry and can never forget and can never forsake.

It is in me for sure; yet it is not 'of me.' I am unable to account for its Origin, to retrace its course. It emanates from nowhere and from everywhere. It dwells in me, in you, in ev-ery one of us! It is the air we breathe; it is our Essence, Life's

---

[21] *See* 'A Course in Miracles.' Text. Chapter 12. II. Ed. Foundation for Inner Peace, Mill Valley, California.

very substance…whose organ, whose place of convergence is our innermost Heart.

You are now invited to go to Volume II, Exercise 7
Re-parenting your 'Inner Child'.
Unfolding a Womb.
Becoming a Mirror to Your wounded selves.
How to use Your first aid Kit.

XIV

The Meeting in the Mirror

At first it happened in the dark, far from these inhibitions born from the scrutiny of others. In the dark—where, like never before—I broke free from my usual me, to fully put myself into the skin, mind and heart of a movie star.[22]

But this didn't happen right away. At the beginning of the film, I found the actress to be ugly. Her nose was too big, her eyes too close together, and her mouth too large for her face—and all this set above a weak chin... But then, something extraordinary occurred: Her face began to change. She had a way of reaching out for love, of delivering something of her soul that slowly rendered her beautiful.

She became more and more intensely present, she grew prettier and prettier, haloed with shining aliveness and I was irresistibly drawn in. I vibrated with her love and with her pain, I moved into her as easily as a leaf taken in by the wind.

The way she related to the man that she learned to love and trust, transformed her, right there, before me, into the most fascinating and unique woman! And my body echoed every one of her feeling states: I shape-shifted as magicians do in strange tales!

Warmth and intelligence remodeled all her traits, and I became aware of her incredible seduction. The Universe embraced her. The entire earth was falling in love with her—from the plants, the animals, the men, the women, the children, the birds in the sky, the waves in the ocean... all the

---

[22] Barbara Streisand in the movie "The Prince of Tides."

way to the tiniest grain of sand. She was their Queen, their treasure, their spouse, their child, and whatever she touched simply blossomed, and so did I! I participated in this miraculous regeneration. I was radiant, intense, loving, loved—I glittered like a star.

I left the theater swept up in a dream, walking over the bridge leading to my home like one who crosses forever into another dimension… Then, with the suddenness of a dark cloud that cuts the warmth of the sun, I realized I wasn't her, just the ordinary *me*. A brutal sadness overwhelmed me. The elation, the trust, I had felt an instant before, drained out of me with the abruptness of a shiver. Doubt took hold. "*Who am I,*" I wondered? Who inhabits this silhouette walking over the bridge? I felt foreign to myself. I didn't know my own face anymore.

I started to run.

Defeated and out of breath, I shut the door of my apartment that protected me from an outside world that had now become disquieting. I desperately needed to look into the mirror to make sure I still existed! In this state of disarray, I looked straight into my face; into my-self.

And there, like shining water that engulfs the one who bends over it, my reflection took me in; my soul called me home through my own tear-filled eyes. And at that very moment I discovered I was beautiful, beaming, feminine. My tears sparkled like dew. I had never seen myself like this before: Transparent, molded not of flesh but of water and light. A timid innocent smile came to meet me. In truth, it was Aurora's smile I saw. I do not know which loved the other first. She rose out of the mirror, naked, fragile and selfless; a frightened child no more, a woman born out of the waves, eternally young.

Flooded with gratitude, and so miraculously close to life, I understood that Love does not depend on our perfection, but springs from welcoming ourselves as we are: in joy and pain, in trust and doubt, miserable and splendid, forsaken and yet found.

I realized that the magic spell I'd experienced earlier wasn't only cast by the actress on the movie screen, but by a Universal radiant Self that is reflected in everyone of us. In this blessed instant, I understood that each Soul blends with every other, regardless of illusion, regardless of despair.

Whenever I recognize you, whenever I recognize myself, whenever we face each other without a veil, we become the Beloved and the Lover.

📖 ***You are now invited to go to Volume II, Exercise 8***
The Experience of the Meeting in the Mirror

Part Three

The Night of the Cannibals

"The feeling of insufficiency is the cause of all desires. When you know that you lack nothing, that everything exists within you, is you, all desire vanishes."
—Nisargadatta Maharadj, 'I am that.'

XV

Where I Discover that I Too Am a Cannibal

When I feel hurt or deceived, a paralyzing net makes me forget, how vast my heart was only instants before. I lose my axis; I lose my unlimited space. My 'field of conscious energy' depletes… like sails gone limp in a sudden shift of the wind! I collapse into a little heap of misery within a bag of skin. Emotional confusion, defensive reactions ensnare me in their web.

Experience showed me that when a friend or loved one is being secretly unfaithful or cooling down in his affection… I glide instinctively into an unexplained depression. My senses numb, life turns colorless, my blood runs cold; my horizon narrows to a slit! Until… the defector himself opens my eyes! Until truth dispels the fog: For instantly the depression lifts, propels me into action, while despair and anger shake me alive in the turmoil of a sudden gale.

Like a surfer overtaken by a dark, erratic wave, I quest the golden thread that connects me to Trust. My fears desperately cling to the past; my hopes soar like spaceships to a would-be future.   Chaos takes hold of me. The *Ark* dismantles! Sensations, emotions, toss me into a number of panic stricken selves: 'Projected selves' that separate me from my inner grounding, delude me, distort my view of the other or wrap me into frozen indifference.

What has happened? How does a Sphere of warmth, of security, transform into such an inextricable and wounding entanglement? Why didn't I see this coming! How did I lose what was the most precious to my Heart? How could the person I love the most in the world, the father of my children, my Indian Brother with whom I smoked the peace pipe, become so unkind; more alien to me than a stranger?

I look at him. I look at me. For how long did I sell myself out to disloyal arms, to my own unconsciousness, to the muffling feel of absent minded embraces?

How long is it since I sailed joyously; since I warmed up at your side, watching our spring bud in your smiling eyes, feeling your hands fill me with softness and desire; how long since I blossomed?

For how long did I stay unaware, bound to a track that should—oh, surely!—keep me safely on rails; bring me straight to the end-station, to a fool-proof cover up, to the perfect companion; to the ultimate answer?

On and on… you and me… you or me… me or you… a dance of grabbing arms, of opposing selves, of averted eyes and flaring angers; a rigmarole of wants and fears. On and on, grain of sand by grain of sand, until a last grain of sand, a last letdown finally jams the complex workings of our life together.

The Day of painful awakening dawns; the excruciating experience of being set free, shattered and undone! My muscles, tendons, bones and nerves, are bared and scattered. This is a Day of cruel initiation. I cannot yet imagine that it also heralds an opening; that this *death* is also a door to my *rebirth*. The passage itself is a trial in solitude and mourning. I don't know how to survive without you, without us feeding on each other. Deprived of your reassuring needs and of my hopeful or demanding expectations, I feel like a dry twig set adrift… a no-thing, a no-body. To perceive that I still exist—meaningful and worthy, I would at all cost recapture you, bind us to each other!

I look at you. I look at myself. Is it our 'Inner Children' that both of us now abandon and betray? Is it my 'Inner

Mother' that you have fed on—before turning me over to oblivion? And what about our offspring, our four precious innocent youngsters, now brutally faced with fear and pain, because we are no more present to ourselves and to each other in the storm?

Whose rapacious hand tore our life apart? Were we just slaves to your hunger, to my famine? Who became our Jailer? Whose colonizing power has consumed our love? Is it mine? Is it yours? Were we nothing more than each other's prey?

Was it a god of feud disguised into the God of Love?

Is it some cruel unfeeling deity in us that leaves me bloodless, exhausts me, or obliges me to extract the juice of life from your throat, from your vein? Were you my Lover or my Enemy? I discover that I—the virtuous wife, the righteous Robinson, that you—the 'fair and tender Knight,' are as much cannibals as those who pursued Friday!

I feel trapped. Threatened by inner starvation, I am in danger of devouring everything! Threatened also by inner starvation, you finally escape without looking back, shutting the door in my face for the last time. I feel cheated. I have to free myself, whatever the price. I turn into a wild and powerful beast—intent to reclaim my candor, my trust, my womb, my heart, the strength of my arms and of my faithfulness.

◆

I vividly recall that beautiful afternoon, when Friday and I ran along the seashore, enraptured with air and movement… like the wings in love with the bird; like birds in love with the wind.

I recall how I felt at one, in the radiance of the now, in its iridescent sphere! But suddenly, the moment I spotted the ship on the horizon, its sails blown full of the wind of deliverance—and saw it bear off—it imploded like a bubble, turning my hope and joy to ashes!

Isn't this the common tale that wanes from our sight when the film ends? You and me... stories on a screen, reflected dreams! I carried your love—and you held mine, but the moment you left me, the moment I silenced my heart, our 'projected story' was swallowed by shadow like a cut off light beam, leaving each of us alone with our own conclusion of the final scene.

Night has fallen; I am sitting on my desolate island. Friday has disappeared. No vessel on the horizon. I am empty, silent, indifferent. The drum of my heart beats so faintly that I can no longer hear it. I feel more destitute than on the day when the storm threw me unconscious onto this beach. Aurora is crying.

◆

And I recall the life after you left. And how, one evening, long after this ship called 'marriage' had gone under, my existence was again shaken like an hourglass turned over.

The children and I were sitting at the kitchen table, and for a reason I can't recollect, what should have been a moment of sharing and harmony, abruptly filled with anger. A sudden storm of bitterness and rage swept over us. Violence took over, until finally my oldest son shouted at me: 'I wish you were dead!' hurling me into an abyss of grief and guilt.

Years of infidelity, lassitude and desertion overwhelmed me. Exhausted from crying, I fell on my bed engulfed by a darkness that seemed to carry no morning. I sank into a somber and bottomless sleep like a stone.

That night Existence showed me, in her own unique way, how she cares for those who totter like infants drunk with tears or fatigue. I didn't know that the abyss I was sinking into would welcome me into strong mothering arms.

Life opens to the helpless, to those who founder when no recourse is left. Providence itself protects the playing child, so unconcerned with death... too light to get caught in the net of time, too trusting to doubt the breast of the Earth, too loving to distance itself from the Heart of God; or too shattered to take hold anywhere.

As if touched by an invisible wing, a weightless hand, I awoke. My eyes opened to... the limitless. Beyond my window I felt immersed in the stillness of an immense and perfect sky; immeasurable like the depths behind closed lids. No rumor, no obstacle, no grief. What I saw, I perceived without eyes; what I heard, I heard without ears. What touched me was formless: Infinite space that contained the soul of everything yet leaned upon nothing! An expanding sphere absorbed me, and in truth I knew it also emanated from me. No hate, no guilt, no thoughts, no distress. I was silence; I was a void. I was peace.

That night I understood that the miracle of our resurrection happens in the epicenter of our abyss, in the instant of utter powerlessness, without past, without future, without desire and without fear.

This peace has never failed me since. This Holy boundless Space where all beings have their place! Heaven and Earth never separate, never close; they live deep within me—underlying everything as a tranquil Ocean underlies its waves.

Virgin Space and Mirroring Bounty revealed themselves in my most profound helplessness; and this secured forever my Trust and grounded the Faith that there is always enough Love. Ever since, I watch over this double horizon where—in-between opposing forces, in-between freedom and attachment—the heart lies open. It is in this discontinuity, in this dismantling of 'all preconceived and projected images of me,' that I know myself; that I know you; that God takes me into His Arms.

◆

Every day I try to be a sailor, to become aware of when I drift into judgment or into neediness, and readjust my route. I will to remember that suffering, my regrets, my errors, my illusions, and all my shadow selves—share the same birthright as my joys, my resources, my certainties, my wisdom. I will to remember that all are forever invited to find their reprieve in our divine Fathering Source; find their atonement in His Grace and their *at-one-ment* in 'The Ark Within!'

When we lose our balance, it is for us to decide to rebuild the *Ark,* to re-deploy the Sphere, to adopt and nurture this Inner world, this Inner family, entrusted to us. For each time we forsake who suffers and hopes inside us, our *Sphere* falters, our *Ark* takes on water, and we find ourselves in a sinking ship; in a 'dissociated self.' And this is what triggers rejection or mutual bloodsucking in our relationships!

The art of self-relating—that 'Voice Dialogue' helped me to discover and nourish—is certainly one of the most surprising ways to acknowledge the wonder we are; to discover and trust others in the same way and to take more and more pleasure in life's and in our own diversity and abundance!

Fusing is not relating: To 'join in and then to dis-identify from—and so separate consciously from blinding self-absorption, is precisely what renders a true face-to-face with ourselves and others possible. An 'Aware witnessing self' naturally emerges from it. Paradoxically, it is this gentle, wakeful and alert relating to our many faces that gives us access to the experience of our Entirety.

Falling in love, partnering, is too often the coming together of our wants and fears; of perceiving ourselves as incomplete, as two halves gone astray; a desperate reaching out for a lost or dormant *me.* We search for what might appease our feelings of lack, unaware that—in truth—we seek to extend and share a Divine Oneness that has since ever been part of us.

Now, whenever I feel hurt or betrayed, when I get pulled into the old familiar storm, I judge myself less. I work toward the Day when I will no longer judge you: The saving Dawn that dispels the Night of the cannibals!

I hadn't understood that love is a bridge. A bridge resting on two pillars, on different banks, where each of us has to stand rooted and steadfast in himself… if we are to sustain an overpass where love and freedom can meet! An overpass to peace where lovers share in the Wisdom of incoming and outgoing breath: Its 'hundred fold hourly rhythm,' teaches us to balance uniting and letting go, closeness and distance… teaches us to cherish each other without losing ourselves.

Just as sunset and sunrise, hot and cold, light and darkness, the full and the empty, are a Dance of Love, I cannot fight my own self. If I fail to hold in my arms my hidden face, my painful face, my condemned face, I will be but a shattered kingdom, and the earth forever a place of war, exclusion, ethnic cleansing. If I fail to hold you in my arms, your hidden face, your painful face, your condemned face, the earth will be forever a place of feud and segregation.

But I must confess that I am hard to teach: Time and time again, it is only when I have spent all my arrows, worn thin all the strings on my bow, reached my wit's end—that lost Wholeness reemerges from Grace, like a Mystery. It rises from beyond all self-images, from a rupture in my armor, clearing the way for the *Being*, like clouds parting to reveal the sky.

📖 ***You are now invited to go to Volume II, Exercise 9***
The Experience of the Unsubstantial Target

XVI

The *Yes* in the Impasse

*"If you want to know your
way, close your eyes
and walk in darkness."*

—St John of the Cross

Quite naturally, we return to our familiar tracks, believing they will lead us unharmed to our goals. And yet it happens that the innocuous path, so clearly marked an instant before, simply vanishes. Suddenly we awake in a different life, in a foreign landscape; in a 'story' we thought could never be our own.

At such times, a cruel and unpredictable hand, throws up a wall before us. The wall can be white or black, thorny, threatening, or smooth and cold as ice… there is no way through!

This is how, during one of those unforeseen darkest hours of my life, I surfaced as a stranger to myself, uttering words that weren't mine. Nothing in the texture of the floor, the odors, sounds or images, in the play of light and shadow upon my bedroom ceiling, reminded me anymore of what—only just yesterday—had been my reality, our bonding, the unyielding hope for the safety of my youngest son.

So often now, I had tried to follow him through the maze of the city, guessing the movements of his troubled being… the beating of my heart tracking his hiding place! So many times I went looking for him, my body tense, my breath suspended, blindly searching for him. So many times I had waited in anguish, leaning out of my window, listening—imploring the great muted space to resound with his steps! Even through the buffers of sleep, I sensed the distant rhythm of his heart, perceived the twist of the key in the door, the comforting sounds; the voice that murmured: 'I'm back, I'll be here for the night.' And then the clink of the glass, the water that runs in the kitchen-sink!

We were both deadlocked in incommunicable distress. He filled my universe with his tenacious self-destruction; I battled with relentless determination to rescue him. The path to his rehabilitation was confusing, strewn with snares, but at least a goal existed.

And then one day, without warning, he disappeared without trace. The world went empty of him; no news, nothing to hold on to. It wasn't as if he'd died. There was no cadaver to mourn, to entrust to the earth, no justified and shared pain. There was only an irrepressible anguish gnawing at me.

My mind became a 'theater of madness,' a rudderless ship between sky and abyss. My entire being was cornered and invaded by absurd divagations. This was my blind alley: To no longer have any traces of my son! Maybe I never lived anything more insane than this absolute powerlessness, this 'not knowing,' that tossed me back and forth between paralysis and a desperate run.

And yet, so often previously, I had reached what felt to be my limit with him, not imagining that worse was still to come. A year earlier, while sailing on a bright blue bay in the New World, when happiness itself should have blown our sails full—for no apparent reason, something within him had turned to ice, had completely shut down. I had witnessed this happening in him before, but it was in such contrast to his gentle, sensitive nature, that instinctively it made me deeply afraid. At first, I silently entreated him: 'Live, re-member yourself, remember life, remember us!' But other words, unforeseen words, incredible words, leaped from my lips: 'Die if you want, but without me. I will not go any farther with you.'

This harsh and foreign language of my own survival had suddenly drawn a pitiless boundary between us. He was losing his footing, and I let him go. My hand no longer caught him in his fall, no longer held back what I loved the most in this world. The unbearable pressure had silenced my heart, had seemingly untied what nothing in Heaven or on Earth could untie.

My own words surprised me like an overstretched rubber band that snaps. I don't think I realized that day that those words, so inappropriate from the mouth of a mother, had un-tethered us, forcing him out on his own, releasing us both from reciprocal constraint and entanglement.

But, autonomy can be painful. For a long time, freed prisoners still carry the stuffy smell from their cells… still bear the marks of fetters on their ankles. For a long time, they will feel their hearts and lungs burn from the fresh air that seizes them by the throat.

In a strange way, the familiar wounds of the past are more comforting to us than the embracing of the unknown.

And then came 'the day,' when without warning—he simply disappeared. The world went empty of him. Every endeavor to locate him failed. All that was left in my life's textbook, were the words: 'I don't know. I cannot.'

At first, my body and my intelligence went blank, drained of my animal-like perseverance, of my persistent loyalty, of my unbeatable resourcefulness. But then, my mind became a circus of delusions, the prey of wild spirits, of obsessive murmurs: 'He'll come back. No, he's lost forever. He lives! No he dies, he kills. No! He is innocent. He is loved. No! He prostitutes himself. No, someone teaches him, guides him, protects him…'

Was this a concrete wall, a bottomless abyss? Sometimes I raged, sometimes I sank into a pit of oblivion, as if forgetting could erase everything.

My sanity, my wisdom, my life experience, love, virtue and

courage exploded against a hidden reef, fooled by a geography I had never explored. Only a miracle could restore and assuage my spirit.

Could this possibly be only a nightmare from which one wakes in the morning? Could this possibly dissolve, like past beliefs, ancient images, projected on the screen of our mental fictions; fictions worn so thin that they fall from us like rags?

Again, it was only when I reached my own edge that a mutation occurred. Maybe the loss of the last recourse, of the last hope, cracked what I'd held as my identity— the very structure of my 'edifice of the self.'

For the condemned there is Grace. Redemption always waited for me in my most somber hours. When you can't go on, it is easy to give up, to let go… to 'die to oneself,' as they say. It is easy to become humble, when only radical unknowing is left. Isn't it precisely there that an Opening is revealed, that we are lifted into another Realm? That the blind wall that taunted us— crumbles?

One night, while my whole being still echoed from the sound of a revolted, despairing *NO*—without understanding how, without hope, without faith, without love—for all had left me from sheer exhaustion… I awoke as I was saying, or was it hearing: '*Why not trust him? Why not deliver him to his own Heart and Wisdom?*'

Someone or something in me uttered it; reversed the flight of the arrow, the course of my erratic thoughts and feelings. In the midst of this night of mind, body and soul, to my own utter surprise, I espoused Trust, my own powerlessness, the unacceptable disappearance, the bewildering destiny of my last-born child. I said YES: 'Yes, why not trust you, Basil?'

I took the unbearable, the unanswered, into my arms; this Shadow that defied my faith and my reason; the Shadow of our 'suffering self!' I took it all; I held it against me like a Loved one. 'Why not deliver you to your own Heart and Wisdom; to the Wisdom of the Lord of Love who encompasses your incorruptible Self? Are you not my Beloved Son? Have I not placed in you all my faith?'

Instantly, effortlessly, the veiling of my peace evaporated like mist before the sun. The *Divine*—He who 'nourishes the birds of the sky and magnificently clothes the humblest flowers,' He who is our most intimate Substance—arose in both of our torn hearts. There wasn't any Wall: The world was wide open, and serene. Peace imbued everything!

It never left me during the eighteen months I lived through, without a sign from my fifteen year old son.

◆

Nobody—not even myself—could understand this so unnatural serenity for a mother in these circumstances. It showed me that the *Yes* to the excruciating, to death, to our pain, the *Yes* to the 'Mystery of the other' …aligns us on the Living God within and without.

Unquestioning childlike surrender retrieves us from the chasm. It is the Vessel that takes us through the Waves; this simple, yet miraculous intent to trust, brought an answer to the Enigma of good and evil and of our suffering.

This is a secret of transmutation: Nothing less than total surrender to the Higher Will in which we are made One— is needed to change our Reality. Nothing more is required to discover that we have a Self familiar with emptiness, a Swimmer in vortexes, a Tightrope dancer without the rope, without the net… that we can navigate through despair and even death without dying.

Had I ever imagined before that I could find solid ground and direction in the Void or keep my balance in nothingness? No, I hadn't really experienced that the Void is the womb of all Births; that Darkness is the womb of Light; Silence, the womb of the Word, and Doubt, the womb of Faith.

There is a world behind the world, a perception behind perception. Losing my last hold revealed a hitherto invisible 'to be' that transcends what we call an 'impossible choice.' But there is one condition, we must diverge from our 'preset orbit' and step into the blind spot; into what we can neither master nor see.

However, there is no guarantee that embracing what scares us most will set us free. Preparing ourselves for such extreme situations is important, and it is difficult. This isn't something you can get used to! A move into nakedness, a break-up, a descent into isolation, into depression, will always be a leap into obscurity. It will always require your courage, even if it isn't the first time; even if you've already survived it once, been saved in extremis or blessed by a miraculous remission before! The risk is real: Our survival, our skin and spirit, our sanity are at stake... or it may be the life of someone else; of a husband, a wife, a daughter, a son. And it is always felt as an injustice; as the intrusion of an insane and cruel fate.

If this time comes for you... may you pledge your Intent! May you brace up your decision and reach out with your bare hands and torn heart for unconditional Trust.

◆

This brings me to what I feel to be the most powerful example of a dead-end: *The Impasse of Jesus.*

The moment comes. Jesus is aware of Judas' imminent betrayal, of the let-down, the denial by those dearest to him; he foresees his arrest, his crucifixion. He, who claims to be the Messiah, the Son of God, He who heals the sick and resurrects the dead, He who dares to announce the *now* of His Kingdom, knows he is about to be rejected, scorned, mocked and condemned.

And he goes up to the Mount of Olives to pray with his disciples.

"He takes with him Peter and James and John. He begins to feel anguish and fear and says to them:

'My heart is full of sorrow, even to death; remain here, and keep awake.'

'…And being in agony, he prays more earnestly and his sweat turns to great drops of blood falling to the ground.'

'And going a little farther aside, he throws himself on the ground and prays that this hour might pass from him.

He says, 'Abba, Father, for you all things are possible; remove this cup from me…'"

Yet, at this very instant, he chooses Trust. He says *Yes*: "…not what I want, but what You want."

As Jesus returns to the disciples "…he finds them asleep. He says to Peter: 'Simon, are you asleep? Could you not keep awake even for an hour?'"

Like each one of us, like anyone trapped in a mortal Impasse, Jesus suffers, he negotiates in anguish, he yearns to avoid it; he feels abandoned in his trial, even by those closest to him.

A few days from there, as if He were nameless and fatherless, Jesus is nailed to the cross; condemned among the outcasts and the criminals. The disciples stay mute or have fled, with the exception of John, of his mother Mary, and a few women. And the Kingdom does not appear. God is silent. The Heavens remain closed.

"The passers-by scorn him, shaking their heads and say: "You, who would destroy the temple and rebuild it in three days, save yourself! If you are the Son of God, come down from the cross." In the same way the chief priests also, along with the scribes and elders, mock him, saying: "He saved others and cannot save himself. He is the King of Israel; let him come down from the cross now, and we will believe in him. He trusts in God; he claims, 'I am God's Son,' let God deliver him now, if he wants to!

Even one of the two thieves crucified at His side, also taunts him in the same way."

Like each one of us, like anyone trapped in a mortal Impasse, Jesus falls prey to doubt and desolation. He trembles. "He cries with a loud voice: 'My God, my God, why hast Thou forsaken me?'"

But God stays silent.

His disciples, his friends, stand far off in fear. Only his Mother, his beloved disciple John and Mary of Magdala, have dared to remain at the foot of the cross!

And it is at this very moment, in this very place, in this instant of the greatest possible pain, of what feels like final treachery, in the midst of powerlessness and unknowing, that Jesus utters the most unlikely words—the most paradoxical prescription of Love and Faith:

"Father, into Thine hands I commend my spirit'"

He says 'Yes.' He trusts.

Mary holds Jesus' broken body. In Him she holds the totality of our 'suffering selves.' There, in her arms, she bears, her Loved One—the Unbearable, the Unanswered, the Son that life has not spared.

Yes. Why not have faith! Why not deliver ourselves and each other to Life eternal; to God who begets and fathers us instant by instant, because he is our timeless Source. Because He whispers inside our own heart: "Are you not my Beloved child? Have I not placed in you all my trust?"

And suddenly, we awake to a different life; a Life we never thought could be our own! Death itself comes undone… like scales that fall from our eyes.

Jesus says 'Yes.' With a simple statement of trust and surrender, he lifts the world into another dimension. He unknots what binds us. We have just crossed with Him to the 'Other side' of ourselves.

We stand in the bright morning before the Empty Tomb. Out of the Light a Voice says: "Why do you seek the Living One among the dead?"[23]

   📖 ***You are now invited to go to Volume II, Exercise 10***
The Experience of Saying Yes in the Impasse

---

[23] Quotes in above Chapter: Mark 14:33-34 / Luke 22:44 / Mark 14:35-37 / Matthew 27:39-44, 46 / Luke 23:46 / Luke 24:5/ The Bible, *The New Revised Standard Version* 1995

XVII
The Sacrifice

"Move your tent farther, bring your heart closer."
—Touareg Proverb

Having faith, while letting go, in times when not a single sign sustains our hope, will be a trying, lasting learning process, from our birth to our death. Life itself will confront us with it, and however experienced we get, it will always be a challenge.

Situations and people, I had imagined would stay forever, were taken away from me, against my will so to speak! And my apprenticeship often was at the price of these disruptions of destiny that taught me—as does a adamant parent who throws his child into the pool to train it to it swim.

Being a fighter and rich of resources, I tend to stay committed and faithful to the end. I only let go, if ever, of a dream, a pledge, a love, when the last recourse has deserted me. For a long time, it never occurred to me that I could give up on somebody or something, by deciding to become a ready partner to an adverse current… rather than battling to rise above it.

I used to find peace only when collapse itself made it easy to drop my arms. Wisdom has awaited me at the farthest end of bewilderment; met me when I gave in as one does to an irresistible Lover, to a paradoxical teaching that transcends even resolve, even the drive to survive.

Life showed me that it cherishes the ingenuous. It offers itself when we least expect it; when one can no longer distinguish the erudition of the wise from the babbling of infants. It meets us where opposites touch. It creeps into our flaws like a perennial plant that takes root in our minutest fissures.

Life also loves those who commit deeply and it didn't judge me for obstinacy! The moment I really listen to it, really risk it, it always presents me with my own Heart's deepest knowing.

To this day I become rich from my trials and losses. A devoted disciple always learns the right thing, whatever, whoever, the master. I keep at it; even though I stumble like a drunkard on my crooked unpredictable path. Audacity and shyness, confidence and doubt, still spin the web of my workings. Inner contradictions, outer trial, like a Hydra, constantly grow new heads—for one sole and unique Lesson: Embracing Trust in powerlessness.

So what is really conquered? What is freely mine? Only maybe what gives itself to me, what I surrender to... what I extend and share, what I release and return to its own path. And this requires of me that I truly face, take in, hold in my guts and heart, every single move in my life.

What I feel mine, is this humanity I water with my tears, I cultivate, plough, and pay for; is this patch of land and soul for which I risk my safety, my faith, my sweat. It is only there—in this fertilized soil of my flesh, of my love, of my intelligence, that I can offer understanding and hospitality. Even though it is imperfect, even though it is only lent to me, even though I will have to separate from it. And slowly Aurora's unvanquished love, together with my persistence to begin anew defuse my arrogance, disarm my rebellion; console my grief.

◆

Quite some years ago, I had the opportunity to rent a patch of garden. It is so minute, only sixteen square meters... that looking down on it from my third floor balcony you'd think you were seeing it from an airplane! But I can assure you that its magic is inversely proportional to its size! This garden called me, I wanted it; it made me wait, and then it became mine... for now, but not for ever.

Was it because it is so tiny, and my desire for it so unexpected... that, to begin with, it spontaneously shaped under my hands into a symbolic image of myself? In it I inscribed my questioning, my hope, the guiding lines that so quickly lose themselves in the maze of existence. Under the watchful and the unbelieving glances of my neighbors and the eyes of the stars, I exposed there something of my faith.

It is inscribed in a square, delimited by pink concrete garden bricks. Four symbolic doorsteps point to the four cardinal directions: east, south, north and west. A spiral—marked out with stones, polished and softened in the coming and going of the waves—unwinds in it. Its trail leads toward the Center or emanates from it... enclosing a step by step of flowers and herbs, dazzling or discreet like my joys and my pains; quickened by the waters from the sky and sometimes those of my sadness.

A 'mandala' of stones and flowers! It its workings, hopes and clear intent flow side by side—purifying, stripping, and baring themselves, under my tending hands; so as not to betray me, hide me or blind me; so as to honor my innocence as well as my falls, my lucidity and as well as my errors.

Like weeds, my projections, the meanders of my thoughts and emotions, continually take over; invade my inner and outer garden. Only vigilance enables me to see what has to go; to make space for free breathing. The dying, the withered, the cut off, are the price to pay for a transparency that I must serve with my back bent, or on my knees; by digging into, wrestling with... the weight of the earth.

With each encounter, with each separation, desire and fear, anger and hopelessness, are sure to show up. I can watch their grooves being dug and dug again by seasons, drought and rain. The weeds spread out at such a speed that they constantly exceed what I just entrusted to a cleansing fire. Life against life! Isn't the jungle of our memories... aren't idle thoughts, rekindled pains, the illusions and errors that take over inside me—also of skin and flesh? Don't they also tremble in the face of death; don't they thirst to live and be loved?

To tear out, to cut off makes me suffer. I've always hesitated to prune plants, shorten stems, discard what has become useless. I've always found it difficult to unbind that and those who cling to my trunk, or hook onto my branches.

It is no easy task to detach firmly but kindly; to feel hurt without attacking, without avoiding; to undo what is still alive within us, but needs to go. Yet isn't this the cost for not remaining a cannibal, for not feeding on possessiveness, for not preying on each other? The price of mutual freedom!

Again and again, I reexamine the teachings, the disciplines of my path. I try to walk my talk, to talk my walk, as American Indians say. Ad infinitum, I point to the moon, but why? For each time I point to the moon I mainly see my finger, and more often than not disillusionment follows. Yet, I do not tire of stalking love and lucidity beyond desire, beyond fear... Such recapitulations help me to clear the way; to make space for the *being* and the *now*...

The Word, Creation itself, arises out of an Empty Mind and the Music out of the Silence between the notes. Things become clear by contrast or thanks to a back-light. Isn't this the 'Virgin Womb,' the 'Intangible Arms' that will hold me to the end? The very place where my tenderness springs from detachment? Isn't this the Space that widens when we look through and beyond obscuring appearances—and suddenly perceive the Love, the Light, the Free will wanting to be seen, to be heard, to be felt?

  You are now invited to go to Volume II, Exercise 11 The Experience of Sacrifice as an Offering

XVIII
A Holographic Memory
A Cosmic Blueprint

'You will know the truth, and the truth will set you free.''
—John 8:32

There is an abyssal difference between recurring un-thinking behaviors, chronic escapism, the digging up of past regrets and failings (and exposing them in our memory's archeological museum), and our choice to fully meet and experience ourselves in the here and now.

Feeling diverse—contradictory and yet One—can happen! It does, as we begin to invite the whole range of our multifaceted *selves* into the luminous empty awareness of deeper *beingness*. It does, for Creation itself—down to every cell, down to every atom—is coherently set in movement and held in an unfathomable Continuum of Intelligence and Love; a Love out of which we are born and reborn instant by instant.

Once we begin to perceive our changing nature—profiled against the 'back-light' of the Holographic Consciousness we partake in—the 'Truth of *Who* Creation is' starts to emerge in our perception.

Let us again try to understand in a nutshell how we can—with the help of a process[24] of Self-remembering—integrate, oneness and multiplicity, wholeness and duality, while also

---

[24] **See also Volume II: "The Ark Within. Exercise Manual."** See Appendixes I, II, III at the end of the present Volume. See the *"Voice Dialogue,* the *Psychology of Selves* and of the *Aware ego,"* developed by Hal and Sidra Stone, Ph.D. USA. See Bibliography.

balancing our needs and our search for care, freedom and security.

   - Step one: Practice an aware listening, a differentiated immersion into the varied expressions of what you used to qualify as: '*That's me!*'

   - Step two: Center yourself by gently stepping back from every subjective emotional, mental and physical experiencing.

   - Step three: Apply lucid self-mirroring and kindhearted relating to whatever inhabits you.

   - Step four: Rest in the Higher and the Deeper Mystery of Peace that underlies and encompasses 'every *form of self* and every *form of other...*'

Instead of experiencing ourselves as 'solitary suffering flesh,' attended by disconnected mental analyzing—this process opens us to comprehensive compassion. We begin to feel cherished and accepted also by our own *Aware self*. At the same time it uncovers in us a sense of one's *Eternal Self* in contrast—as well as in connection—with the changing selves that compose our complex personalities and psyche.

The past events and stories of our life, are always yesterday. But our whole creative and sensitive potential is constantly ready to evolve; and this quite independently of time and space. The baby, the child, the youngster we were—but surprisingly also the mature, the elderly, woman or man we will be—the Wise Seer we may become... are permanently available within us. They partake in a 'cosmic body-mind awareness' of the universe! It is up to us to clear the way for their healing, their learning, their flowering. But this transformation can only happen through the live empathetic relating we create with them.

Every time we perceive these 'persons from within' as a burden or a source of suffering, we tend to discard them! But they never tire of calling upon us and we can never bury them for good. Yearning to be recognized and loved they wait. They wait like these wheat grains, sealed away in the ancient Egyptian tombs: Rediscovered, watered, thousands of years later, they do sprout and bloom!

All it takes is holding them in the palm of our hand, in the fertile ground of our attention. All it takes is a womb of warmth, of water and light, so they can unfold. If the *Sower* comes and cares, millenniums of latency weigh no more than a single season!

As stressed before, our stories do belong to yesterday, but the *selves* impacted by them endure in isolation, as long as we remain unaware of them. They cannot be set free unless we release them in the attention of our love.

All can still hatch and be brought to completion, if we transmute our 'vistas, our defense mechanisms, complexes, conditioned reflexes, reactivity, co-dependency, neuroses, depressions, mental and emotional disorders' into *Inner persons*. For to know without love is sterile!

Inner strangers, concealed in our depths, do step out unrequested: out of our daydreams, of our night-dreams, of our unconscious. It is their way to remind us to reconnect with them. They defy or enchant us; irreverent like children stamping into every puddle after a rainfall. The organic messages that ferment in the folds of our digestion, burst forth in our chests, rant and rave in our heads, are an Inner Humanity that demands its salvation. And we can contribute to its healing by welcoming it in the Weft of the Heart, by picking up 'Love's tiny lost ends...'

If we can do this, we will no longer stay frozen in iced up bygone fields. We will thaw; we will flow!

◆

Saving blueprints guide us through the meanderings of our human destinies! We find them mapped in myths and wondrous tales; in the Journeys of the Gods and the Wise as they descend and rise between heaven and earth, between heaven and hell, just as we do.

Ours is indeed a Heroic Quest, a Divine Roundabout. But the moment we forego our cosmic calling, our ego ensnares us into something akin to the dance of 'Living statues...' where the dancers must transfix whenever a mischievous spell interrupts the music. Children and even adults enjoy it because they relish in the tension of being briskly petrified and then released into resurrecting aliveness.

You do experience this intensely when unexpected criticism, fear, aggression or pain, suddenly freeze you still, mute your song... as if some cruel, invisible hand had pressed on the button *pause* of your life.

Aren't there too many dormant castles in our psyches; too many *Sleeping Beauties* entangled in the meshes of ancient curses; trapped in our subconscious or handed over to the nets of our fears and pains... every time the *Witch's spindle* wounds or deadens us?

As in the Fairy tale, hearsay will not suffice to rescue our Sleeping Princess, or win her hand. Many a pretender will only get scratched and held up by thorny hedges. To get through to our freshness of being, we must have the determination of a *Prince-Aware*, the will to revive our own loveliness with a kiss!

To understand and not condemn lifts the spell; appeases our inner and outer conflicts; becomes the foundation for our true maturity.

Now, if you have forgotten the way back to your Heart, remember that it is always magically close: No more than a few inches away from your head so full of wrestling thoughts! It waits right in your Center, in the Womb of your chest, precisely in the place where you feel your heart-breaks and your joy.

As in the Brothers Grimm's tale, everything quickens the

moment your 'Aware Love' breaks the curse. One hundred years later, life reawakes. The Princess, the castle and its inhabitants have not aged at all!

We can at all times free our spirit, our body, our heart; revive what has been silenced or hasn't fully lived in us yet. A woman in love is always a virgin. Each love is the first love. And no matter how late it comes to you, you will be fifteen years old!

The whole universe is accessible inside us. And that is how we can be Robinson, as well as Friday, Aurora, her Teddy bear, the Grasshopper; and also this age-old woman in the deep forest. She rocks the infant born from her tenderness. A knight in shining armor stands guard over this child.

It is a gift of Holographic Consciousness to clothe into the skin of a stranger, into the hand of a friend… to enter the hell of an abuser, to inhabit the anger of Genghis Khan; to pulse within the heart of matter, to become the rose or the lion, the breathing of the metal or the 'say' of the stone—so as to relate to them all in ourselves.

Let us burn like fire, espouse like water, take wing like air, be patient like the seed in the belly of tombs. Let us grow all the way to the vault of the sky, deepen all the way down to free sacrifice. Discover, breath by breath, heartbeat by heartbeat, that our Spirit knows all the signs, all languages… that we are not victims, but divine children; that we have the choice.

Happy and prosperous voyage! In our veins, in the cavities of our brains and hearts, in the labyrinths of our thoughts, in our meandering lives… lies a Fulfillment that hopes and waits for us!

📖 ***You are now invited to go to Volume II, Exercise 12*** *Embracing, Breath by Breath, the Moment of Now*

XIX

The Eye of the Needle

Insights dwell, hidden in the vibrating jungle or in the arid monotony of my days. Insights that surprise me like fish jumping on a summer lake. I almost saw *it*, but I didn't! So I wait and watch, but they never leap out when and where I am looking! I continuously lack the quality of attention that would allow me to catch a glimpse of a parallel universe; it just flashed by… at the farthest edge of my field of vision.

Sometimes, for a split second, *it* lifts me beyond my rational horizon; tilts me over—as if by a strike of wing or dorsal fin—into something that doesn't need my permission to come and go. I barely touch its fleeting opening. It is as if *it* lived at a different speed, too fast or too slow for me to grasp; or in some other realm, too elusive, too fathomless, to measure... It speaks a murmuring language; traces signs deceptively familiar and yet so easily missed.

It leaves me with a taste of intense nostalgia. In a shimmer, in the span between two breaths, I sensed my very essence, a sunken, forgotten world that lies just under our surface. It rushes in and out of nowhere, through a profusion of sounds, images, smells, tastes, and touches; through the innumerable doors and windows of my soul. Windows as countless as the pores of my skin: fragile skin, naked selves, unveiled body. My skin encloses me and yet unfolds thousands of sensors. My skin sees. It drinks the light. It breathes like a giant lung. It probes with intangible antennae. It hears like a giant ear. It vibrates and resonates like the tightly stretched membrane of a wondrous human drum. Skin of the Being!

By night and by day, the mystery of Life entrances me. Though I remember being but a frail speck in the immensity, it happens that Love and Spirit suddenly lend me their wings. At the detour of my path, that just an instant earlier obeyed time and space, I become a *passage*. An invisible Archer just hit a target that I didn't ever know existed within me.

My joy explodes, my faith soars. My body—matter itself—becomes sensitive like a photographic plate; malleable like the hot mud of origins; pervaded by a wind of particles; dispersed, multiplied—and yet holding together.

So, I watch, I wait. But I am almost always too slow, or too impatient, too early or too late… to seize such unpredictable *in-gates.*

◆

Jesus says: "It is easier for a camel to go through the eye of a needle than for a rich man to enter the kingdom of God."[25]

And I see it so well! I am too rich of self-protections, of prospects, of knowledge and of skills. Too often, I am driven forward, blinded by my certainties, pressed by my pains, lured by my expectations, disoriented by my fears and restless memories! Unable to recapture the fleeting magic experienced an instant before. Empty also. Empty of the Love, of the Lover, that doesn't come.

Are we not immensely laden, adamant to retain what deserts us, to amass what we lust after? One way or another, we cultivate and store our sicknesses, our neuroses and our preoccupations. In our gardens we grow flowers of worry; in our nights we ride the trains of our anguished thoughts.

And yet, the elusive passage that is always ajar, the narrow door to the Kingdom that so easily sidesteps, lies at hand. It is embedded in our heart and vision, in the 'here and now'

---

[25] The Bible. Mark 10:25

the Wise speak of. It is the 'Eye of the needle,' *that* which lets us through when we are naked and humble, stripped of past and future; *that* which offers itself, but demands that we knock unceasingly at its open door.

Is this rich man at the gates of the Kingdom, not my overloaded *me?* We do not polish the mirror of our soul. We only busy to upgrade our credibility: w*ell* off, *well*-adjusted, *well* meaning, *well* preserved, *well* behaved; *good* child, *good* spouse, *good* parent, *successful* provider, *forever* young…

And if—in this first round of 'show me who you are, what you possess, what you know, what you do,' we fail to measure up—we may venture to stage it on the dark side: *King* of thieves, *Queen* of whores, *Don* Juan, *Marquis* de Sade; *good* tyrant, *good* terrorist! And if we even don't rise to standards there, we can finally play it third hand, by clothing ourselves into shame and guilt: *no-good, good*-for-nothing, *good* slave, *good* victim…'

Don't we nourish a never-ending chore: The furbishing of our *me,* of what we have to pretend in order to be in the parade; of what we must dress up with as rulers or drifters—to prove we exist. No wonder it is so foreign to be simply trusting. No wonder we feel like strangers in a strange land!

To cross the Threshold, we need to stand unclothed and empty handed. We need to bear in mind that we came into the world naked, through an extremely narrow door. So will we leave it also: Through a tiny slot between two breaths; dispossessed. Carried through the 'Eye of the needle;' weighing almost nothing!

◆

I remember a certain summer festival in my hometown and how, as a very young woman, I was standing midstream of the crowd, feeling like the prow of an insecure and yet audacious ship. People moved toward me like rolling waters. Face after face I watched my solitude; I saw aging in the passersby.

Decades later, in this same festival, standing at the point of tide reversal, laden with years of oceangoing storms and ventures… wave after wave, people now seemed to grow younger and younger. And me, still trembling; still alone. Was the ebb flow now baring my wrecks, carrying off my joys and soaring ideals? I suddenly felt exposed like a badly placed island. I saw cadavers in my roots, debris and stories I thought outgrown, still sticking to my soles. My audacity faltered. How I would have liked to disappear… give it all back to the Sea!

If only I could make it all One: the real and the false, the old and the new, the harsh and the tender, the lost and the found; this world and the other. And so, at last, stand bare, ready to dive into the inspirational Waters of Life.

To Aurora, the heart is never a secret. She moves from shadow to light like one skips rope. She slides effortlessly through the Eye of the needle: She just slipped her hand into mine! How I love you, Aurora, and how much you redeem me, transmute my nightmares, provoke these gaps that wake me up.

◆

Little by little, I learn to cross the boundaries of my limitations, to take some steps beyond safety—not out of rebellion or provocative acting out as I used to in earlier years—but to shake my slumbers into leaps of faith.

One night, as my curious restless mind stalked untried tracks, I dreamt of myself, sitting in midst of the rush hour traffic like a motionless torero amongst wild bulls; eyes closed, on the concrete, offered to sudden death or to slow tearing defilement. Or—could it be—to a miraculous uplifting? So often, I had yearned to release all questions, all desires, into the Hands of weightlessness and void: A breathtaking anticipation, like strong wine after a fast!

Soon after that, to confront my fears of exposure, test my courage and unchallenged sides of me, I decided to attempt one of my own narrow doorways. I dressed in clean, simple clothes. Taking with me a small flat cushion, I rallied the bustling touristic streets. Without haste, I chose a spot in midst of the flow of shoppers. I sat down. I closed my eyes. Immediately the whole world changed. Was I now a 'jungle being' in an unknown hunting ground? Was I the hunter or the hunted?

Even though this experience in the animated whereabouts of a small town was far less daring than the scenario envisioned in the night… it felt outrageously scary at first as well as totally new to me! I could feel the people were startled and uneasy. I could feel them try to ignore me or bend their course in a wide arc. I used to dread what now happened more than anything else: Mistrust. They isolated and excluded me!

However, as I settled into myself, my heart calmed its beat. Gradually I began to sense a sort of swirling emptiness around me. Much to my surprise, my anxiety subsided: Peace descended. Silence in midst of rumor; space in the midst of constriction; safety in the midst of the unpredictable. Time stopped. Comments died.

Did Inner Eyes open? After a time that I could not assess, I had a feeling of gathering birds, of a soft flutter, settling at a distance but strangely close. I could intuit their unspoken song; feel their wings folding almost soundlessly to take a rest.

When I opened my eyes, I saw a bunch of small children and adolescents sitting in a semicircle; and behind them, some parents and adults stealing glances—with *Inner children* in their eyes. Enchantment, a sense of buoyancy and lightness took hold of me.

As I fully came back to the outer reality, I saw that most passersby still bent around me, hurrying to accomplish their errands; but my perceiving had shifted. Fear had waned. Youth was budding and smiling inside me. People were human.

And I wondered: Is this enough to amend one's world?

◆

I noticed that summer, walking along my childhood path by the side of the lake that the moment Aurora is with me, I effortlessly catch the flash of the jumping fish, the flight and song of the birds; that when I look through her eyes, I seize embers and sparks on rippling water. Maybe she has a contract with the birds and the fishes! Almost without knowing it, I can simply enter into her innocent gaze… and there it happens: The Other Shore. The Land of Now. The Land that the Children, the Lovers and the Wise, tell about.

The wind of Spirit here is disconcerting! Sometimes it carries our souls and bodies like whirling feathers, sometimes it cuts through reason like a blade and upends our thoughts. Here the infinitely large and the infinitely small blend; opposites are one. Inhaling, exhaling, take on a rhythm of waves; lift our entire self towards a High Sea, a High Chamber, an overflowing and grateful Place. The gap between breaths drops us into the unbounded. All desires, all expectations, all worries miraculously dissolve. I am, I live, I die, I am. Even in death, even when time betrays me; even when everything collapses and disintegrates into nothingness… I am.

No need to beg for a future, to carry burdens past. Suspended, I taste simultaneously the ephemeral and the eternal. I encompass the virgin space where the birds soar. I sense the tranquil foothold of the earth. My body and my lips are dipped there… intimately One with what meets me.

Elsewhere is right here. What I thought lost rests securely in my heart. Why question? Why solve? The time of our Awakening, the time of our Love, is solely now: A holographic memory. A stroke of an immaterial wing. The sound of one hand clapping.

📖 ***You are now invited to go to Volume II, Exercise 13***
The Experience of Transgression
Stepping through the Eye of the Needle

XX

A Tale of our Many Faces

A pale dawn shines through the light rectangle of our door. At the bottom of the cliff the sea rolls and grumbles. Wrapped into softness, Aurora and I drift between waking and sleeping; our glances float away on the low bushes just outside our bamboo and thatch hut.

Out of the corner of my eye, I notice a furtive movement. Despite our human scent and vibes a wild rabbit unexpectedly stops just beyond our doorway; its soft nose quivers, exploring every fragrance, every inch of the ground. Aurora holds her breath; her heart skips a beat. I can intuit her every feeling. I know how deeply she is touched by the rabbit's innocent trust, by the sweetness of its composure. How natural to love such candor. How easy to destroy it. Beyond its instinctual fear, the rabbit offers itself, picking up on our silence, on the rhythm of our hearts echoing its own. A few breaths later, the rabbit has gone, leaving us aware of its gift.

Now, we head for the beach, as we do every morning. I believe Friday runs there already. The west wind blows, pregnant with rain; hollowed rocks, carved out by surging waters, cast gloomy silhouettes. Nature turns fierce. Should we become more vigilant? Does it warn us about a foreign world, where love and candor bear other names; wear other faces? Faces sometimes so alien, so scary, that the humility and the faith one needs to take refuge in them, is a constant challenge.

Is there a way to trust in spite of hurt and fear? Is there a way to see through the *Face of evil* and to recognize beyond it the *Face of Light*?

Under the spell of the ingenuous presence of the rabbit, I walk strangely undefended. My private world retains the imprint of a childlike morning where no ill has yet shown itself! Have I lowered my guard, dropped my scales—now being dangerously bare... delivered to the slightest caress, but also to the slightest brush off?

The beach is deserted, very humid. Aurora and Friday skip about, looking for shells and shiny stones. A high chair, painted in white, stands in the middle of this empty shore, like on a stage. Tempted, I climb up... no audience though, only the clouds riding the wind; only the chair and me, overlooking the sea.

Should I have known that we cannot remain forever in a secluded personal realm; that no one goes into the open without skin, without armor, without tokens of credibility? Far off, I see a man approaching. It dawns on me that I might be sitting in his towering seat. Have I, unwittingly, just become the lamb of the fable, drinking from the wolf's private spring? As he draws near, I attempt a smile, hoping for his. But, immediately, wooden-faced, he curtly reproaches me for trespassing!

Conflict surprises us. A judgment, a rejection, a tiny grain of sand in the gears of our needs and prospects is enough. In a split second our world collapses or blows up. Our millions of cells shift. I am the lamb of the fable no more! A suit of armor, a skin hard and smooth, solidifies around me. With a sharp snap, my facemask clamps shut like a cutting jaw. The morning abruptly darkens, as I close up to secure Aurora's scathed heart. Friday is nowhere to be seen.

Unmet expectations, lack of awareness, can be deadly. They feel like the door I thought would open... hurled back into my face. To the blind, on a flight of stairs they are the missing step. Now sadness surges up like an unruly wave. Anger rumbles inside me like loads of pebbles tossed by the sea!

All it took—for my world to change face, was this sudden minute splinter in my heart. From one moment to the next I am deprived of vision; trapped in my hurt, in my wrath; exposed in my error; unable to detach from the antagonistic response of this Life-guard, of this Supervisor of empty sand and empty sea!

In the past, I would have just retaliated, satisfied to hit back. But now that I have learned to listen to *who* stirs and cries and whispers inside me, inside you... I cannot go on ignoring my tightening throat, the blush that rises in my cheeks. I cannot disown the irreversible pact of solidarity concluded with a wild stranger named Friday, with a sweet little girl called Aurora. How could I betray their feelings or abandon them?

And since I have come to know them in my flesh, how could I forego them *in you*, Mister Controller! My enemy? My brother!

Compassion rises from awareness.

◆

Such a trifle, such an innocuous event! The tip of an iceberg that sinks our proudest vessels; the story of one's lost position; of lost wholeness, of betrayed good will! Do we explode or go slowly to pieces on the hidden reefs of our frozen memories, of our power games, of our wounded selves? Is this the reason why we act like lone wolves? Is it because we feel fooled, misunderstood, dispossessed of our most legitimate birthright: security, respect, trust, welcoming love?

Is this why a tidal wave of rage and despair overtakes me when you shut off and disconnect? Is this why my dike collapses under the pressure of a single drop too much, of one more let down, one more silence or unkind word? Is this why I break under the strain of an invisible flaw in my heart—now brittle like glass; why my strength, my joy, my hope, so abruptly turn to ashes?

Don't such absurdly recurring scenarios call for an awakening? But as much as we would like it, our awakenings only last until the next slumber and rarely propel our lives into a once-and-for-all state of awareness and peace. Enclosed in matter, our capacity for consciousness wavers like fading ember light! We continuously have to re-kindle it; and this, not only through the burning blaze of our trials, but with caring attention and resolve—throughout our cooling off relationships and our ordinary lives. Everyday issues are the most difficult: It may be so easy to be heroic and so hard to move out of our entrenched reactions and routines. Their *thresholds* have to be traveled again and again, from hurt to awareness, from revenge to compassion, from 'fight and flight reflexes' to chosen assertion, to chosen distance or embrace—until the rupture between *Me* and *me,* between oneself and the other, bridges! The torn apart sides of our wounds and contradictions need to pull close and touch, uniting to heal.

This requires recognition of one's pain and anger as well as the setting of clear personal boundaries—without withdrawing, without raising our sword in hate, without slipping into an abyss of discouragement. If we work at it, if we espouse what is, if we call our disoriented and afflicted *selves* home into our sheltering heart, we will reconnect—faster and faster and more often—with our inherent depth of being, and with it to inborn Oneness and Love.

At first it is never easy! On the high seas overtired birds have to land, risk and trust the deck of unfamiliar ships!

Even the gods choose to descend. Buddha at first bears the failure of all his human efforts to solve mankind's suffering until he finally collapses from exhaustion. Yet, at this very instant of utter powerlessness, He trusts. As he surrenders to the Divine Spaciousness that gives us unending birth—He awakens! And we with Him! He frees us from the fears and the desires that submit us to separation and pain. He becomes the way.

Jesus, like any man, sweats in anguish and in doubt; He stumbles under the weight of his unfair and cruel fate. Yet—not foregoing compassion and forgiveness—in the midst of mockery, deathly pain and abandonment, He straightens and trusts! He gives himself over to verticality, to His Divine Father who births eternal Life in Him and in us. At this very instant of surrender, He becomes the Door. He frees mankind from guilt and from death. He resurrects—and we with Him—in the Sacred Relating that dispels all darkness, that soothes all sorrow.

◆

Sitting on the sand in the gray morning next to a scowling silent man in his high chair, I consider how quickly I have shut down, reverted to ingrained schemes, to old masks and dormant weapons.

Even though our hearts learn to open, our spirits to lift… our ego remains a double-walker on double paths: One of profound self doubt and self defilement, and one of mammoth self importance and deceptive superiority. We shape shift, from victim to abuser, from vulnerability to arrogance, from enslavement to tyranny. Are we only this *little me* needled by fear and guilt; only this stained self-image that we try to fix up at all cost; only self-worshipers?

Each Power game is the *Replay of our Fall from Grace*, is Paradise lost. Again we become the pitiless 'surveyors of the right and the wrong'! Again the temptation to know better, to accuse, to make guilty, deprives us of Peace. Again we hide out or attack to escape a Judgment that henceforth houses inside us!

Because we take God's Law and Wisdom into our own hands, we mistake our egocentric feuds for holy wars; the devil for our father; Lucifer for a saving angel; terrorism, ethnic cleansings and sadistic righteousness, for Justice, Reason and True Faith.

Yet, if we could weigh 'the blood, shed by the *righteous*' against 'the blood, shed by the *sinful...*' wouldn't the balance tilt down heavily on the side of those who deem themselves righteous; those who kill in the Name of their concealed power schemes and abusive ideals, throughout History? Wouldn't it tip over under the mass of innocent flesh sacrificed to pitiless values and murderous principles? A far higher price than obvious plain sin could ever justify.

And this is also true of our family and couple disputes and of our conflicting inner world. Criticism rages: Inquisition without and within!

"Do not judge, so that you may not be judged. For with the judgment you make you will be judged, and the measure you give will be the measure you get."[26]

If we understand, if we become aware—of how and when we move away from our Source and from each other, will this not show us when to turn around?

Are we not endlessly redeemed, re-created in God's likeness and in relationship to Him—the moment we remember Him calling us 'His sons?' Are we not endlessly yearning to meet our True Identity? But failing to search for it in the depth of our own Soul and Heart, where our divine Source forever dwells?

Our Life cannot disconnect from its Source; what if we dropped the reins and trusted its natural wisdom inside us;

---

[26] The Bible: the New Revised Standard Version. Mark 7:1-2

trusted what spontaneously germinates—even in devastated fields, even in the entrenched recesses of our knotted guts and our congested hearts?

God Himself rejoices in our wombs, the moment we commend ourselves to His Living Hands and Spirit!

◆

Hurt and confusion still surprise and overrun me for trifles. Storms still happen, diverting my course. Only the time I need to return to the Light and Warmth in my heart and in yours, has lessened! Can it be that someday only a few hours, a few minutes, a few seconds, will suffice to surrender and recognize that I am free and you with me?

"Emotions, behaviors, beliefs, images of me, images of you… is it possible to realize how harmful and deceiving you can be—and yet to love and care for you, because you inhabit sensitive flesh; because you are full of human sap, full of atoms gravitating in search of Love?

'Energies, fears and desires, that dance inside me, inside you… is it possible to acknowledge you—yet not identify with you?

'Can I be touched, because you struggle, because it is your pain and your concern that drives you; because it is your anguish that makes you destructive—and yet not follow your dictates?

'Can I embrace in you the *Say and Deed of Mankind*— submitted to trial, submitted to slowness, submitted to its yoke, to the duality of birth and death—and yet not lose hope, not despair of our release?

'Will I forgive you? Because our faults themselves are subject to Mystery; because we 'know not what we do,' nor *who* we are; because we are God's children, forever innocent in Him? Is it possible to weave the threads of our contradictions into the weft of divine Equity and Love?"

Detachment and compassion: The reverse and the obverse of the "seamless tunic, woven in one piece from top to bottom."[27]

'Forms of me, forms of you, will I acknowledge and console you, because you carry our suffering, our strayed *selves...* yet not let you take me into custody, jeopardize my life? Can I cease to idolize or reject you? Can I cease to confuse the behavior and the Person, the wave and the Sea?

'Is it possible to become your Host; to invite your *many faces* into the *Ark Within,* knowing that you err, that you feel separated from me, from the other, from God; that you feel forsaken, in solitude, in unconsciousness, in hatred and in guilt? Is it possible to grasp how illusory you are—and to call you back; back to the forgiving Shelter of my Heart?

'And to say to you: I see you deeply. I will to love you; with tenderness, with humor, with unwavering firmness. Beyond the multiple and sometimes repulsive appearances you take, I will to meet you—as God meets us: With unending compassion and clarity.

'And to trust... that every time I see your Deeper Self beyond your shadow, you do come home to Consciousness and Love; you do start to let go of your dramas.

And then... to cast off from my moorings; to untie my Ship, so inhabited, so full; to steer and secure it in Faith; to slip it into the life-current—surprisingly serene and spacious."

◆

Can I listen? Will I bear in my heart the answer of the Healer: "Father, forgive them for they know not what they do?"[28] And say: 'Father, forgive me for I know not what I do.'

---

27 The Bible: the New Revised Standard Version. John 19:23
28 Luke 23:24 The Bible: the New Revised Standard Version

Will I remember my Divine Soul, the Wellspring of all Love; the 'God-Child' in every one of us?

Seated on the humid ground, I consider my many faces in the grains of sand always brought back, abandoned, transformed by the recurring flow—knowing that only a Divine Father can lift us together, as his sole Child, into His merciful Hands.

The Life-Guard sits on his re-conquered chair, supervising a deserted beach, useless and insignificant in the now drizzling rain. Both of us are lost in the immensity. 'Who am I? Who is he?' I wonder.

And as naturally as a ray of sunlight illuminates the room once you open the shutters, the Universe answers: 'Wasn't he with you at the Source of the Original River, when its waters were still as clear as baby's eyes?'

The same clear water that now rises in my own eyes! The chasm of distress and violence that had separated us becomes insignificant.

Touched, undressed of my importance, of my righteousness, returned to nakedness, I walk up to him and speak the words: 'I am sorry.'

The guard looks up. A smile comes to our lips!

📖 ***You are now invited to go to Volume II, Exercise 14***
The Experience of Communication in Relationship

Part Four

'Voice Dialogue' From Sensitive Body-Self To Universal Self

> *"If the foot were to say: 'Because I am not a hand, I do not belong to the body' that would not make it any less a part of the body. And if the ear were to say, 'Because I am not an eye, I do not belong to the body' that would not make it any less a part of the body.*
>
> *If the whole body were an eye, where would the hearing be? If the whole body were hearing, where would the sense of smell be?*
>
> *…There should be no schism in the body; but the members should have the same care one for another. If one member suffers, all suffer together with it; if one member is honored, all rejoice together with it."*

—The Bible. 1 Corinthians 12:15-17; 25-26

XXI

The Weft of the Heart

I find that my life is connected to all those who preceded me and to all those who will come after me. Is this why, at Noah's example, I try to steer an *Ark* through wind and flood? I really don't know why I hold onto it so. It simply seems to be my lot, the only solid patch of ground available on high sea.

The perceptions of my Journey are discontinuous. For long stretches of time, they present themselves like the unrelated elements of a gigantic puzzle or weaving. The articulate picture they hold is still indistinct and requires my perseverance and my blind probing. Sensations, emotions, thoughts, scattered images and events float up on a vast canvas. The elements of my awareness are patchy; they elaborate a scene that I never completely recognize.

Sometimes I belong to a detail, to some specific experience that absorbs all my attention! Sometimes, through this faculty that permits man to look upon himself and to rise like a balloon above the web of his own existence—a much wider landscape surprises me! It randomly takes shape, puts on flesh, creates a fresco; weaves itself into a living tapestry. I suddenly notice an unforeseen segment of coherence where I thought there was only a maze. Like a network of veins or nerves, conducting threads tie up the jumbled themes of my life; and I discover that fresh avenues have just opened, when and where everything seemed to be held up.

Often it is precisely when reaching a dead end, at the very edge of my wits and patience... that appears—as if by enchantment—an embranchment or an odd piece that makes all the difference!

I accompany the soft, the intoxicating back and forth of my life-threads; the meandering edges of unions and separations. I offer myself; I take myself back. The thread is cut; the thread is knotted. Sometimes I am the happy captive of a colored pattern… only to brutally realize that I am been sequestered. Sometimes I am the free bird soaring toward the sky; sometimes the bird shot straight through the heart, falling like a stone. But whatever the signs and pictures, I am led by something outside my control. I am not the Designer, only the blind servant; servant to a completion I do not fully grasp until the last piece, the last thread, falls into place, revealing the utter simplicity, clarity and truth of the whole.

Tirelessly I smooth out the creases in the bright and dark fabric of my life, laced with the intense blue of the sky. Will I finally know how to be the Lover and the Partner of this Work? Know how to intuit and further its movements? Become a symphony? Dare a succession of chords… contrasts and harmonies! What does it mean to be in relationship without craving allegiance, without dependency; without defending oneself; without excluding; without colonizing? How to be autonomous without rejecting, without feeling abandoned? How to connect and stay free? Receive freely. Give freely.

Nothing wants to be lost; every scattered 'wisp of flesh and life' yearns to be related, returned to its original Oneness. All insist on being separate and yet complete, in the likeness of each fragment of a universal hologram!

What does it mean to be two, to love each other, to unite, and yet to keep one's integrity as well as one's singularity? Can this be done without gathering up our being?

Shouldn't we embrace the world in the likeness of these blankets made from juxtaposed odds and ends; made of old torn and now useless remnants sewn together; a Patchwork of the Heart, born from our attention and our love, from the work of our hands, from our acknowledged pain and wear?

Shouldn't we assemble the lost, the discarded, the imperfect, the lonely, the meaningless… like the dismantled pieces of a giant supernatural enigma that Life delivers into our hands? Shouldn't we enclose that which was severed into a token of warming, shining beauty; honor what now shimmers in the oneness of its diversity?

Each little square, each circle, each star, each lozenge, each triangle, can stay purely itself, while at the same time being rejuvenated in connection to others! Now each fragment reflects a Totality imbued with gentleness, with happiness, dancing in its colorful contrasts of dark and light…

This is a Weaving so generous that it gifts us from its shared poverty! Whoever decides to wrap it around his shoulders, around his brother, will wear and bestow the robe of a King! Whoever places it at the feet of another as a token of gratitude and trust, honors himself and honors his guest.

Life then blesses us with a unique, weightless and exquisite shawl that graciously falls around our aging shoulders, woven only from delicacy and tenderness.

XXII

The Alchemy of the Self
Our Quest for the Holy Grail

"Jesus said to them, 'When you make the two into one, and when you make the inner like the outer and the outer like the inner, and the upper like the lower, and when you make male and female into a single one, so that the male will not be male nor the female be female, when you open an eye inside your eye, a hand inside your hand, a foot inside your foot, a likeness in place of your image, then you will enter the Kingdom." [29]

Aurora's and Friday's affection, the discovery of a kinship within and without, the resolve to never lose touch with it again, have been among my most precious steps toward a hitherto unsuspected universal connection. How fascinating and joyous to become a Womb to all there is, to be all at once the Giant Gulliver and the minute Lilliputians, Noah's Ark sheltering every species, a 'Matrioshka doll,' a Cosmic patchwork!

Evolution itself I regard as a giant Magnet of Love that pulls life toward Life, consciousness toward Consciousness, the breath of survival toward the Breath of Knowing! A magnet that attracts and joins us in the *'me* and *you,'* that multiplies and unifies us in the *we.* A love-lore in which the narrow yearns for the wide, the shallow for the profound, the low

---

[29] 'The Gospel of Thomas,' Logion 22. See: 'The Nag Hammadi Library.' Scrolls discovered in Egypt in 1945). James M. Robinson Ed. Harper and Row S.F. 1978.

for the high, the empty for the full, and vice versa. A divine Wholeness that extends *Itself* in the kaleidoscope of Creation in which all forms are birthed; in which all forms will be ultimately lifted back into Love as their Source, and simplified in it.

Life urges us *to be!* Let us develop courage, awareness, trust into inborn intelligence, with tireless curiosity and appetite for life. This requires the guts to descend into what scares us most: A naked newborn delivered to change, to separation, to helplessness, to the unknown; a naked newborn who accomplishes his journey from Paradise lost to Paradise found.

This endeavor is an alchemic process. It demands our Presence: In the burning of desire and the hurt of disconnection; in their decanting while we cool down in the release of our attachments. We need to reconcile, to purify, to redeem, what wells up, what deserts us—with caring and gentleness; with patience and with faith.

Our ego feeds on rejection versus approval, but our Being extends through cherishment! In truth, we yearn to transmute—in the crucible of our heart, in the mortar of our pain—the base matter of our fears into the gold of Conscious Love. We thirst for aliveness, for awakened relating; for a Flame that will neither devour nor abandon us!

Each of us harbors an ever exploring divine Spring-child. Aurora is this Child in me. She never tires of probing the hidden, of peering into the chasm. The moment she heard about the '*Emerald Tablet*,' she questioned me, she insisted that I read it out to her again and again, like a mysterious love poem in the old language of fairy tales. And at each reading—as if in resonance to her simple faith—I could feel a faint yet liberating sigh, a stirring in the depth of my chest... responding like a buried seed to the promise of the light.

"In truth without doubt, all that which is above is as that which is below and that which is below is as that which is above. All there is proceeds from the One and by the mediation of the One, of the Unique… The One fathers all miracles in the world. His strength is perfect when it turns to earth. Thou shalt separate earth from fire and the subtle from the gross, delicately, with extreme care and caution. It ascends from Earth to Heaven and again descends from Heaven to Earth and receives the strength of what is above and of what is below. So thou also hast the glory of the whole world and all obscurity flees before thee. Therein dwells the Force containing all forces, overcoming the subtle, penetrating the solid. So the Universe was created. And our small world in the likeness of the Universe."[30]

For a long time this remained Aurora's field of query. I owe it to her that I never renounced it; that I let myself be surprised… by signs, messages, distilled by my blood, born out of an Invisible Organ thriving inside me, revealing itself in the very process of living. With time, I understood these alchemic propositions, and in particular this 'circulation of the One in the multiple,' better. But understanding the principles was only the first step. I had to incorporate them! Was this something other than a seductive myth?

Things changed, became observable and helpful, as I began to realize that the alchemic process… its fire, steps and parts, all take place within our own body. The whole universe is contained right there! Our embodied self is the alembic; is the *sole locus* of our transformations… through union and separation, death and rebirth, *solve et coagula.* I saw and felt two hearths, two crucibles: The cavern of the womb, the cavern of the heart. Higher up, there was my head, this third chamber—alas packed full with the unprocessed matter of

---

[30] The '*Emerald Tablet*' is an ancient text purporting to reveal the secret of the primordial substance and its transmutations. It claims to be the work of Hermes Trismegistus, a legendary Egyptian sage, variously identified with the Egyptian god Thoth and/or the Greek god Hermes. This short and cryptic text was highly regarded by European alchemists as the foundation of their art.

tangled thoughts and judgments; of upsetting memories; of the unloved, unburned and unforgiven. It felt as if I was constantly processing my contents upside down! Under such conditions, things couldn't correctly simmer, decant… before evaporating and cooling down—thereby serving an efficient distillation.

The earth itself, cries, storms, trembles, explodes! Becomes tender, becomes a Mother, abandons itself like a Child; dances like a Youth, full of mirth and laughter. My Quest had first to take root in the everyday soil: Within my body, my womb, my heart… and a lucid balancing of my sensations, feelings and reactions.

Every star, every beast, every plant, every stone, simply expresses its inbuilt nature, simply submits to its innermost calling. No one and nothing—except man—tries to start from another place; to skip the path, forego the growth; to be something or somebody else!

Have we forgotten who we are? Have we forgotten to be the Holy Children of divine Consciousness? Have we forgotten that the Universe is a Holy Person? A person who murmurs in the wind, whispers in the rain, sings in the thousand voices of birds; dresses in the colors of sunrise, turns to dark velvet when night falls.

Is such Self-remembering not the true Path on our Quest for the Holy Grail? Can this Grail be anything else than a Living Chalice that unfolds inside everyone and everything? It is said to be carved in a miraculous emerald—made of the overflowing green radiance of the Heart. Could it be *The Ark Within?* The Ark we uphold in the Body of Love, in union with the earth and with every creature? Such fullness comes with it… that it doesn't appear to belong to us. And yet it does ascend from our innermost; it permeates and encompasses every atom, every cell.

If I remembered that God *created man in His likeness*, that He loves me as Himself—wouldn't it be easier to care? To love myself; to love you! Wouldn't our wombs and hearts unfold in *His likeness,* holding the Universe? He who is the servant of this Chalice unifies the Embracer and the embraced; shelters all beings in the memory of their Source: Friends, enemies... welcoming them back into their innate sanctity.

Even though this is a Mystery beyond our grasp, we understand and do feel that even the smallest flower of love blooming in our chests is of the same nature and beauty as the Mystic Rose.[31] In alchemy, the rose is a symbol of the operation of Conjunction, of the Marriage of opposites.

Spirit imbues our flesh, outshines all separateness, discloses our radiant undying nature, the moment our heart opens. Is this the *Great Work* the alchemists spoke of... this embodying of the Infinite into the finite; this absorption of the finite into the Infinite? Would I have the heart to turn destructive, if I realized that each aspect of the inner and outer Cosmos is a mirror to our Soul?

Aurora seems to find all this quite natural. She always knew that the world of matter mirrors the Kingdom of Spirit; that all together we are—the Divine Offspring of the Divine Source. And this proves itself: Every time we return who we are to sacredness, the Divine suddenly unveils in our everyday humanity; in the step of the Beloved, in the harmony of mathematics and geometry, in the arms of the River, in the belly of the Mountain.

And from this Spring I quench my thirst. I nourish the certainty that creation is the visible counterpart of an unseen Realm, that macrocosm and microcosm are One, that the created includes the Creator.

Shall we not turn round like the Prodigal Son; call on the

---

[31] See: The Wolfram Demonstrations Project; a simple design, sometimes called the Mystic Rose. A number of equidistant points are placed around a circle and then a line is drawn from each point to every other point, forming a mandala design evolving at each addition of an equidistant point around the circle.

unconditional love that Fathers us? Isn't this our freedom of choice: To acknowledge in awe and wonder the *Sonship* we have discarded!

"In him was life; and the life was the light of men. And the light shineth in darkness; and the darkness comprehended it not. …That was the true Light, which lighteth every man that cometh into the world. He was in the world, and the world was made by him, and the world knew him not. He came unto his own, and his own received him not. But as many as received him, to them gave he power to become the sons of God… which were born, not of blood, nor of the will of the flesh, nor of the will of man, but of God. And the Word was made flesh, and dwelt among us, and we beheld his glory, the glory as of the only begotten of the Father, full of grace and truth."[32]

📖 ***You are now invited to go to Volume II, Exercise 15***
The Experience of Holiness in the Body
'The Ark Within' as a Sanctuary

📖 ***Followed by Exercise 16***
The Experience of Lowering Your Head into the Body
Discerning the World and Yourself from There

---

[32] King James Bible." John 1. 4-5 & 9-14

XXIII

The Caravanserai of the Heart
From Egotistic *Self* to Universal *Self*

"The universe is an infinite sphere
Whose center is everywhere and
Whose circumference is nowhere."[33]

In my recurring haste to flee into illusions or self defense—be it out of guilt or self-importance—I usually fail to take time; the time to acknowledge my sensations, my feelings and my beliefs—so as to allow them to evaporate naturally, letting their purified essence be returned to me like gracious dew.

This calls for a proper distillation of my egotistic self; for an aware filtering of what stagnates, ferments, heats, mixes, fuses and separates, within me. It asks of me to break the law of a 'psychological *omerta*' that keeps my underground *selves* in hiding; selves that only conscious love liberates from their insulating crust!

'Voice Dialogue'[34] is the best tool I ever experienced to help us with such an alchemical practice: to clarify the perception, to condense, drain, dissolve, what storms, competes and fights in us. It ensures the necessary undoing, the necessary

---

[33] Blaise Pascal, in 'Thoughts.' Cambridge University Press 2013.
Selected and translated by Moritz Kaufmann

[34] *See also* **Volume II: "The Ark Within. Exercise Manual."** See Appendixes I, II, III at the end of the present Volume. See the "Voice Dialogue, the *Psychology of Selves* and of the *Aware ego*," developed by Hal and Sidra Stone, Ph.D. USA. See Bibliography.

burning; the stripping that leaves us alleviated and aware enough to embrace our concealed sensitive selves—as had been the case when Friday rushed into my heart and womb, like a long forgotten nurturing rain after an endless drought!

'Voice Dialogue work,' not only helps us to probe into what weighs upon us… it uncovers an 'inner spaciousness,' cleansed from its scoria; it returns us to transparency, to openness and presence.' Only the empty space that surrounds all shapes in this world, allows us to distinguish them! Be it in my room, my garden or my psyche, without the gap that separates one object, flower, feeling, from the other, I would be blind to their moves and singularities.

Even seemingly solid objects are mainly empty space. In my kitchen I look at the wall, I look at my table. I try to envision their dancing particles floating in emptiness and nevertheless contained, nevertheless related to each other in a totally precise and coherent structure! What if they were assembled by Love, by a non-possessive involvement; by a Law that does not need to enforce itself by constraint, exclusiveness and punishment? In this vision I discover Joy. I feel vast, and yet deliciously inhabited! This allows me to direct my attention beyond my usual limitations, beyond hit and miss thoughts and overbearing emotions—yours and mine!

I become like leaves, while a soft wind makes me quiver; like water just before it turns to vapor. Substantial, and yet intangible! I breathe better. I feel connected; to the tree, to the sea, to the earth, to you, but without any coercion. I find forgiveness in me for what submits me to form. I find faith in a void that sets me free. I belong and yet have enough space. Not a space I must conquer or defend… but a loving luminous space, inherent to my own nature! I find Peace.

A sea of energy surrounds me, expands me, uplifts me… no longer in my mind only, but in the exultation of my cells, the jubilation of molecules.

"Molecule: The smallest part of a pure body that can

exist in a free state without losing the properties of its original substance."[35] (Undoubtedly, I like the dictionary!) 'The quantum theory, created by Planck in 1900, affirms that radiant energy has, as matter, a discontinued structure; it can only exist in grain form or quanta, of the value hv, where h is a universal constant (...) and v, the frequency of the radiation."[36]

To say *radiant energy*, is to say light! To say *grains*, is to say *void* in which they move or settle. To say void is to say freedom!

Even without really understanding this, my heart soars, and all of a sudden, I find that *being* can pass through walls, dive into solids... where *it* can swim, sink, unite, vanish and be reborn. And yet not lose its apparent shapes: The wall, the table, retain their outline, and my body its contour!

Could it be that everything proceeds from conscious particles that are independent of time and space, smaller and faster than anything we can fathom... imperceptible, unimaginable. Could it be that they effortlessly infuse all existence? That they generate and assemble out of darkness, out of nothingness, out of the abyss—an Earth and a Sky; a man and a woman; a thought, an angel... And who knows, in finality, bear evidence to what we call God!

I contemplate Nature, its sovereign acceptance, its multiplicity, the abundance, the inventiveness that it displays without ever betraying itself. The seed sinks into the ground... cracks open or dies, with perfect reliance. And Earth feeds it! It sprouts toward the light, toward space, where sun and rain combine to quicken it. Sky and Earth thirst for each other. The tree grows. The bird nests in it.

Wavelengths interlace, reaching for each other, weaving their threads into an unending design of extending and interrelating Consciousness. This is a holy dance; a blending of

---

[35] *See* Webster's Dictionary under ' molecule.'
[36] Translated from French. Petit Larousse Illustré, Paris 1985

opposites. Doesn't this make us partakers and disciples of an extraordinary divine in-and-out-breath?

In its time Noah's Ark was most likely made from the great cedar trees; a large womb of wood, and Noah knew to handle it in the Flood by the strength of his arm and his Faith. However today—if we are to survive the floods of meaninglessness, if we are to save our communities from social cannibalism, our couples and families from disruption and our children from callousness and despair, we need an *Ark* directly born from Consciousness.

Every woman, every man, every child, is to open up as an *Ark* that shelters and carries us in our daily lives. Our 'conscious body-self' is to prove spacious enough for wings to take flight; stable enough for children's first steps, weightless enough for love not to be suffocating. Let us unfold an *Ark* that breathes and pulses; a Sphere of Presence that can bear our innumerable faces; bear mankind and creation itself in its flanks.

Love can only be Love when it is without judgment—empty even of itself. For Love shares without depleting; revives without exhausting.

I am you. You are me. You are me in your tears, in your violence, in your fear. You are me in your innocence, your freshness, the fragrance of your unexplored garden. You are me, but not mine; and I do not belong to you.

Union: The ultimate reduction of two dots, three dots, a myriad of dots—into a S*ingle dot.* Union, an *Infinite Space* that welcomes and frees all dots in *Itself.*

A way to be limitless in our diversity; and to still be *One.*

"Be fruitful and multiply,"[37] yet not in number, but in *Beingness!*

---

[37] New American Standard Bible. Genesis 9:7

📖 ***You are now invited to go to Volume II, Exercise 17***
The Experience of 'The Ark Within.'
I. The Experience of 'The Posture of the Aware Self' and its Triple Body-Womb, in Connection with a Difficult Relationship or Issue.
II. From Aware Body-Womb to Infinite Womb. Dissolving into the Void.

XXIV
Moon and Sun

At the edge of dawn, I watch Aurora sleep.

In me, she is the love, the Spring-child that never dies. Her heart beats to the rhythm of the flight and the song of the birds, murmurs like running water. In the most somber moments of my life, she is the one who believes in miracles, who lives in trust, in faith. She is the Unprotected Child also, who passed through fire, whose torn heart gave back its very sap.

Yet like the phoenix, like the shaman, she resurrects from the ashes, from the ordeal, from the winters of the soul, like thawing rivulets. Sometimes one would say that suffering glides off her like raindrops do all night long on the foreheads of Watchmen! Yet in the morning her blue eyes sparkle afresh like mischievous forget-me-nots. Her blond hair plays with the first rays of sunlight that filter through the forest. And when she flings herself at me, to meet my tenderness for her, I see her fragile splendor: A corolla of white poppy petals dancing in the light.

As if feeling my gaze and thoughts resting upon her, she wakes up. Still surrounded by the veil of dreams, her spirit a little disheveled… her glance resting on the window. There, a gracious insect like a young girl—long members, transparent wings, interminable antennae—moves up and down along the glass, vibrant, sometimes knocking against it, sometimes motionless.

Behind the windowpane the dawn glitters through brilliant leaves. The trees breathe, bathed, caressed; mysteriously translucent. The insect resembles an Angel having mistaken this world for the *other*, lost the key to his return, to the *passage*... the passage between the worlds.

I sense how Aurora feels stirred by the insect's dilemma and how much she would like to make it understand... Beyond the window there is a mosquito net, precisely to keep insects out! The unexpected is that the insect is inside.

Observing this miniscule day fly, I have a feeling of kinship, aware that the very essence of our being reveals itself in our most burning desires. The insect palpitates there like my soul: So weightless, so miraculously frail and powerful! And, my soul, like the insect, isn't able to renounce its nostalgia for open space; it craves for the light; it hungers for the ocean of greenery! And this cannot be found between squared walls, trapped in this hole of shadow. It waits for us beyond the window, where our rightful abode is calling; on the other side of the *opening*.

A clear pane of glass, a net so fine as if woven by the insect's own slender legs, does not appear to obstruct the way! Passionate desire can be the blinding focus that renders all saving alternatives invisible!

To find a way out, the insect must defy its instincts, turn around and dive into the dusk of the house, pass the shadowy landings; follow a hidden thread that runs deep underground. Descend rather than ascend! And therein lies the answer... and this is neither the easy nor the obvious way. To find Peace, Freedom, may depend on relinquishing our survival drive, on leaving our familiar universe behind!

'Inner Light' waits on the other side of shadow, on the other side of trial. Inner Light reveals when we do not evade our fears; for when we face them with lucid compassion, they dissolve like clouds veiling the Sun.

Remain vigilant behind your closed doors, the opaque doors... the mysterious doors. Remain patient when you cannot, when you know not. Trust the uncertain, the risky, while your narrow path winds like a drunken guide who seems to take you the other way… farther and farther from you had imagined.

Our descents may show us a lowlier route than our blinding certainties! To venture the stairs that lead down—where it is so difficult to envision that a sky could open at the bottom of the steps—we need unshakable resolve!

I feel that Aurora follows my thoughts. I take her hand as if to say: 'We will be together on this path.' We are both apprehensive, though determined to risk it; to enter the labyrinth, to plunge into the well; to turn away from illusory escapes, from the brightness that provokes us behind the window and attracts us to glass walls so insensitive to our hopes!

The powerless insect has made us aware of the necessity to uncover a different threshold, to find another door, more humble… the threshold that one crosses like a defenseless infant on the wings of faith! Not with the wings of stubbornness, not with the wings of our tireless ideals, not on those that carry our fascination. There we only exhaust ourselves. The sun burns us when courted from too near!

I have to close my eyes, to open interior eyelids; I have to let darkness take hold of me, before I can distinguish the concealed Path, its Radiance obscured by my beliefs. Real life eludes us in the raw light of preset understandings.

Indeed I have to morsel myself first, turn to sand, grain by grain; disperse and abandon myself, where I neither can, nor know. I have to quiet the persistent chatter of my panicked thoughts, the erratic movements of my limbs against the unyielding glass, before I can faintly recognize the echo of another pulsing, of another truth, in the hollow of hidden ventricles. No doubt, Real Life waits in my own depth. It palpitates in these Nights of the Soul that other stars govern!

I can feel Aurora's sadness, her need to find meaning in all this; together we search in our old dictionary for the name of this insect. We have to smile! It is called *ephemera*, like the vain surge of desires and fears! We are from the same vulnerable and stubborn family; captive of closed windows and of mosquito nets; caged between our wants and our self-protections.

The point is not how to get out of it, nor how to master it, but to begin by staying with it; by following one's fear line. We can learn to watch and forego our automatic reactions, to attempt the unfamiliar steps, the ways never or seldom traveled. We can learn to espouse our discomfort, our suffering, and so realize what holds us there, and how we perpetuate it!

◆

As if by magic, the day has gone by. Night has fallen. We are sitting, huddled together and silent. A sigh from Aurora brings me back from my thoughts to my heart. She touches me lightly and shows me the moon that looks at us, consoles us with its soft rays from beyond the window.

Aurora's face begins to glow; a smile awakens fireflies in the depths of her eyes. I guess her connection with the moon. Spontaneously, something unknots, is set free… the Message of the Moon also resounds in me:

"I do not burn and yet the Sun is the source of my brightness. I do not doubt, even though I do not shine of my own light. I guide the steps of the traveler; I enchant the soul of children and poets. I imbue the embrace of lovers with shimmering softness!

My splendor is the merciful reflection of a Fire too ardent to unite directly with my Moon-body. To be reborn in the glory of *Light*, I need but turn toward it—virgin still of Knowing; to let myself be inflamed by its rays. It is enough to orient the Eye of my Heart towards it; to offer myself to its glowing touch… Never will I lack Clarity, Truth and Grace; never will I disbelieve, as long as I draw from this Life-giving Source."

Aurora's eyes glitter in the penumbra, as if all worries,

all questions, had dissolved. She is serene; a little elf. The Wisdom of the Moon inhabits her. An invisible finger comes to rest on my Heart, on the precise spot where a sigh of sadness still lingers. It rests just where love hurts, where love is stronger than death—so fragile also, that it is there that I break, that I collapse into my own depth.

I take Aurora into my arms, into this Mysterious Core where I know 'I am.' And through her the God of my childhood returns, like a living seed, rediscovered where forgetfulness left it, where remembering finds it. Intact!

Without fully understanding this alchemy of the self, right here in the middle of my chest, at the bottom of this crypt, so empty, so painful inside me… I feel a disk, an eye, something of a celestial body! There, in my ephemeral flesh, incorruptible and timeless.

The moon passes and passes between the trees, saying:

'See, it's so simple. You only have to let yourself be lit when your night is at its darkest.'

◆

Ever since, like a seaman in his submarine below somber seas, I try to align my Inner Well… so deep, sometimes so lost and so desperate! I adjust my periscope. I try to orient myself toward this unimaginable Sun with my body, heart and soul; I become a large telescope, squeaking at its base, unfolding its segments reaching out for the Sky.

Lover and Beloved, Sky and Sailor, Sun and Moon, You and Me… need but turn toward each other—bare and empty of themselves, smooth and polished like mirrors—to be gifted with divine Ardor and Glow. Mankind also is of the nature of Stars!

To align is to heal: Trust. Open yourself; become a passageway for the Light and it will rise out of you!

'I didn't know that we are like the Moon; I didn't know

that God is like the Sun,' Aurora whispers. The whole Creation tells it. All stones rise to the surface, all plants turn toward the brightness; all men seek enlightenment in the jungles of their lives! I remember that in the dream time, a miniscule Pygmy, almost insect like, with black, wrinkled skin, once told me so. And the alchemists of the past always drew moon and sun side by side and face to face!

Ephemera, I thank you for having touched our soul with your heartbreaking obstinacy, with your powerlessness, your incoercible nostalgia for clarity. I thank you for having conjured up for us this Strange Voyage, where what is at the bottom of the well shines like a torch on the mountain. Maybe you were an Angel after all!

📖 ***You are now invited to go to Volume II, Exercise 18***
The Experience of the Meeting between Moon and Sun
The Alignment of Our Heart with the Heart of God

XXV

The Twin Brothers

"I asked my Heart: 'How do you feel?' It answered:
'Growing, for by God, I am His House of Images.'

The Divine Image penetrates the Heart
Discloses in it a new Spirit, a shape so vivid
That if its radiance were to be reflected on a wall
This image would acquire a soul
And would begin to speak and to see"[38]
— Djalāl ad-Dīn Rûmî

To know is to love. To love is to know.

Once upon a time there were two twin brothers, Jon and Tan, born from a distant Star, who knew nothing about the Earth. They lived in a world without images, devoid of colors, smells, sounds, shapes, or tastes. Everything came to them instantaneously, which didn't provide any leeway for creations to be born and to die. Theirs was a blank, uniform world, without sadness, but also without pleasure: Neither shadow, nor light, neither desires nor regrets! Time—that would have made a past, a future—didn't exist; nor did Space that would enable them to unfold or contract, to discover a form, a temperature, a volume to their bodies! Their senses, their feelings, bore no connection to the vibration of one's nerves, the beating of the heart, the impulse of muscles, the pumping of the blood, the opening or closing of one's arms. Theirs was a

---

[38] Djalāl ad-Dīn Rûmî, Balkh 1207 - 1273 Konya. Sufi mystic and poet.

universe where all was immediately given, without having to ask for it or conquer it.

Without having ever heard about Adam and Eve, but pushed by a seed of curiosity undoubtedly blown in from elsewhere, they decided one day to let themselves drift into other fields. It is in this mindset that they left their planet on winged horses. A current, accomplice to Fortune, attracted them to Earth and delivered them there at nightfall, each one in a different place, though only a short distance from each other.

Jon found himself on steps leading up to a kind of giant Vessel of stone that seemed to rally the sky, leaping forward in arrows, vaults and arches. Fires glittered in the high windows… as if they had just captured the light of the stars! He entered. The pillars, the stone ribs around him, rose like immense trees; far above, branches connected and intertwined in a man-made firmament. Jon felt himself filling with a strange inner silence. His body emptied, made room to encompass this awesome space that now vibrated inside him like a note devoid of sound, like a vision beyond sight.

Almost without being aware of it, his body started to stretch and expand; his feet still walked upon the marble floor but his head touched the nervures of the highest arches. His hands spontaneously joined in front of his heart—as if cast in a mold of the same shape and movement as the nave. An unknown feeling surged within him, a shining, agile joy, like quicksilver! It ascended from his entrails to his eyes, blossomed through all his pores like soundless fireworks, vital and yet composed, lifting his own radiance far beyond this ship of stone, all the way up to the sky!

Jon had never known any other body than his own, had never vibrated with such exuberance. He stood there, surprised like a little child in a new self, a cathedral-self. His soul burned like the altar candles, transfigured by intensity, imbued with a nameless fervor. He felt as if his flesh had become transparent, his skeleton luminescent, and his heart aglow with a soft, dancing flame.

He fell to his knees and for the first time in his life tears rolled down his cheeks, like stars rolling on the body of the night. And in his soul and flesh, he willed never to forget the miracle of that moment.

Subsequently, Jon discovered Earth's innumerable faces and chambers, shapes and structures, countless other forms and figures. He became their disciple. And, as he welcomed them like a student welcomes his Teachers—finding delight and meaning in all sorts of transformations—he became a Sage. And if you haven't heard of him, perhaps it's because he leaped out of time and space. Or, because we humans have disfigured the Earth, shut our eyes to its images, closed our bodies to its breathing, cut our sensitivity from its love.

Yet, like all Sages, Jon secretly lives in everyone, in one's own Heart, and it's up to us to meet him there.

As for Jon's brother Tan, he landed in a dark lane in front of a building, signaled by a red lantern, where a pretty mouth beckoned to him, where beautiful clear eyes full of stars shone through small windows. To his surprise, he felt an urge to go inside, to rest there from his far off journey, to ease a new nostalgia that he couldn't explain. He entered. His heart beat faster. Here, perfumed lights appeared as flowers that he'd never seen before: diaphanous, pink, orange… Their velvety skin enchanted and attracted him. And as he plunged his face into their depth and fragrance, a strange drunkenness took hold of him—his mouth wed their forms, drank in the semidarkness of their corollas. One by one, he lost his scales. An unsuspected softness and frailty began to unfurl from the tips of his fingers, from the tip of his toes that now resembled young sprigs full of tender leaves. He was shedding his body as born from a fresh mold; became a fish in warm waters. He undulated, magnetized by a rocking of the seaweed; he resurfaced with strength and voluptuousness in the current. A force, hitherto unknown, stretched him in the riverbeds, breathed him into the belly of a sea. His chest broadened with great sighs; he felt his arms lengthen, bend like the streams of water in the valleys. Tan had never known such sensations, had never felt his whole being, his very heart swell to the beat of a Universe.

Tan became a man full of tenderness. And like his twin brother Jon, he willed to never forget his strange metamorphosis. He learned to Love, to shape-shift in all embraces, and—allowing them to be his intriguing and enchanting Teachers—he became a Sage.

And if you haven't met him, it may be because he returned to his planet on the other side of the sky. Or because here, unconsciously and without understanding, we have disfigured and blinded the body of men, the body of women; we have ceased to marry Heaven and Earth, closed our eyes to their probing, closed our hearts, our sexes, to their divine gifts!

Maybe we lost the taste youth, of fruits picked by a thieving hand, still wet with dew at sunrise on a summer morning. Maybe we turned Creation into a no-man's-land, formless and dull; without fragrances, without murmurs, without savors… forgetting to lie down with the Earth… in her arms, in her entrails, in the infinite spectrum of her colors, that set us alive!

And yet, like all Sages, Tan has secretly embedded his seed in everyone's soul and womb and it's up to us to join him there.

◆

The story of Jon and Tan invites us to make ours a marvelous Creation; a Universe that doesn't refuse itself; that doesn't stop nourishing, teaching, loving, those who drink from its Body, listen from its Ears, see from its Eyes, speak from its Mouth.

Maybe Jon and Tan became wayfaring Pilgrims to honor in each woman an incomparable flower, in each temple a God; or else, they refresh, they quench their thirst along the way, by entering into the 'spirit of things.' And, if this is so, they never feel bored or despaired in their life! I even believe that—despite their totally new capacity to feel—they do not suffer... as long as they espouse the essence of *now*, embrace all states of being without judgment and without fear. And this is not a matter of imaginary marriages; it comes from a sharing with all otherness. A sharing that intimately roots in our sensations, merges with our feelings, melts into our flesh! It originates in a soul-to-soul closeness—similar to what Jon and Tan experienced during their initial adventure on Earth—when the *other* takes shape inside *us*, when we take shape in *him*.

Is it not a gift of Understanding to slip into the spirit of things? Into our own fatigue—or the fatigue of another—into solitude, betrayal, anger, sickness, transgression... into aliveness, laughter, love, joy; to clothe ourselves into the thousand fold moves of Creation; to make ours the oblivion of the night, the stone matrix of Michael Angelo's slaves. Or to feel that the bark of a tree is becoming our skin; that its roots are growing from our feet, that its branches are rising from our hands, sheltering birds nesting in our ten thousand arms?

Is it not a gift of Relating, to recognize inside ourselves the determination of Robinson, the desperation of Friday, the innocence of Aurora; a gift of Consciousness, to become aware of the Unseen, of a shimmering Grasshopper, of Noah's Ark, of the Emerald Tablet, of the Grail—heralding Insight and *At-one-ment?*

Is it not a gift of Compassion, to hold in our heart an old hungry man; a soldier frozen in the snow, a woman who cries for her child; a small girl bloodied and dirtied; a little boy whose eyes close in powerless misery?

Is it not a gift of Wisdom, to look through the quiet eyes of old age, to offer ourselves to our dying, to be reborn in the smile of a stranger?

Encounters are rivulets in which all beings, all situations, always show the 'One and Only Face,' the Face of God, the Face of the eternal Beloved, transcending time, space, our own limitations. They unfold an endless, sacred Meeting that one breathes in, that one breathes out, with a profound respect, a profound tenderness for all there is.

Yes, surely Jon and Tan became Wayfaring Lovers. And yet they didn't neglect their far away Planet akin to the Void, where '*being*' remains serene and Life suspended in waiting like a Virgin Womb: A Rest, before or after the Movement.

Together with them, from up there—as if we had risen in a spaceship or slipped into another dimension of consciousness—we can recognize it all in a single glance. We can behold our multiple selves, from above and outside; become our own Witness! And return from these out-journeys... like the Shepherd at dusk. We can choose to lead our flock to the haven of a familiar stable... to be reborn there like the infant Jesus in the warmth of the straw; to be held there, like holy children, in our own consenting arms and breath! For only like this can Oneness descend.

It's been a while since Aurora has been tugging at my sleeve, preoccupied to not see me come down from the galaxies... 'Jon and Tan are down here,' she whispers. 'They have been waiting for you for a long time, they're hungry!' I had to smile, say sorry.

Maybe, right now, Jon and Tan are standing on your doorstep, or waiting in your bedroom! Maybe they have prepared a cathedral for you, or a vast bed where love cascades and bubbles! Don't forget that like them, with them, you are invited to journey; that what is below is like what is above, and what is in the other is what is in you!

Maybe you will be tempted to slip into some new shape, to let yourself merge into its rhythm, its color, its weight, its density; its light; tempted to bathe in it, to breathe through it. Maybe all you have to do is espouse it with all your senses… to discover how totally it becomes yours, without holding back, without greed, without secret.

  You are now invited to go to Volume II, Exercise 19
The Experience of Relating to the 'Spirit of Things'
Part I. An Outline of the 'Voice Dialogue' Process
Part II. Relating to the 'Spirit of Things.' Self-facilitation
Part III. Guided Facilitation: A variant of the Part II

XXVI

Little Stories and Attunements
From the Satchel of the Wise

"Jesus saw some infants who were being suckled. He said to his disciples: These infants being suckled are like those who will enter the Kingdom."[39]

Are we not, deep down, in search of a *Homeland* imbedded in our Being? Are we not the rebellious and famished children of a *fathering*, a *mothering* that links us to our Source, to each other and to all there is, in a sacred brotherhood? And *It* visits us!

When I let go of my preconceived images—about 'who I am' or 'who you are,' or should be!—I come back to a simplicity of body, heart and mind; I return to an original state. The moment we allow unknowing—be it because we trust, or owing to despair and exhaustion!—we are suddenly graced with unforeseen replenishment.

Try it!

'Close your eyes. Relax like a suckling infant at God's breast!

And as you remember these words, be still. Let them seep into you. As you listen, as you wait—in childlike innocence and faith— feel how they slowly become true... how the Kingdom begins to stir in the middle of your chest, swells like a warm soft current of love, a breath of release. It gifts

---

[39] The Gospel of Thomas. Logion 22

you—like a parent his offspring—you start to brim over... to extend this nectar into the world.'

And as I share these words, I can feel it too! I can feel our hearts, yours and mine, and all the hearts of past and future realms—uniting outside time and space. It is together that we fill with humbleness and joy; that we bow in awe; that our wings open, that a shiver lifts us into freedom like birds! And you and I will ask in wonder: 'Can we so easily stretch into a weightless widening... in which all men can rest and find their deliverance?'

Beware of greed, of doubt, of fear and judgment: As we deny our safety in God's Love, we immediately sink under. We sink like Peter walking on the water toward Jesus; we fall from the boundless and timeless recognition of Grace, like stones.

Check it out in daily trifles! Watch how your mental projections take hold of you and turn your world upside down.

"One evening, during a great wind, a young man hurried home afraid of returning after nightfall. Inextricable foliage and high grass rendered his path barely passable. Thick clouds prematurely darkened the sky. Nature—that earlier hummed reassuringly in the brightness of a summer's afternoon, now hovered like a ghost. An indefinable hostility crouched in the underbrush. He quickened his pace.

Darkness was falling fast when a short span ahead of him, he sighted an undulating, slithering shape. Ever since he was a boy he had dreaded snakes. All at once he felt utterly exposed, helpless against a venomous attack that, he knew, could strike as lightening. Panic knotted his stomach. He stood paralyzed, holding his breath. And as he remained still, so did the snake. To retreat a step, to turn to run, could provoke his death. He now thought he perceived a shift in the snake's posture, but no sound accompanied it. Leaves fluttered over the path, the world began to spin, he almost lost his balance, yet his sudden movement provoked no reaction. Was this a trap? Never taking his eyes off the treacherous beast, he kicked a stone toward it. Nothing He kicked another. Nothing! As quickly as morning mist lifts, he could feel himself emerging from the throes of fear. His eyesight cleared, his breathing eased, his heartbeat slowed! Still trembling, he inched forward, closer and closer to the snake … Be it through magic or pure deception—it revealed nothing more than a dark sinuous root!"

Our thoughts rule over what is true or false to us; they induce or modify our emotions and even our perceptions. They are the stronghold of our interpretations. The undulating shape that blocked his path, the young man's experiencing, were a spell. A spell cast by obsolete records. And yet, his millions of cells, his entire interior chemistry, his muscles, his nerves, his blood circulation, his breathing, his reasoning, his feelings, all went on emergency alert, just as if he had faced a real threat! This can save our life in the face of actual danger, but will poison it if we forego 'here and now self-awareness.'

Yet, independently of being founded or unfounded, fears and pains' do affect our mental, emotional and physical health and balance. It remains crucial to examine and question their validity. At the same time, it truly matters—even when they prove imaginary!—to show compassion to such *Inner selves* who suffer from bad day-or-night dreams. Let us awaken from our speculative beliefs and 'self-relate' with lucid tenderness and say: 'I acknowledge your fear and your pain, I am not ashamed of your frailty; I stand at your side with love, with strength, with trust.'

Sometimes Aurora, my Inner Child, wakes in the middle of the night in tears. Because I love her, because I know that negative thoughts and hurting emotions—like roots in snake disguise—create real damage and sickness in our minds and bodies… I immediately—prior to any rationale—hold and comfort her! I listen to her story; I murmur softly into her ear, I stroke her hair.

As I accompany her breathing with my own, the color returns to her cheeks, the fireflies resume their dance in her eyes. 'I am here, Aurora, don't be afraid. All the snakes in the world, all the nightmares born from darkness, the werewolves that feed upon children's feet, the sharp beaks of ravens, and all the other scary things… can do no harm in the presence of shared Love.'

Of course, then… but then only, will we get up together and check the room, and the shadow beneath the bed, to make sure that imaginary threats and sorrows have been dispelled by wakefulness, like dawn dissolves nocturnal ghosts.

Aurora has fallen asleep against my shoulder. She sleeps in the arms of her trust in me, of my care for her. It would have been cruel to laugh her nightmare away because it was just a dream, without soothing her first: Our delusions always involve suffering!

Whenever your heart, your throat, your plexus, contract— they signal a *little person inside you,* calling out for your affection and reassuring presence; a little person who nests at the exact place where you can feel the sadness or the pain.

Is it not inhuman and dangerous, to disregard the messages your heart and flesh send out? Don't we despair because we have distrusted or withheld love, inspiration, sharing? Don't we get sick, or deeply upset, from believing in depressing thoughts and feelings rather than in the 'True Self' we all share? Is there anything to gain from being so merciless with ourselves and others?

Do I forgive the *Woman in me* for failing to make an *Ark* of her marriage; for not rising like Aphrodite, seductive and weightless, from the crest of the waves? Do I absolve the *Mother in me,* for not being wiser and more attentive to her children; for not having saved her son from self-destruction? Do I bring my *Inner Child* solace, for not having transformed over night into an Indian chief or a heroic Knight? Do I pardon myself for not retaining the true eternal Friend; for failing to be a lighthouse for fleets of sister ships, for my children, on the ocean of darkness, of solitude, of self-defilement; for being suddenly the aggressive wave, the hidden reef that sinks our life-boat? Do I forgive the other for these same misgivings; for rejecting or abandoning me?

Aurora woke up in my arms this morning, happily laughing and lively. Life is not a two-dimensional story, a blind train on a one way track, racing from A to Z, from past to future, from 'not good enough' to perfect. Life is a three-dimensional blooming, an extending of God Himself: 'Aurora, you are—since ever and forever—whole, loved, innocent and free!'

Once Aurora had built up enough faith in my love… I told her: 'To grow up means to watch in wonder our Deeper Self outshine even barrenness, even mud and tears, even pain and blood. It means recognizing that we do exist in a Holy Self, in a Holy Now—whatever ache we would flee, whatever joy we would preserve, whatever our mistakes. It means embracing the continuous dying of our transient shapes, while never distrusting our eternal life and freedom in the Spirit.'

Aurora fell silent, her face went white. I thought she was going to cry. But she simply slid her hand into mine and said: 'Then it's true! I can give life to my Soul, share what is deeply mine, give birth to God in me and be born of Him!'

'Yes, Aurora, the Kingdom of Heaven lies within your Faith and within your Love!' She smiled at me. I could see quiet wisdom in her eyes.

Ours is a wondrous Journey! Every human re-condenses billions of years of Life's evolution in nine intra-uterine months. In this minute period of time, in this fragile and magical cellular love story, we grow from a unicellular into a miraculous babe! And more! In the unique and brief 'span of sensitive immersion' between our conceiving and our death—we are presented with countless possibilities. Every being, every psyche, is both distinct and universal. We host a fathomless diversity of life forms.

A universal 'Loving Intelligence' unfolds in and around us; nourishes us, teaches us—if only we open our eyes, our ears, if only we put our jars on the roof… to collect its blessing rain of insights. It offers itself without any avarice, without any judgment… to the rich and the poor, to the cultivated and the ignorant, to the wise and the insane, to the young and the old, the healthy and the sick, to the innocent and the guilty.

Is it not our responsibility to acknowledge our thousand faces as they meet us? Is it not our spiritual assignment to reach out to them with ten thousand compassionate hands—like the Bodhisattvas; to offer them a multitude of breasts, brimming with the milk of love and abundance—like the ancient Mother-goddesses?

If we assume that we originally proceed from One Love, why not trust that our seeming separateness dissolves in the same One Love? Why not postulate that each time we cherish and forgive ourselves, a chain drops from us, setting us and our neighbor free. For no one unfetters alone. It is in relationship that we separate and suffer and it is in relationship that we heal.

In our search for meaning, for our core-identity, the slightest occurrence, encounter, holds the opportunity of an immersion into the Self. Each shared present moment is a door to it; instant by instant, we can—as all Lovers do—cross its threshold; become Whole.

Our relationship to Life, to mankind, to the human psyche, to God Himself, is a Love affair: Undress of your preconceived mindsets; hold everything and everybody in your arms… and the world transforms! And the world gives birth to renewal. To Love, is to love all the way; for the Knowing exceeds the sum of the known and the Love surpasses the sum of the embraced.

Isn't this precisely what the most invisible of insects, the most hidden of flowers, serves and demonstrates? Look at them. Listen to their teaching! They offer their splendor, their colors, their seed… to the unseeing eyes of the sky. They surrender to sleep or to death, in winter or at dusk; they wake and resurrect with spring, with the rising of the sun. Humbleness of love; absence of fear; generosity of being; desire of Life and Love for Itself!

'Voice Dialogue' practice brings into perspective the holographic nature of Consciousness. By shedding light on the manifold angles of our physical, emotional, mental and spiritual expressions, it assembles them into a coherent three-dimensional experiencing, allowing us to integrate opposites, multiplicity and differentiation. Thus we outgrow duality, the restricted vision that splits us off from ourselves and from each other. What is outside is like what is inside. He, who recognizes in all things 'One and the same Self,' encounters *Himself.*

Can it be that Consciousness breathes in 'the embracing' and breathes out 'the dissolving' …loving, unbounded and free? *Solve et coagula,* a practice of alchemy.

"In truth we are one soul, me and you
We come into sight and we hide, you in me, me in you
This is the profound meaning of my connection to you
For in-between you and me, there is neither a you nor a me

We are at the same time the mirror and the face
We are drunk from the eternal cup
We are the balm and the healing
The Water of Life and the One who pours it"
— Djalâl-ud-Dîn Rûmî

XXVII

The Nesting of Desires
'Voice Dialogue Facilitation'
A Process of Self-Inquiry & Self-Connection

In the past, I often denied or made light of my qualms and of my weaknesses. Repeated loss, failure, sorrow, but also nascent wisdom, have gradually subdued the arrogance of my bravado and of my judgments. To meet myself, to meet you, and to uphold empathy, has now become vital to my human journey.

The practice of 'Voice Dialogue' has shown me how our thoughts, emotions, perceptions, actions… take form inside us as a 'Tribe of living selves' that battles to survive trial and threat. 'Voice Dialogue facilitation' helped me to sustain a double approach: To feel deeply touched by human suffering, while at the same time remaining lucid and firm, regarding reactive behaviors, mental dictates and emotional confusion that shut off our natural intelligence and sensitivity.

Equanimity leads to peace: 'I see your error and keep an open heart.' I embrace the shivering of the flesh, the bewilderment of the heart… and yet exercise detachment and clear-sightedness.

Understanding how innocuous roots become venomous snakes shows us how irrelevant our interpretations and our competing about the right and the wrong usually are. And this discernment liberates inner space, makes room for open exchange and good will!

Our vision depends on our perspective. Inner and outer world, oneself and the other, are rarely what we believe them to be. This raises the question: 'From which frame of mind or mood-setting—based on what—do I look upon a situation; upon you; upon myself?'

The moment we identify with an 'Inner move...' *this* becomes *who* we believe we are; becomes one's transient or more lasting *identity*. And immediately a number of related projections take over; they do so by *personifying* in our psyche as our 'Suffering or Efficient or Defensive selves;' they trigger opposites. Inner contradictions abound; our world fills with guilt, disapproval, self-enhancement, illusions and ache. We literally *become* the given response; we shrink to just *this particular me!*' We suddenly shift from trust to withdrawal or anger; or revert to submission. We lose our balance; we oscillate from deflation to inflation. Reliance turns into rejection and bliss into despair. It is our own array of fixations that prompts our dysfunctional behaviors and rekindles—ad infinitum—the same misery in our minds and bodies; in our feelings and relationships!

When conscious and chosen this shape-shifting can become a fabulous richness. The problem is that these scenarios, these changing focuses are almost fully involuntary and prone to excess: 'I was the best an instant ago and now I am a naught! And *you*, my 'dearest for twenty years,' are now who hurts me most; a sudden stranger, an enemy!' Our 'survival personality,' our Inner Critics and our Judges, our Controllers, take possession of our lives.

Who did this? Was it God? Was it the Source of our being? Was it me, was it you? Was it both of us together—abruptly cut off from self and other; from what we truly want?

How will we restore our broken connection, mend our exploded hearts? How will I find the way to myself? How can I reconcile love and freedom, vulnerability and strength, gentleness and boundaries; gather in an 'Ark Within' the *selves* that inhabit and surround me; remain serene in the midst of injustice and hurt?'

Who am I really? The answer awaits us in our own depth: From one's conception to one's last breath—under the guises of our countless desires!—we do thirst for our Oneness and Freedom. The Truth of *who* we intrinsically are lies in this simple fact of our 'deepest longing.'

Your Core-identity is at hand. You can check on it:

- Name one of your specific and quite ordinary desires…
- And ask yourself: *'How would I feel, what would I sense… if it came true?'*
- Give a simple answer in one or two words…
- Use exactly the same process with a few more of your desires, as they come to your mind, and name, each time, the feelings and sensations, you imagine it would bring you…

. . . .

- Now, ask yourself: *'If all this were granted… is there something more important, more essential to me that I might still desire?*
- Name it and ask again: *'What would I sense… if this too came true?'*
- Give a simple answer in one or two words…

. . . .

- *And so on…* Investigate deeper and deeper wishes you might have and the inner release they convey… until you find nothing more essential to wish for.

. . . .

- Finally, name clearly, in one, two or three words, the fundamental completion you were in fact reaching out to, via countless substitution desires.[40]

◆

---

[40] *The nesting of desires'* An exercise I experienced at an 'Enneagram Seminar' with Eli Jaxon-Bear.

'When we examine our human wants—all the way down to our core-longing—we most probably find that *Peace, Love, Freedom,* are our ultimate desire. And this may well prove true of everyone; all the way from the Saint and philosopher to the terrorist; from the most self-destructive to the most serene of men; and even from animals and plants to inanimate objects when we tune into them.

Aren't *Peace, Love, Freedom,* not our most sought for Treasure? And ask yourself: 'How could I possibly imagine and pursue something utterly alien to me? Could this even arise in my consciousness, be intimately recognized, if it were not already imbedded in me?

As newborns, we still reflect essential reliance. Yet, very quickly—as we sense aloneness, suffering and constraint, we develop a 'survival personality' and thereby lose contact with our innate nature of trusting innocence and selfless love. Instead, we set up an ongoing struggle to find relief, to summon up the oneness we deem lost—and yet intrinsically possess and couldn't mislay! Our Treasure-Self has never been lost. It waits in perfect consistency as one's undying *Seed,* ready to sprout, to bloom, to extend.

Why do we always see ourselves deprived of it? Why do we search for it in myriads of substitutes? There is no substitute for Love, Freedom, and Peace, for they are enough unto themselves. Whilst we complain, feel dispossessed and impoverished, whilst we endeavor to snatch it all back from each other, by fighting or pleasing, by bettering or criticizing—fulfillment awaits us within our own Heart; within the Heart of all there is.

It may not be easy to see how we have obscured our Innate Intelligence. It can even seem absurd—considering our destructive and suffering world—to evaluate man from 'inborn Innocence and Love' rather than from 'inborn fear, lack and guilt.' But we can observe that it is our ego that veils and silences 'who' we more truly are. To proceed on our journey of self-inquiry, to revert from automatic to aware, from driven to intentional, from rejecting to compassionate, we need wise tools.

◆

'Voice Dialogue' is a process of psychological and spiritual awakening that wonderfully combines empathy and boundaries. Our first guiding steps lead us to discover our 'Inner family of selves;' we learn to *identify with* and *dis-identify from* what we feel, think and enact—in a now conscious way. Our second steps teach us to relate to our different selves with attentiveness and care. Such mindful connection to our own suffering, to our contradictions, qualities and diversity, entails inner peace and healing and the experiencing of underlying Oneness.

'Voice Dialogue facilitation' invites us to slip into the very skin of our various *selves*. As we move in and out of what hurts, pushes or hinders us, we come face to face with our fears, guilt and pains… and can begin to respond to them with kindhearted containing. We realize that the workings and motivations of our *Inner selves* are mainly dysfunctional attempts to love and be loved! Touched by our own predicament, we will call them home; home to an *Aware self process;* home to forgiveness, to solidarity. At the same time, we take distance and detach from our limiting and often negative self-shielding. Unmet affliction and blind reacting will gradually cease to govern and overwhelm our lives.

I can believe that my identity proceeds from original sin, from exclusion, from disunion, and thus multiply distress, shame and strife. I can believe that my identity proceeds from biological foregoers, from surroundings and education and make them responsible for my ailments. Or I can think that I am called to be a self-made creature… and therefore—hating or mourning my failures—repeat wars against myself and others and persist in furbishing and worshipping self-images. I can also build on a spiritual option and place my identity in a Divine Source of *beingness,* in a fathering consciousness, in a life path that leads from ignorance to awakening, from separateness to oneness.

Our ego's projection of a perpetually 'lacking or grandiose self' can be terrifying; they breed self-sabotage and power abuse, false assumptions and ruined relationships. Our fear of insufficiency is a delusion. Let us become aware of it whilst also exercising compassion for our failings.

As we undress of our *persona,* our egocentric self-images fade. We develop a more timeless, formless, spacious, welcome of *who* we are. We reconnect with the Inner Peace that sets us free, with a Love comparable to the quiet bottom-layers of the Ocean, changeless and supporting—even while waves and storms upset its surface. We begin to meet inner and outer world with tolerance; with boundaries that safeguard mutual respect. We relate to others with more honesty, kindness and appreciation, and with less correcting, criticizing and expecting. This assists us in nurturing our partnerships, in raising our children, in finding our way to joyful living and serene dying.

There are two sides to the Coin of Relating: The first is to comfort and console; the second bids us to let go of the behaviors and projections that perpetuate suffering in ourselves and in others. The moment we do so, we serve Love. Realizing that attitudes of withdrawal and attack are always a plea for love, we gradually cease to confuse the behavior with the Person. We awaken from our nightmare of aloneness, guilt and accusations.

To remember my 'spiritual genes' in God's extending Love and unconditional Forgiveness, I need to acknowledge my Source in Him. I need to put to the test that whenever I commend myself into His hands, together with all creatures as my brothers, I am graced. At least for a split second—removed from egotistic time and space—I feel, I know: *"Loving God above all else with all my heart and all my soul and all my mind, and loving my neighbor as my Self,"*[41] is my true wish and reality.

📖 ***You are now invited to go to Volume II, Exercise 20***
The Experience of 'Voice Dialogue'
The 'Aware Self Process.' Self-facilitation.

---

[41] "The Lord is One; thou shalt love the Lord thy God... with all thy heart, and with all thy soul, and with all thy mind. Thou shalt love thy neighbor as thyself." Mark 12:18-34

XXVIII

'Voice Dialogue'
A Unifying Cosmic Dance
The Awakening Self

Because we are not aware of our spiritual reality, of being both the Lover and the Beloved, we persist in hiding from ourselves and from one another. No wonder we sometimes perceive our lives on earth as a curse, seek solace in artificial paradises, believe in islands of solitude, fusion or rebellion—only to recognize in the end that we have failed to cure our sores; that painful separateness and questioning still prevail!

We bury our childhood dreams, our most intimate hopes; we bury the Kingdom, the Original Garden, the *Ark Within*. We forget who we are and the treasure we carry. Our makings turn seedless; man and woman become enemies and our children prey to hopelessness.

Let us risk the love, sustain forgiveness, include rather than exclude, outgrow our limiting self-protections. Credit life; embrace it fully! One of the most efficient and rewarding ways to recapture our aliveness, is to practice 'Voice Dialogue' as a psychological and spiritual Exercise, an *'Energy Dance'* in which *all we are*—regardless of right and wrong—can be embodied, understood and honored. The art of 'Voice Dialogue' is the art to integrate our diversity and to recognize the hidden Fisher King and the invisible Grail in ourselves behind all appearances.

We need to unveil the fascinating inner cosmos we harbor! What we feel, imagine, express, fear, desire, hope and despair of, has to be recognized as our sacred and challenging trail towards awakening and inner peace. We need to embrace our 'Inner world;' to envision it as a world we can take care of, that feels human, precious, redeemed and blessed.

Our *Inner Selves*, our *Inner Voices*, are specific and autonomous 'energy fields.' They come and go at often high speed, so that we do not really relate to them. Each *Inner self* characterizes by an emotional weather, a personal body feeling. Our 'psychological and biological meteorology' conveys our needs and necessities: the hot and the cold, the fair and the rainy; high and low pressure, season changes and sometimes cataclysms inside us.

If we don't become aware of our defenses, if we don't embrace our anxieties, our anger, our helplessness, we stay encaged in them; we repress the flow of our life stream. And as we obstruct it, we start to be in danger. If the inner pressure amplifies, it can turn violent and destructive—like an earthquake, a flooding, a vortex that sucks us in and drowns us if we resist it. It can entail sickness, burnout, inflation, depression. And by all means will keep us unhappy and extinguish our liveliness and our joy.

Yet even such extremes contribute to save us: Miracles are the unexpected release in our darkest hours. They wait in the collapse of our dam, in the deathly pull of the current, provided we have the courage to let go—be it because we are too exhausted to resist! When no alternative is left except abandoning ourselves to a descent into the unknown— it becomes easy to say Yes! Freed from our faithless control and resistance, we are suddenly lifted by Grace into Peace and Light!

'Voice Dialogue facilitation' is a cosmic adventure in which our impulses compose a 'Living Mandala.' Our survival selves, power selves, vulnerable selves, disowned selves, will successively take place in the consultation room. There they will revolve around the central pole of one's *Aware self process*—furling and unfurling the 'minor dance of me.' This opens us to a more respectful and healthy balancing of 'inner opposites;' it gives our 'suffering selves' the space to be heard and seen. As such, this procedure results in a growing *dis-identification* from our mental, emotional, and somatic patterns. Their ego-focused dance will gradually loosen up; move into an essential quality of presence and connectedness.

Facilitation is a selfless skill:

'I give you my full attention, with an open mind, an open heart and a faithful reflecting back. I will not judge you. I will not interpret or correct you according to my own views. I will commit all my empathy and intelligence to understand what you serve and who you are. I will put my full trust in your meandering ways and in the uncovering of the treasure concealed in your twists, bends and folds.'

This caring face-to-face will free and appease inner reactive drives or pains; it will assist every *Inner self* in finding its own deeper truth. When our moves are acknowledged, they come to rest. Those who are listened to relax: They belong; they feel human again! Once we call our 'Suffering selves,' our 'Defensive selves,' home to love, understanding and forgiveness… we can abide in the eye of our own cyclone.

A feeling, a person, a situation, a *subpersonality*, we turn down or deny, acts as a retaining chamber in our 'castle of many rooms!' A castle in which each chamber only leads us further if we first explore it; if we walk through it. Each has a *door in*; its proper use and furnishing. We can stay caught inside it… or experience it fully and reach the *door out* to step into the next. This leads us naturally from the first to the last ring of an 'Inner spiral;' from the first to the last movement in which all our being states find freedom from themselves.

All have to be attended—before we can finally settle into a reconciled 'Inner widening.' The laws of energy show us that espousing the current is the only way to survive when caught in a vortex. As we go through the succession of our reactive and emotional states, we approach deeper and deeper levels... until we finally reach calm water: the Quiet of our Shrine! Its door is always open.

We become the 'faithful disciples' of a Temple of Consciousness. And this is always a disclosure we will never forget: We come home to the stillness of our *Aware self process*; home to the Love of the *Ark of the Heart*. We access the threshold of our Innermost Chamber, the Holy of Holies embedded in our depth.

'Voice Dialogue practice' invites us to a pilgrimage that teaches us that divine selflessness is alive at the hub of who we are. It is a process of surrender and liberation. It can be compared to the whirling dance of Sufi dervishes, called Sama. Suddenly we are part of the very movement of Creation. Each atom, each fragment of self, whirls and melts into both its beginning and its end; into an experience of Oneness we can only dimly foretaste.

'Let us watch the dancer who celebrates the 'Sama.'
He turns around himself;
He is both Point and Circle.
He is the Axis of the World.
Through him Earth links with Heaven
And they get into motion.

The Self becomes the Hub around which
The 'Making of the Worlds' expresses itself.
The Dancer moves from point to point...
Yet, in reality, he never leaves the Center Point.

As 'Being' goes only from God to God,
Man only moves from the Center to the Center.
In other words, all what is exterior to the Center,
Is merely an aspect of the manifestation.

Each point of the circle represents
A possibility of our being…
But, at the same time that it expresses a movement,
It also exemplifies the immobility of the Center;
That which is unchanging,
That which existed and will exist forever:

The Central Point in which
Being and Non-Being are One. "[42]

📖 **You are now invited to go to Volume II, Exercise 21**
'Voice Dialogue' as an Energy Dance
The Experience of Following Your 'Inner Spiral'

---

[42] Quote from "Mawlana Djalâl-ud-Dîn, Rûmi, Le Soufisme et la Danse" by Michel Random. Sud Editions 1979

Part Five

The Gift of Sorrow
The Unveiling
The Epiphany of Love

'Ultimately there is a Place
Of Union with the Beloved
A Place where all images are erased
Where all forms of self
Dissolve in God

All representations fade
The entire Ocean is but infinite blue
All arrogance falters, only
Glory remains.'

—Djalāl ad-Dīn Rûmî

XXIX

The Well of Sorrow
The Unveiling

"Can you be hurt by the energy of others?
No, never by the energy of another,
You are only hurt by the way in which you sustain
The relationship in your own consciousness. "[43]

To give birth in this world to an *Ark Within* is not devoid of hardship. We must clear our way through jungles, sever what entangles our path, reclaim our most intimate truths and joys; let go of what we cling to… An endless decanting that only discloses its entire significance when we trust our life enough to risk it.

Attachments, pains, grudges, the servitudes born from them, seep into our flesh and bones like a tentacular memory. They adhere to our cells; permeate our organs, our muscles, our skin. Past conditionings well up in our slightest movements; rule over our energies, over the expression of who we believe to be.

When abused… a body, a gender, a person, might numb or pervert. We re-experience misuse and violence in nightmares, flashbacks and daydreams; we may become incapable of healthy relationships. We bear our past on our shoulders and in our wombs! The heart of many a child breaks again and again on feeling abandoned, invisible, disfigured. Who

---

[43] Richard Moss. 'Words that Shine Both Ways.' Enneas Publications Ca 1998

is isn't recognized; who perceives himself as a mere object to the other—fights against his own annihilation.

Where does our contribution lie? Doesn't Life weave our canvas without consulting us? What will we offer to it, if not a Consciousness in search of its own awakening? Dying to bygones is essential to our rebirths; forgiveness is crucial to our peace; to our freedom. How can we face a new love, take a new step—being neither locked up in our past nor harshly disowning it?

I didn't always know that to mourn, that to bleed, before detaching the last fiber of what keeps me in bondage, would engage a descent into myself; allow me to touch much deeper levels of who I am. Our tears, our blood, our errors, are the fertilizers of a harvest to come. But to dig the furrows, lift out the stones, loosen the clods of our physical and psychic substance, hurts: it is our body, it is our heart, it is our hope! Who is this *Link-cutter* who clips down our young shoots in the merciless run of Time and clicks on 'repeat' until we get free of its wheel? Who undoes our workings; who separates us from those we love; who throws our old bines on the fire?

What agitates and touches us so is really a flock of unappeased ghosts—calling from without, calling from within! Should we not listen, respond to their query; quench their thirst for love; pray for their wandering souls? For what is left unanswered, will fail to find rest; persists to knock at our door. What isn't absolved is not set free. On the contrary, it will devour us like an undetected wound, a drying out of the soul, a stubborn recollection of our frustrated flesh and psyche.

Are we not blinded by a strange madness that turns our lives, our relationships, into a ruthless jungle that little by little devours the Temple of Love? Slowly its shrine dismantles; prey to iconoclasts and to vandals, dislocated by the creeping liana, swallowed by the virgin forest, abandoned by its devotees. Slowly it sinks into its living tomb, sacred only in the memory of the dead and the gods: split-up lovers, broken limbs, scattered couples… Who will honor them now with blessed offerings? Who will reestablish their sanctuaries?

Have we not sold for little our precious embraces? Haven't we—indifferent or powerless—watched *Time* obscure the lively flash of our joys, deliver us to conflict or to silence and stupor, erase the paths that lead to each other?

Haven't I seen myself at fault and forsaken—rather than cherished and beautiful?

Haven't I condemned you as the unfaithful man, as the uncaring pillager, while forgetting the architect, the trembling traveler—who without knowing how or why, had to build a destiny elsewhere, without me? Didn't we both disbelieve our love? In younger years, I wasn't aware that—in you as in me—opposing forces coexist. In me a wife who forever loves you, a blissful amorous woman… but also a bleeding victim and a relentless accuser. In you, a spouse ready to die for me… but also an adulterous man, a deserter!

Comes this daze, this debasing, this hatred in which—to justify one's innocence—each finds it necessary to blame, to disavow what was sacred; finds it necessary to make of the other 'someone else.' Someone, neither you nor me is… or ever wanted to be! The blameless and the culprit, the beloved and the rejected, the faithful and the traitor, the weak and the strong, the wise and the fool… live side by side in the same '*human me*,' in the same absurd and painful dream. All yearn for Oneness; but all compete to keep up their little 'separate self,' dreading and defending its possible loss or defilement.

Like a mythical figure from ancient tragedies, I had let myself be led to the doors of the City. I had taken, almost unconsciously, albeit with courage, the path of banishment. Not knowing… that in doing so, I turned my back on myself; not imagining that the woman, the mother, the lover, the child inside me, would stand guard alone and famished—without the comfort of my tenderness for them—over the dismantled sanctuary of my life.

And yet—except in one's own condemning mind—no one can be truly sullied or forsaken; for no one is guilty or adulterated in the Memory of divine Love. Once we rely on this, judgment becomes meaningless.

Because I doubted Love, whole parts of me stayed trapped in past or future tales. My Inner child was orphaned. My Inner woman was living in exile; her heart, her chest, weathered away in the jungle. The paths that led to the temple disappeared. The Lovers are returning to sand.

Attachments, rumination, selling out, do not credit love. They are not a blessing for the journey. Denials, amnesia, are not a worthy way of saying goodbye. If we end up judging that what we felt never was true love, we deceive our children—making them believe that they were born from deceit and not from cherishment! Should we not respect both the richness and the precariousness of our relationship; let go of the reproaches? Honor what was, and remains the truest: The Holy Instants we shared! Or do we prefer to turn our treasure to dust, our knowledge into ignorance—because the loss of the other as our object is too cruel for us to bear?

Why assess love in terms of expectations, success, duration? Love is eternal—not because it endures, but because it is by nature a Totality.

Only relating saves; sustains love's healing flow, what needs to be reborn into caring, but fails to do so …unless we redeem it in our conscious wombs, in the tenderness of our gestures, in the warmth of our words, in the attentiveness of our gaze. If we don't search out our lost, our broken thread and hold it dear; dear like the hand of a long missed friend, we fail to reconnect.

◆

Isn't winter always followed by spring? Let us look with compassion on our loneliness, on our fear and with patience on our errors… rather than flee them; rather than stay their victim or become their angry champion.

Sometimes we wonder at an insidious spleen, at some lasting, unexplainable depression that sticks, that thickens: We wander in the gray. Low-hanging dismal clouds shut out our light, dull our understanding, stifle our joy.

One day the clouds will burst and the inner dam will yield. Indeed, each time one of my dikes gave way, the collapse I had so feared and so stubbornly avoided, in reality salvaged me from an overburdened, barren or mistaken life! What weighs on us is not so much the load of a given trial as the load of our vain efforts to master it. The repressed spit up of what I cannot digest. It is the bulk—not of tears cried, of conflicts met!—but of those I shunned. It is the storms that haven't broken.

Sometimes, it is a 'stillborn *me!*' An ashen horizon, black motionless waters, upon which I let myself glide—like a funeral boat between two worlds! It is my love frozen in the midst of summer; the natural consequence of sealing off the source of my bliss.

I came to understand that immobility … this incomprehensible entrenchment of the being, this unexplainable fatigue that overwhelms me, is the awesome stillness before the gale. The dams so cautiously erected start to rupture… slowly at first, along a fine fissure that imperceptibly widens. Trust and love dwindle while judgment grows like the crack beneath the water. Will the strain lessen by simply exhausting itself? Or will it suddenly destroy what we so carefully constructed, within one giant murderous wave?

One day, under the pressure of a single drop too much, the crack explodes leaving all that was hidden exposed. Fury growls, echoes in the mountain; a cloud of grime obscures the sky. As if released by an over tight rubber band, one's life and love is propelled into nothingness. How long will it take to forget? How long for grass to sprout in devastated fields? How long to forgive?

Can it be that each break up will also bring the clean washed sky that follows lightening, thunder and rain, fragrant and fresh like the skin of a newborn child; carefree like Aurora's dancing steps?

Salvation doesn't await us in our highs, but at the bottom of our well. And years later, it appeared to me that it was Grace itself that led me along this endless fall into darkness—until nothing was left to risk, or to learn, but unconditional surrender; until nothing is left, but this 'rift in our consciousness' by which the sky opens on the other side.

This Holy instant came, as if by magic it seemed. Beyond my own limit, beyond my headstrong *no's*... at the bottom of the lake of tears, just where I died into the *yes*, into the letting go of my story; ready to seize my own hand and your hand!

I suddenly found rest, in a deep place, a secret place—only revealed because my reservoirs were empty, because my anger and my hope had proven powerless; had stranded at wit's end.

Solely the Wings of Faith remained—wings of which I had long lost the feel. But now, sounds, colors, perfumes, awoke; gestures unfroze; muted words were heard and spoken. A whole Sunken Realm miraculously uncovered in my deserted abode!

And there, in the Forsaken City, in the empty House, in the shrouded Heart, a surprise awaited me. Because my wrath and my sorrow had exhausted themselves into a '*yes* to what is,' into a *yes* to a forgiven life, I rediscovered—intact inside me—the Woman, the Mother, the Child, the Husband, the Father, the Friend. Betrayal, error, pain, guilt and fury had unlocked their grip! No need to wind back, no need to bear or to undo; to better or to avenge: Each Heartbeat, here, still gushes forth from Innocence, from Love!

The laws of good and evil, of right and wrong, are suspended by Mercy. It is by *at-one-ment* that we are healed; that we are returned to our *Self* as God willed it.'

So it is true! There is a Holy Conceiving, a Sinless Birth within God's Love. There is a Resurrection: Luminous unbounded Presence in which we originate and root; where we are never separate, never alone, never cast out.

📖 ***You are now invited to go to Volume II, Exercise 22***
The Experience of Sorrow
The Rising of the Star in the Well of the Heart

XXX

The Star of the Solstice

Once more, it seems that light and energy dwindle. Right in the middle of August things were already paling. Robinson clenches his teeth; locks his eyes on the horizon. The Grasshopper no longer sets my imagination ablaze.

I ask myself: Is this a sign of aging, of sickness; one of those things that undermine you well before the pink fades from your cheeks and the sparkle from your gaze? I rub my eyes. I take vitamins. Aurora says nothing; we just hold hands.

Although I already mourned many a trial, my heart sometimes still wells up with loneliness and sorrow! This time, I have decided not to torment myself, not to blame myself, but to wait, humbly, without searching for an answer. I take refuge in this unerring patience known mostly to animals and plants; the patience of dormant seasons, of dams that fill drop by drop, while the torrent below empties, while its bed dries up and becomes solitary.

The scenarios we rewind in our minds, replay in our lives, seem endless! What is their purpose? Do they bring us closer and closer to consciousness? Do we ask better questions about ourselves, rather than accusing the other? Do I now give myself permission to cry? Do I, at last, remember to seek out who turns to stone within me; who again feels trapped and hurt in 'long-ago;' who is suddenly silenced, denied? By raising such issues, I have progressively opened the door to fair self-love and caring. A climate of solidarity and friendship has grown roots deep inside me; roots that survive winter! I can now hold in my warmth and understanding *Inner selves* I had previously ignored, condemned, or abandoned in some dead angle of my psyche.

Fortunately, nothing can suspend the law of renewal. After the draught, comes the rain; after frost, comes the thaw. I vow to stay trusting. I can sense Aurora, Robinson, Friday, the Grasshopper, the Teddy Bear, gathered around me. Together we are silent and watchful, like Vigils from a Lost Kingdom, from another Chamber of Time. Together, we rest our hands—the Grasshopper his wings—on the door of the Heart; attentive and listening.

Aurora, who intuits everything, turns toward me and smiles. Her gaze is so penetrating, her heart so sensitive, that nothing remains hidden from her. Her smile tells me, reminds me: 'It's never too late; it's always the Holy instant of now; the *now* of shared love, shared pain and forgiveness.' Children never lose hope! She is the one who always brings me back to myself; and it is precisely in the midst of winter, in the time preceding Christmas, that one of these blessed openings she foresees, is about to take place.

It is December 10th during Advent. I sit in my room, face to face with a friend and colleague. While she holds for me the Mirroring Heart of 'Voice Dialogue' facilitation, I dive once more into my grief-stricken venture—that re-condenses again in this single afternoon. I cry for each second, each hour. I cry with Aurora. Friday almost believes he is back in the jaws of the night on Robinson's Island. Only the Grasshopper already unfurls his flickering robe; discretely, so as not to disturb us.

Slowly, the lake of sorrow empties… Below, the held up river begins to flow again and timidly resumes its course. And something amazing happens. In this emptiness left by the draining of my tears, in this abyss of more than twenty years, at the bottom of the dam, I myself become the Mirroring heart: I see a young woman, her newborn on her knees, her beloved facing her. Both lean over their child.

In the 'Aware self process' that emerges from facilitation, Love claims our Immortal Spirit. Forgiveness attests our Innocence. Awareness pre-exists and outlasts the rising and the sinking of our scales, of our credit debit balance, of our opposites; of our destiny upturned by a dire spell; of what we deem to be our personal drama and our need to retaliate.

I reach out to this woman, this man, their child. I lead them back to the City. I give them an abode in the Caravanserai of the Heart. It is this 'calling home' that marks all our steps towards undoing and reprieve. Not to brush it all off! Not to will it different; not to justify or regret... but to rehabilitate all facets of *'what was and still is...'* as a part of our life; as so many translucent windows to consciousness—some shining, some dark—juxtaposed in a dance.

This dance is the Divine Wheel that whispers the Name of God and it is up to us to recognize Him in every spoke, at every turn. Neither our erring ways nor our contradictions have the power to misguide it. Its Truth lies in its Hub where all spokes originate; in which all our moves are held safe. Our journey has never left the Center, because our faults, our misconceptions, cannot alienate Love as our Source.

But we remain free. Free to choose from where we look on our destiny and free to choose how we participate in it. It is my responsibility to remember who I really am; to take this woman home. A woman safe and whole, that no judgments—neither yours nor mine—can alienate, even if they sealed the door to her room and obscured the way to the deserted temple for so long!

Consented tears and joys disperse our clouds; we discover the rain-washed sky, the inner Spring-child when winter subsides. Water murmurs, the sap rises, the Source is released. And it is easy to pardon, once we realize that no atom of love will ever be lost: I was wrong in believing that you had taken something from me!

This afternoon of thawing sorrow has brought us peace. Time itself has become motherly. Huddled close, Aurora, Friday, Robinson, the Grasshopper, the Teddy Bear and I, nest in each other's arms. Together we have fallen asleep, but this sleep is not anymore the lone and naked sleep of orphans. Creation itself is redeemed. It is December 10th during Advent. The earth is awaiting the arrival of Christ, the rising of the Light, the return of Love. Animals, plants, men, our millions of molecules and cells turn toward the Ascendant.

As if touched by an invisible and weightless finger, we awake to an unexplainable radiance. The night has begun to glow. The Grasshopper is almost phosphorescent! Aurora gets up first; her frail silhouette seems that of an angel framed by the window. 'Look, she whispers, just above our garden, the Star of Christmas! The Guiding Star that stops above the newborn Jesus in Bethlehem!' I hesitate to answer. This evening Star... hasn't it always been there?

It shines through my window with growing intensity; surprising and yet familiar. And in the depth of my chest, I feel like a flame that responds to it. There, in my heart, in my being, a light arises. A sudden simple evidence: Wherever our steps lead or mislead us, whatever our detours, whatever we choose—on the crest of the wave or in the abysm—always the Star of the Self has preceded us.

In this blessed moment I do not know... that exactly two years later, on December 10th, during Advent, a few hours before dawn, I will sit at my dying mother's bedside, listening to her uneven breath. The Star shines on the Book of Time and Fate. I take refuge in its Wisdom. I do not know... that at the instant of her passing, she will turn toward me, one last time, with open eyes. I do not know that I will behold the Star's otherworldly glow reflected in her eyes; partake in her vision of the Beyond: A Realm of awesome brightness and beauty.

Her last gift to me, her child!

Two thousand years after the birth of Jesus, two years before my mother's death, at the vanguard of Time and Space, the Star shines upon the ever present moment of *at-one-ment*. It rises in the thickest of our fogs, the deepest of our despairs; in the very time we would so much avoid; in the time we dream to join.

Be it in our escape or in our return, we can never forego the Star of the Self, the Star of the Christ-Child. It waits for us in the Feeling Heart. If you can't see it, every Heart will clear your sight. If you can't find it, listen to your Heart step after step. When you love, it burns, it expands. When you cry, it distills a reviving juice. When you are lost it flutters like wings; when you die it gets quiet. It strikes your first beat and surrenders your last. And when—against all reason, you trust… is it not in your deepest Heart of hearts that God shows Himself? Is it not precisely there that you recognize Him?

Know that Pain is an initiation. Sometimes it calls with a tearing gentleness, like a first shower that announces nurturing change. Sometimes it spreads unnoticed and silently. Sometimes it gets crazy like a spurned lover; turns murderous; shapes into an assault, a war, an insurrection. Better we listen in time! Better we open the door of the Heart before it seals shut or breaks apart…

The *Self* is a Mystery, like Sorrow, like Love. What's to be done when, prisoner of our fortresses, of our leaden insulations, we no longer perceive *It* in this body? A body in which we wait and hope, like in a long-deserted house, for the Master's return! What's to be done, but keep an open Heart, an open Mind, an open House?

The *Master* returns unforeseen, like a Stranger, like a Pilgrim, like an unpredictable Brother; a Traveler on invisible trails. He appears when everything within us is ready to receive Him.

If by adventure He comes to you at dusk or in the fearful night, while you keep count of time by the distant ringing of a bell… know that He just clothed Himself into a 'Naked Child' that trembles inside you at the far end of your own darkness. Approach Him softly, humbly, for He carries the holiest of your pains, the holiest of your joys, your most priceless wisdom. Get down on your knees, warm Him with your breath; wrap Him into your most beautiful robe. [44]

Know that He has healed your wounds and carried your cross. Know that—by forgiveness, by faith and surrender—He has transmuted evil into innocence and death into eternal life.

Know that His Nakedness has set you free.

📖 ***You are now invited to go to Volume II, Exercise 23***
The Experience of Uniting with Your Inner Star
Meeting Your Angel, Your Celestial Friend, Your Essential Self.

---

[44] A tribute to Og Mandino, 'The Greatest Salesman in the World.' Bantam 1983

XXXI
The Twenty-Fifth Hour

The Twenty-Fifth Hour! The Hour we never expect.

And yet we do wait for it, we know it to be there, like an invisible door to the other side of ourselves. The Hour we cannot foresee … The Hour we discover like a small child. It can only surprise us, evade us—even though we have packed our luggage and think we are ready to leave everything, to give everything… when it comes!

It follows us at every step; it offers itself between one breath and the next. It draws us into its elusive Mystery between two dots of time; between this day and the morrow; in-between you and me; in-between the before and the after… in this imperceptible, timeless space, called *Now*.

It doesn't show on the calendars from which we feed our certainties. It sends ambassador after ambassador; yet we aren't alert to it. It just struck like lightening. It approaches barefooted and silent. We neither saw nor heard it. It is always through the little door, the back door, the side door, that it comes. Too early or too late, we think! Or, could it be that it doesn't exist—because we have not outwitted it, never retained it? Because it keeps all of its secrets and can neither be avoided nor rushed. It tirelessly returns to meet us and yet is never marked in our diaries.

The Twenty-Fifth Hour; the Hour that should come later… and comes before. Sometimes I believed it to be the last hour, far away from this day, in old age. But no! Every time it suddenly catches up with me, it feels as my first and only hour. Traceless, spacious, it arises from the Void, from the Unknown, from the Wisdom of the Heart. It is the Hour we so intensely desire and fear.

◆

It always sets its seal on a virgin page; the Virgin Page of Love, of Birth, of Death. When the target isn't set, the blinding arrows cannot strike. On a blank page we are new!

But in my youth, I wanted to challenge the target, to master my arrow and my bow; to fill out my life-book in my own personal way. And as I did… the number of arrows grew; I could no longer see any white on my pages. As for the target… it was my flesh and blood. And the target had become a wound and the book a go-round of cyclic crossroads.

My days have repeated themselves, twenty-four by twenty-four steps in the cellars and attics of time. And the carrousel ceaselessly twirls! So much to do, so much to learn, so much ache: Minds packed full with shelves and drawers; chests heavy with stifling nights when the storm doesn't break. Wasn't it only yesterday that I realized that I have grown old… startled by an unexpected strike at my body's clock? Now sometimes, in the evening or even in the morning, a strange fatigue comes over me. All awareness, all relating, the slightest movement, feels like a burden. I have to close my eyes! Like Esau, I would even sell my birthright for an alleviating of my hunger; my hunger for unconsciousness.

So quickly, we succumb to fevers or to indifference! Shouldn't we question ourselves when our cravings for food, sleep, pain, anger, sex, youth, money, power, security and love… leave us answerless? Shouldn't we get alarmed about our self-dazing; about our blindness toward others?

If we don't—getting really old, really sick, facing our ultimate powerlessness and mortality, might feel unbearable; our doubts, our despair, our loneliness, so naked, so exposed.

◆

Sitting at my father's bed; looking upon the ending of his days, I reflect: '*Who* is it that summons these images we do not invite; that digs up our old bones, our lost trunks, our miscarried dreams? Who fans the embers of our delusions, of our hurting memories, of our guilt and regrets?' And then, there are these nights… nights that drag numbly and strangely, that spin and mill our disheveled thoughts.

Sitting at my dying father's bed side, I question myself: 'Is this how he felt; did this happen to him, without me ever being aware of it?'

I look at my father…

Surely, this Hour we cannot avoid will come! It lies in ambush in what is so perfectly arranged and organized and suddenly sidesteps. His gears still turn, but not like before. Perhaps the clock in his head speeds up, or moves its hands in jerks: '*It seems I do not see, I do not hear that well anymore. Why don't I remember your name? Have I lost track of time?*' Disappointment, bitterness, anguish, become the very substance of these endless hours—counted by this far off bell: '*Why is this bell no longer the bell of my familiar neighborhood? Or do these hours strike in my own chest so irregularly? Is it always night and dark? Aren't there any more birds?*'

Sitting at his bedside, I look at my father…

My father, who loved to talk, to tell us stories, to share of every book of human venture, of wisdom and poetry, stays silent. My father who knew everything about the gods and about men, about the flowers and the trees, in the sky, on earth and in the heart… my father says nothing. And me—me who had wished so often to stop the flow of his discourse—I now lie in waiting for his faintest word!

I look at my father.

I remember his inquiring spirit, so brilliant, so dependable, so precise… so imaged and powerful, that to me it resembled those marvelous machines, those giant turbines in the belly of the old steamboats on our lake. His Tales were full of these chromed nuts and bolts, of the soft flash of the brass, of the hiss and the sighs under the steam's pressure. And when the story left its moorings, it was picking up speed, like a giant lung that breathed faster and faster! And then... the reassuring rhythm, the paddle wheels that turned on each side of the boat, churning the water like massive mills that I admired as a child. And the arms of my father in which I felt safe.

I look at my father.

Something is broken, something is out of order. The big engines in the head hesitate, disobey. The captain no longer recognizes his course; the boat is no longer on schedule.

Is it also this... the Twenty-Fifth Hour? The Hour we want to forget; the Hour in which we didn't want to be born? Destination unknown. Time unknown. And my throat tightens; my eyes sting. All of a sudden the past seems so real, so precious, so close, so lost. Often, he had reminded me, how as a tiny child I always insisted that he hold my hand at night until I fell asleep... and how he finally inched out of the room on his knees so as not to wake me.

I look at my father.

The Grasshopper is perched at the end of the bed; he doesn't dare to rub his wings. The Teddy bear sits in the corner, patched all over, my father's red scarf around his neck; he also looks very old now, but his little bead eyes are alert, full of this enduring kindness that soothed me when I was small, and still does, even now! Aurora and Friday lean close to me.

Around us, inside us—as if suspended in the hush—hangs everything that could not, knew not how to express itself. An epistle of the heart that neither of us had truly dared; that each kept bottled up inside: A song hidden in between the lines of the stave.

Without me realizing it, Aurora has slid her little hand into my father's hand; a handsome hand, peaceful on the white sheet. And now it's me, who seizes both their hands into mine—the little girl's and the old man's… watching over his breath, over what falters, disconnects and sighs in him, while darkness grows and leads him to a closing sleep.

In this reversal of time, the little girl of long ago bravely stands by her father—as he himself of old had stood by her, squeezing her little hand until she fell into first sleep.

I look at my father.

How it must have hurt and scared him to no longer be able to harness his thoughts; to go blind, to face the unknown without the reassuring glitter of images and words; without the precision of the wheels, of the gears, so unremitting but so sure in the infallibility of their order. To no longer master. To no longer find refuge. How it must tear at him, leave him stripped!

Is it in moments like that, when we lose all control, all solving, that we reach the Twenty-Fifth Hour; that it carries us at last, gives itself over to us; bestows us with something miraculous of its own?

I look at my father.

His ideals, his loving thoughts, his clear-sighted trenchant views, had been his tools and weapons.

Now that the tumult of the great wheels subsides, that their revolving slackens, that his mental pools no longer fill with inspired turquoise waters… all of a sudden—a *small ancient voice* becomes audible again. The voice no one wanted to hear: The voice of a 'little boy' who cries; who has cried all along; cried his sadness, his fear. A little boy who feels alone and at fault; whose voice was drowned by roaring anger; silenced by the resolve to be good, to be better, to never inflict on others what he had to bear.

Now that the white waters of my father's thoughts and feelings ebb out, that his pages go blank… that the weight of his arguing, of my arguing back, falls silent—only my father's

Inner child is left; its faint, intermittent *voice* that doesn't really know what it is doing here.

And me too—now that the rumor ceases—I can hear *it*!

Aurora understood it first, for children recognize each other. She rests her hand on the 'little boy's heart' that beats within the heart of the old man: *'You are good, Papa; God lives inside you; here, in the middle of your chest. You are not alone.'*

Aurora's little hand knocks gently, timidly, but with certainty, on the door of the Heart… in the center of the body that dies. *'Here, Papa! Here, in the Hub of your Heart, God uncovers his Face. Here glows your Essence; the Real Presence of the Living Christ. It is soft in your chest, like the crimson flame in the choir of churches.'*

Maybe I did not pronounce these words; maybe they only resounded in the Sanctuary of the Heart, where all beings find their place and oneness.

Aurora said it with such simple words: *'Do you love me, Papa?'* And he replied, *'Of course.'* And she said, *'Me too, you know, I love you.'*

And because I remembered all the moments of resentment, hopelessness and anger that had separated us, all the regrets, all we had left unsaid, I added:

'You see, we love each other, Papa, that's already something good.'

And he corrected me, saying: *'It's much more than that.'* There was a single word left: *Love.* And this word said it all.

God's Presence unfolds in the shared Love that cannot be taken from us. And together we knew it. Like plants and birds know the dawn, know migration, know springtime, know impending death.

God unveils inside us when we return to infant-like nakedness—be it in spite of ourselves. And my father knew it. We both knew it, even though we had evaded it again and again!

And in this Time, this Space that was not on our dials, we found it fully given: "Surely I have composed and quieted my soul; like a weaned child rests against his mother, my soul is like a weaned child within me."[45]

◆

Having witnessed my father's decline and journey into dying, I asked myself: '*Who am I?*' What is left, when the trains of our thoughts and disciplines run off the line? When the body dismantles? When the mind goes astray? When the great weakness takes over? What is left when we can no longer protect ourselves, no longer direct who we are and what we do; no longer set and decipher our clocks? Who will I be, when the wagons of my certainties, of my skills and wisdom, the locomotives of my ideal, will start to diverge towards open country; ignore the railway stations and the safety of familiar tracks? Will I disappear in the great blue?'

Or will I be free, safely held in the arms of Love?

📖 *You are now invited to go to Volume II, Exercise 24 Holding Hands with our Selves and One another before we Die.*

---

[45] New American Standard Bible. Psalm 131:2

XXXII

Open Sesame: I Love You

In the hospital ward, I look at my father.

When I was a teenager, I sometimes hated him for pouring himself out so much. The flow of his words seemed endless. Later, I thought of his unhappy childhood; I said to myself: 'Theses streams of words are a call for someone to listen, someone to pay attention to him.'

And now I realize—somewhat late—that all his erudition, the teaching, the eloquence, the rising tide of his thoughts… were not just a call for someone to hear him; that there was much more to it.

Do I recognize this because knowledge abandons him, because it is finally Silence that speaks for our hearts? Now that our 'expectations of each other' are laid bare—in an unbound book that sheds its leaves—the child in him, the child in me, look up between the fading lines, the scattered pages, out of the stillness between the words.

Feeling how tormented he is, I take his hand. I read him some passages from 'The Way of the Russian Pilgrim,'[46] without knowing if he understands them or not.

Suddenly, he says: '*I can't stand all this noise!*' I ask him: 'What noise, Papa; the noise in the room; the noise of me reading? 'He says: '*No.*' 'Is it the sound in your head?' I ask. '*Yes,*' he says, '*in my head.*' Without a transition, he tells me about the life of the Empress Theodora. Already I imagine one of his long historical digressions that I never could stand.

---

[46] 'The Way of the Pilgrim,' G.P. Fedotov, Courier Dover Publ. 2003

But here, I try to listen between the lines, close to the heart. I try to listen only to the 'voice of a little boy' lost in the jumbled riverbed of his thoughts, now almost dry. My father says to me: '*You have no idea what her life has been like... An edifice of falsehood!*' 'Who, Papa? Theodora?' He says nothing, but begins again: '*An edifice of falsehood.*' I ask: '*Who, Papa? Are you talking about... yourself?*' With anger and impatience, he answers, '*Yes... yes, me!*'

Aurora begins to cry. How can we assuage the mind; pacify the heart? The old man expresses his fear and his truth... "If I speak in the tongues of mortals and of angels, but do not have love... I am nothing..." The little boy has always doubted his own worth; feared to see his Treasure lost to looters and vandals. He never really trusted that a Loving Hand might lift him up, without any price to pay for it—invite him in, as he is... into the Light!

The little boy has lost faith in his own worth, in his own love. His earthly father abused him by violence and shamed him. The little boy has desperately tried to become a good man; a man who so often grasped at Love and seized only shadow. "If I speak in the tongues of mortals and of angels, but do not have love, I am only a resounding gong or a clanging cymbal. If I have the gift of prophecy and can fathom all mysteries and all knowledge, and if I have all faith so as to remove mountains, but do not have love, I am nothing. If I give all I possess to nourish the poor, and if I hand over even my body to be burned, but do not have love, I gain nothing."[47]

My father is tormented by his inadequacies, his untruths. And I sit next to him in this dreary hospital ward. Me who always wanted so badly to tell him better... now that I finally have the room to do so, I find nothing to say! Long, crucifying

---

[47] The Bible. I Corinthians 13 (1-3)

moments, where all my words are still-born, as they so often were in the past. And my father's words are silenced… swallowed by the abyss of his abandonment; drowned by the noise of guilt and wrath that thunders close to his suffering, like the roar of a lioness that can't save her cubs!

Did he ever realize that he is, always was and will be—like every one of us!—a good and worthy man in the eyes of Love?

And now I do recall how he always forgave my anger, my missteps, my negation of his gifts; how he never bore me grudge for rejecting him; how he always supported me, always responded to my needs—even before I was myself aware of them.

So does God Himself act toward men! And so are we to remember Him and to practice in his likeness when relating to each other.

Aurora, who safeguards the hidden and the beautiful, has taken my hand and placed it over my father's heart. Aurora has taken the tear that pearls in the corner of his right eye. She has set this tear into my own eyes like dew, and the true words into my mouth: '*You are good, Papa, and God lives in the midst of you, right here inside your chest. And God does not leave you.*'

I felt the 'child in him' relax. I thought: All through his life my father tried to uphold justice, beauty, spiritual values; tried to help, teach, console… while the child in him was so lonely, held captive by bitter memories, below the rising tide of wise or irate words. And me, I fled from his words, from his wisdom, from his love, from his anger, like I would from a torrent where I can't keep my foothold; turning my back on my father, but also on myself.

I try to make peace within myself, to kindle the flame of love inside me. I try to assuage his anxiety and despair within my heart. Aurora and Friday show me the way. And then it seems to me that my father has grown quiet. He doesn't say *no* anymore. He no longer roars. A little earlier I had said to him: '*You are right, Papa, to roar; what you are experiencing is too cruel.*' Now his breathing is calm.

My father has just died—at the twenty-fifth minute past one in the afternoon—in this brief moment when I left him to call my mother from the phone in the hallway. The large curtain around his bed, now shields us like a sacred isle in this crowded unit; a motionless ship in the current of the hospital-river. Something like a Silent Song unites us: closeness, reconciliation. We are both at peace.

And, for a few moments—removed from the mesh of oncoming agitation and of the social urge to quickly dispose of the dead!—we keep watch together over his passing; over this threshold to another Life. Around us, ordinary living carries on. Strangely, in the background, a radio broadcasts 'Tibetan psalmodies; *chants* that my father so deeply revered. I can also hear a patient who ceaselessly begs someone over the telephone... who repeatedly threatens to throw himself out of the window: Anger and despair that my father had so often voiced as his own.

The serene litanies of the praying monks mingle with the bitter litanies of a sick man on the other side of the room. An uncanny convoy for this final moment! Absurdity and splendor, helpless protest and quiet recollection escort us. No heavenly canopy! Only the bare hospital ceiling and the beggarly curtains insure us a short span of privacy; of intimate togetherness. For a few instants more, he and I are alone to know that his boat, that his *Ark*, has just gone through the sluice; has just been lifted up to the gate-lock; and from there into the River Beyond.

"Everything on dry land in whose nostrils was the breath of life died... Only Noah was left, and those that were with him in the ark."[48] And me, I'm just Robinson—the would-be sailor, the apprentice islander. And I survey the horizon, the sea—so immense and empty with my father gone…

In this final 'Ark of earthly time', in this Twenty-fifth hour of my father's life, we shared the secret language of the soul, of angels and of children; the love of Friday, the trust of Aurora, the song of the Grasshopper, the softness of the Teddy bear. All of us held safe, for a fleeting instant—or is it for Eternity?—in the Ark of the Heart, in The Ark Within.

◆

Once my father's corpus of forms, in body, emotions, thoughts and reactions, had been lifted from our battlefield—lifeless now in our ego's biased grips and sights!—forms ceased to be an obstacle to our bond. It has become easy to share with him how dear he is to me; to ask for his forgiveness and to forgive him. It is so effortless now, to accept that he could never stop the flow of words that held me back; that I could never listen to him without finally getting angry and without feeling guilty about it. For, indeed, I had fought him with all my might! I realize how obviously futile it is, to lead—against myself and the world—the same kind of war we had always led against each other. The war with those we love.

It is so undemanding to accept that we had both cherished and hurt each other. It is so undemanding to comprehend that whatever the past, whatever the circumstances, we need but align our Inborn Will on God's Will: The Will of Oneness and Love that joins the above and the below; the you and the me; the Pole in our Heart with the Pole in God's

---

[48] The Bible. Genesis 17: 22-23

Heart. "I am the Beloved's and the Beloved is mine."[49] This simple insight heals us.

To a God who's Love fathers us, our errors never will, never did… matter. Freedom is our birthright; we have always been free. Blindness is lifted by a volte-face the moment we envision the world, our neighbor, our Lineage, our Name, from the other side: Born from *Love* instead of *Fear;* born from *Innocence* instead of *Sin.*

When we deem ourselves enemies, fathered by separation, unloved, unworthy, poor and guilty, we forget the miraculous statement that opens our jail and highlights our riches. The walled obscurity that holds us trapped when we forget the password, so easily dismantles! It is enough to remember and pronounce the *Open Sesame* in three simple words: '*I love you.*'

---

[49] New American Standard Bible. Song of Solomon 6. 3

XXXIII

'Voice Dialogue' and 'The Tibetan Book Of the Dead': The Bardo Thödol'

'After the peaceful Deities and the Holders of Knowledge have ceased to appear, ...will come the wrathful, blood drinking Deities, surrounded by flames, who are in fact nothing else than the peaceful ones in a different guise. [50]

The Tibetan Book of the Dead, the Bardo[51] Thödol, describes in detail the experiences of our dying body and those of our soul thereafter.

It says that immediately at death—prior to anything else— our soul beholds the 'Clear Light of Ultimate Reality.' It states that therein lies our first chance to free ourselves from the delusions of one's egoic mind, provided we recognize in this 'Clear Light,' the 'Divine Consciousness' we share in—and fully unite with it!

However, if this is not recognized, our soul will then be challenged by terrifying figures, by dazzling images and daunting sounds, suggestive of dark sides, projections and il- lusions we carried in life. Our guilt, our anger, our sufferings, our cravings, will flash across the screen of our minds like a scary motion picture run wild. They will frighten us, confuse us, overwhelm us—exactly as they already do in our everyday

---

[50] 'The Tibetan Book of the Dead, The Bardo Thödol.' Transl. W.Y. Evans-Wentz, Oxford Univ. Press 2000. *See* excerpts in this chapter.

[51] *Bardo* means "in-between;" here the transient span after death in which the soul can recognize its immortal spirit or be captured by delusions of its 'egoic mind's projections' and be reabsorbed into the 'Wheel of Time.'

lives... lurking within our daydreams and our insomnias... in the guise of our wants and fears, of our inflations and depressions!

Yet, says the Bardo Thödol, at this point, we have a second chance to free ourselves from the 'Wheel of Time,' from our 'cyclic re-embodiments,' if only we envision and embrace with total Trust— behind the thousand masks of such Wrathful deities—the Radiant divine Essence of all outward show!

The Bardo Thödol invites us to pray as follows:
''May I acknowledge, whatever vision appears, that it is the reflection of mine own consciousness... May I not fear the bands of peaceful and wrathful deities: mine own thought-forms...'
And it instructs us thus:
'O nobly-born, when thy body and mind were separating, thou must have experienced a glimpse of the Pure Truth, subtle, sparkling, bright dazzling, glorious, and radiantly awesome, in appearance like a mirage moving across a landscape in spring-time in one continuous stream of vibrations. Be not daunted thereby, nor terrified, nor awed. That is the radiance of thine own 'True Nature.' Recognize it. That is the natural sound of thine own 'Real Self.' Be not daunted thereby, nor terrified, nor awed.

Since thou hast not a material body of flesh and blood, whatever may come—sounds, lights, or rays—are all three unable to harm thee: Thou art incapable of dying. It is quite sufficient for thee to know that these apparitions are thine own thought-forms.'

'...O nobly-born, those pure lands are not anywhere else—they abide in your own heart within its center and four directions. They now emerge from out of your heart and shine onto you! The deities themselves do not come from anywhere else: They are primordially created as the natural manifestation of your own awareness—know how to recognize them! So do not be attached to them! Do not be terrified of them!"

Such a vision of the 'ephemeral and the eternal' in us is not restricted to Tibetan views. Religious traditions as well as philosophies exemplify that our living and our dying, that our daily little deaths and rebirths—are our Teachers in the unveiling of our Deeper Reality. Socrates puts in a nutshell when he says: 'Know yourself and you will know the universe and the gods.'

Let us not wait for our last hour or for our Beyond! Trains of obsessive thoughts, whirlwinds of energies and emotions—embodied by our *subpersonalities*—stage our plays and dramas in the here and now of our lives. They do appear to us, as attractive or repulsive, as blissful or unbearable, and indeed in the manner of peaceful or irate deities: I feel burning impatience, irrepressible desire... I feel listless or fearful, or joyful, or despairing; buoyant, angry, guilty, innocent, loving, hateful... bewildered.

Who am I in Truth?

Am I only the oblivious actor of 'conflicting roles made flesh;' tempted to believe them all to be *me*? Could I become their Witness—rather than letting them co-opt and subvert my free will, toss me from artificial paradises to imaginary hells? Will I become their compassionate Friend, as they show me their contradictions, their suffering, their alarms, their successes and their failures—thus touching my heart?

'Voice Dialogue' is a particularly efficient consciousness tool; a spiritual discipline: As we release our mental and emotional responses, as we detach from our behavioral scenarios, we also uncover our intrinsic underlying Unity.

Let me evoke briefly how this works.

Step one: I leave my chosen Center place to embody what presently inhabits me as fully as possible…
- I take a seat for this particular 'self.'
- There, I voluntarily 'identify myself with it;' I take time for inner listening, time to enter its skin, mind and heart:' I state aloud what I feel and sense; I recall related actions and situations.

Step two: Once I have fully expressed this specific 'self…'
- I consciously step out of this 'form of me' and return to the Center place.
- I 'separate and detach' from this 'self.' I welcome it as a *person in me*, but without believing that it is 'who I basically am' or that it is 'all I am.'
- I observe whatever has changed: Liberated from what I could share and release, I now naturally perceive an 'inner widening; an increased rooting and vitality; a serene presence in the body.'
- As I tune into this 'centered, silent, freed inner space,' I access an experience of the 'Unchanging Peace' that underlies all manifestation.
- I become available for new vistas and alternative choices. I can decide to take care of myself and others with more compassion and equanimity. I can begin to relinquish self-criticism and judgmental attitudes.

'Identifying with' and 'dis-identifying from' our defenses, allows us to meet our hidden vulnerability. We become more caring! We resent and react less. And deeper still, we can envision the Light of the True Person—in both self and others.

The Bardo Thödol states:
''If the most humble of believers, as soon as he sees the blood drinking deities… recognizes them as tutelary divinities… their encounter will be like the one of human understanding: He will believe in them and dissolving himself in them, will attain in union the state of Buddha. If you can

recognize them, exercising your faith and your affection towards the tutelary Gods, and believing that they came to receive you disguised in the tricks of the Bardo, think this: I seek refuge in them..."

Every relating, every conflict, confronts us in this way; challenges our trust, our commitment. Each attraction, each divergence, can build up into a saving love or a condemning exclusion. We can be the artisans of peace or of warfare, of union or of disconnection.

What will I see when my death comes, if not what I already see today? What will every one of us see in the Bardo?

We delude ourselves if we don't seize the opportunity in our lifetime to develop a more heartfelt clear-sightedness. Our reactive behaviors, our mental, emotional, judgmental, interpretations, will torment us until we cease to believe in them! They prefigure what will exacerbate, once our powerlessness increases. They will persist until we cease to mistake our ego for 'who we are.'

We will have to question, to discern, to choose:
'Who in me, what in me, styles and molds my identity; has just conceived this particular thought, feeling, deed?' We are currently governed by our fears and hopes, our fixed values and hasty shielding. Unless we invest our full attention to remember our deeper Source of Being, we remain prey to distress and unconsciousness.

A postulate, a hypothesis, is confirmed by testing it. Moment by moment, we may assess what fathers us, whose child we are, what we create in our image. Do we proceed from the Fall; from its subservience to judgment, sin and guilt? Do we rear separation and suffering? If so, it is left to us to turn around; to remember the 'Divine Self' God bestowed on us, and how He willed it:

In His likeness! And feel it come true—on earth as it is in heaven—whenever we ask for forgiveness; whenever we answer God's Love with our Love—breathing in His Spirit.

    📖 ***You are now invited to go to Volume II, Exercise 25*** *The Experience of Detachment, of Dis-identifying from the Ego.*

XXXIV

The Epiphany of Love
The Bridegroom

Our inbuilt Memory of God is our homecoming! A homecoming that delivers us into His Grace; dissolves all self-images, frees us in Him; in Him who encompasses all beings without possessing them, who eternally redeems and cleanses us in His Love without judgment.

Yet we need to give up our ambition to become 'self-created masters.' The masters of the right and the wrong—and therefore soon breeding guilt; competing for justification; forever dependent on proving our worth, and yet disbelieving it.

We need to return to infant-like trust; and this is in no way a regression into some original bosom! It is the choice to reclaim our *Is-ness*. It is the mature act of acknowledging our true Source. It is the decision to release our 'drops of water' into the Ocean of God, who receives and transmutes them in His unbounded Self—regardless of their bitterness, regardless of their limitation.

'My skin and my bones are changed into gold. I am the basin of Love; aliveness like waves. A single drop of water has become an Ocean. Un-navigable..."[52]

Love is un-navigable... We can neither force it, nor control it, nor keep it, nor lose it. Love is a Mystery that bids us

---

[52] Lãlan, 1775-1891. His songs were popular among the Bauls of West Bengal.
In D. Bhattacharya. 'Songs of the Bards of Bengal.' New York: Grove Press, 1969.

to become its fervent ones, its disciples. Not to claim it from each other!—but to serve it as transcending us both; to give ourselves to the Divine Lover who perpetually invites us to a lighthearted and selfless embrace.

◆

"Be fruitful and multiply..." says God to Adam and Eve in the Book of Genesis. But let us not understand this as a two-dimensional 'accumulation in number,' but as an 'Expanding Volume of Consciousness;' a volume of unfolding intelligence, of joyful differentiation, of creative flowering.

Are we not thirsting to evolve from the quantitative to the qualitative; from slumber to awakening, from self-entanglement to Selfhood? What if... it was only our ego pretending that we originate in sin, scarcity and separation? An ego chiefly interested in locating culprits!

For how could *Consciousness* destine us to a merely consumerist increase;' abandon us to our judgmental one-track mind; to the deep-seated shame we are caught in? Isn't this rather our self-made nightmare?

What if Consciousness originated in the Loving Breath of God; in the Spiritual Rebirth we foretaste—scales falling from our senses!—whenever *Love calls us by our Name?* Are we not suddenly serene, even in the midst of feud and hunger; suddenly bathed in innocence, in an unconditional accord? Are we not lifted into Union without cause or merit or hard work or tribute of sweat and blood?

Even our modest transitory human love is a Witness to this 'Holy Memory' embedded in us. Every love invites us to a holographic blossoming, rather than to a daily grind, via fractured opposing selves, circling on never joining orbits. Do not believe incoming clouds to be truer than the open sky. Do not believe in shadow instead of Light. Do not postpone: Will to remember and reawaken the glow of shared bonding.

Choose the spring you drink from; for this is the water you will taste and hand out to the thirsty.

Arising Love illumines our horizon like the *Clear Light* experienced after death: It requires surrendering everything to it.

◆

Let Love teach you its Song:

'Do not hide from yourself or from the other. For what is insufficient suffices to Love. Recognize yourself and the other as infinitely free and gifted. Tune into your bodies, tune into your feelings; tune into your souls and spirits; share your human sensitivity with playful and joyful tenderness. Exercise mutual comfort and forgiveness in your trials and in your failings. Do not take advantage of each other's worldly hungers and needs.

Do not blame yourself; do not accuse the other. For you are God's children; both perfect in His Love and carried in the 'Cradleboard' of His Creation; both blessed with His abundance and equally precious to Him since the beginning of Time.'

Let Trust teach you its Song:

"Feel equal in your hearts; equal in the giving and the receiving; for what is shared belongs to both. Exercise mutual care, but do not give yourself to be carried; and do not carry the other as if he or she were powerless! Lopsided loads rear angry claims, reproaches and mutual liabilities; blame validates beliefs in abandonment and incompetence. And this doesn't serve Trust! Embrace all conflict, all rebuke, as a disguised call for Love; a call to be reborn in gentleness and warmth! But also trust self-reliance in each of you, for even the smallest infant knows how to face suffering and to stand its ground with innate wisdom and courage.

Let Faith teach you its Song:

'Risk the relationship. Risk the forgiveness. Risk the practice of Love: the touch, the word, the gaze, the radiance, the holding, the surrender. Know that in this discipline, it is not your perfection or your efforts that matter, but your Faith in the perfection of Love; Faith in the Love embedded in both of your souls! In the midst of fog and darkness, seize the hand of Faith; seize the hand of the other, as if it were an Angel or God himself leading you securely through the unknown.

Let Hope teach you its Song:

'Stay close. Close to yourself; close to each other. Do not despair of yourself or the other; it would be, 'doubting God's presence in your lives.' Do not require from each other—or from yourself—to be better or different. Melt rather than freeze; open what closes; stay instead of fleeing; communicate instead of shutting down. Let the relationship flower in your coming to the Rendezvous!

Take every 'suffering' and wrap it into your tenderness like a shivering babe. Release gently what burdens you—fear, pain, guilt, failure. Relinquish your righteousness, your aloofness; return it all to Love. For what we give ourselves to… gives itself to us."

◆

Isn't inner peace restored the moment we let go of our suspicions, of our chiding and control; of our neediness? Isn't our healing revealed, when we return to simple bonding?

And yet—as if we were on the alert in the wild—we react to the slightest offenses and hypothetical dangers. We fail to disclose the warmth of our heart, the innocence of our flesh. We do not put down our weapons in front of each other.

Beyond our self-images, there is only One Person; One Love, One Face. We might recognize it more easily hallowed in brightness than disguised and impaired. Nonetheless, will we decide to be its vigils, its faithful, in the immediacy of each encounter? Will we pray to stay aware of it when we feel hurt? Will we decide to disbelieve our ego's fearful interpretations?

'The stone that the builders rejected has become the chief cornerstone..."[53] says the Psalmist. Instant by instant, if we so choose, we can be born again within the Virgin Mind of Love; within the Virgin Self of the Resurrected Healer; within the virgin gift of every godsend; within a virgin space in ourselves. This is the saving *god spell*, the redeeming Gospel, the everlasting Alliance between the Love of God and its Memory imbedded in us.

This Memory is touched every time we remember the primal innocence behind the guilt, the pain concealed in the attacker, the hope alive in the despaired, the powerlessness in the abuser. The Mindful Heart becomes a Witness to the flawless core in us, so easily obscured by our fears and judgments. The Art of non-blaming, the Art of Trust, is a giving over to the 'Master of Love;' He establishes our being in His Being, our love in His Love, our forgiveness in His Mercy, our gestures in His Gestures, our limitations in His Freedom.

◆

The 'Master of Love' sends for you, sends for me and says:

'You are welcome. You can lay down your armor; lay down

---

[53] The New Revised Standard Bible, Psalm 118:22 and Matthew 21:42

your faceguard, your helmets and weapons. Take your emotion, your nakedness, your solitude, by the hand… Take each other by the hand. And come as you are.

Know that I ask nothing in return—save your coming, save your saying *yes*, for I have already given My Self to you.'

If in your deepest Heart you know this to be true—answer:

'Here I am. I unlock, now. Worthy or unworthy, wearing the bridal dress, the cloak of innocence that God's Love has wrapped around my shoulders—I come! Holding my brother by the hand, I come.

Not because I know, not because I can, not because the other… but because the God of Love calls me, calls us, by His and Our Name.'

The 'Master of Faith' sends for you, sends for me, and says:

'Whoever you are, whatever you feel, come! But come right away; do not postpone! Do not lose precious time: time to change face, time to improve on. Because I request you as you are; because Love, because the Bridegroom, because the Celebration… is ready for you since beginning of time; is ready Now.'

If in your deepest Heart you know this to be true, call upon one another— and sing:

'The Master of Hope invites me, invites you! Even though we have nothing to offer, except our coming… except the little spark He has put in me and you; except the inextinguishable spark of His radiant Love gleaming in our bare hand, in our ephemeral cells and bodies, in our trembling hearts, in our confused minds.

Any say: I am, we are, on our way to the Gathering!'

◆

'…We shall not cease from exploration
And the end of all our exploring
Will be to arrive where we started
And know the place for the first time.

Through the unknown, unremembered gate
When the last of earth left to discover
Is that which was the beginning;
At the source of the longest river
The voice of the hidden waterfall
And the children in the apple-tree
Not known, because not looked for
But heard, half-heard, in the stillness
Between two waves of the sea.

Quick now, here, now, always—
A condition of complete simplicity
(Costing not less than everything)
And all shall be well and
All manner of things shall be well
When the tongues of flame are in-folded
Into the crowned knot of fire
And the fire and the rose are one."[54]

---

[54] T.S. ELIOT, in ''Four Quartets''

Epilogue
The Raven and the Dove

"Everything on dry land, in whose nostrils was the breath of life, died... Only Noah was left, and those that were with him in the Ark."[55]

Life has taught me that without God's Love holding us all in His Heart and Vessel, without Aurora and Friday, the Bear, the Maple tree, the Grasshopper, without my family, my friends and all those who called on me, without you who read this lines—I would have remained a reckless and rebellious Robinson, a shipwrecked sailor, an islander.

And even now, when doubt and discouragement take hold of me, I am again just a solitary Robinson who surveys the sea—so immense and empty with my mother gone, with my father gone, with my youngest son gone; with no seafaring knight on the horizon... And I cannot disregard that sooner or later, I will follow in their steps. I will leave this patch of home I cling to; entrust my frail bottle to the sea; commend my hope and all my loved ones to God's safeguard. But even in dim hours, I can sense innumerable beings from Beyond and around—like Tender Vigils at my side. Together, we rest our hands on the door of the Heart.

Be it at night or at my desk, I can feel it: The Grasshopper has just jumped upon my shoulder; he already unfurls his flickering robe, readies his wings! Maybe he is an Angel in disguise! Aurora, Friday and the Teddy bear are gathered around me. They tug at my sleeve and ask: When will the

---

[55] The New Revised Standard Bible, Genesis 17: 22-23

nightmares that overshadow man and his planet dissolve at wakeup? How will the Earth be? Will it be an innocent Garden again? Tell us how the journey ends.

"Then God remembered Noah,' who took continuous care of all those who were in the Ark, animals and men... 'At the end of forty days, Noah opened the window of the Ark that he had made and sent out the raven; and it went to and fro until the waters were dried up from the earth. Then he sent out the dove from him, to see if the waters had subsided from the face of the ground; but the dove found no place to set its foot, and it returned to him to the Ark, for the waters were still on the face of the whole earth. So he put out his hand and took it and brought it into the Ark with him. He waited another seven days, and again he sent out the dove from the Ark; and the dove came back to him in the evening, and there in its beak was a freshly plucked olive branch; so Noah knew that the waters had subsided from the earth. Then he waited another seven days, and sent out the dove; and it did not return to him anymore."[56]

Noah knew to be patient; to shelter every being within the 'Ark of his Love,' until the time came to deliver them to themselves! Will we follow his example? Will every one of us become an Ark for inner and outer world? Will we "Love the Lord our God with all our heart, and with all our soul, and with all our strength, and with all our mind; and our neighbor as our Self?" [57]

Aurora and Friday, the Grasshopper and even the now very old Bear, skip with delight and impatience: 'Us too, we will, like Noah, build with God's help a Boat that survives

---

[56] The New Revised Standard Bible. Genesis 8: 6-12
[57] The New American Standard Bible. Luke 10.27

the storms! Whatever happens on this Journey, we will regret nothing! We won't go backwards! We will take the same care of the dove as of the raven. They will be our ambassadors. And as long as there will be floods, and as long as men and animals will feel solitary and threatened, we will invite them in, with gentleness, with patience, like Noah. We will hold them close within the Ark; the Ark of the Heart.

Until there is Peace on Earth!

The young unruly Robinson I was, who left his Father and denied his inheritance, has now grown old and somewhat humbler. Waves, adverse currents and gales have worn and smoothed my spiky shell. And there is reason to wonder! With every flood, every disruption, Life has also offered me one of its virgin shores where all can thrive anew. And every time—as my sight and hearing cleared after the turmoil!— the waning waters left me with tender grooves filled with the finest clay, smooth and peaceful among disheveled thoughts and rocks. Soft and untouched clay: Clay born from endless sieving and filtering through love and trial.

Clay of the first Day of Creation: Clay in the Hands of the Divine Maker who insufflates His Spirit into us! Clay that takes shape in His living Hands and Words, embodying the Light, the Joy; awakening the Soul at the core of matter!

Whenever we meet our life with the simplicity of an unclothed Heart, cleansed of all judgment and of all pretenses, our being becomes a mirror. A Mirror reflecting Grace. The Mirror in which we discover ourselves and the other, as God Himself sees us.

"The Sufi's book is not of ink and letters: It is nothing but a heart white as snow."[58]

Our healing is the healing of the blind and the deaf: We suddenly see and hear what was already there.

---

[58] Djalāl ad-Dīn Rûmî, Balkh 1207 - Konya 1273. The Masnavi: Book Two.

I look at Aurora, at Friday, the dark skin, the light skin. Haven't they just told me that this story is no longer a tale of ancient lore, but one of Our Time? Let us not regress, let us not mourn Paradise Lost, but rather go forth, forth to each other until every child of man recognizes its Source, quenches its thirst with Living Water.

Lausanne, March 2nd 2018

Verses of Aurora's Love
The Name of Our Love

Your love for me, my love for You,
I would shout it from the rooftops,
Call it forth in every passer-by like a sun!
May no one be deprived of it.

I would toss it like a golden rain
Upon the leaves, upon the wind,
Upon the crest of every wave,
At every door and window in the city.

To what spell do I owe such bliss?
I can only fall to my knees
Like a rider in the desert,
Because the liquid Sky reflects in the Well.

Wherever I turn, there is Your Face.
Each of my steps espouses Your Trail,
Precisely where and when it seems forever lost.
Each land is the land that waits for us.

My love for You, Your love for me,
I would launch it from the tip of my fingers,
Like a laughter that rings,
Like a flight of swallows escaping from my hands;
Uplifting You into the rustling of wings,
Living arabesque on the page of the sky,
Carried by their cries.

Each source is Your Spring,
Every stinging Your flame,
A leap into Your Tenderness.
Newer, fresher, more soothing
Than the birth of leaves,
Than the evening rain
That touches my dried lips.

But this Secret, though ablaze in everyone,
Who recognizes it?
Who submits to the 'Judgment of God'?
Who places his bare hand upon the Fire of the Heart,
Beneath the skin of matter, without being burned?
Who contemplates the Radiant One
Beneath the veil of shapes and is not consumed?
Love, if You are not my Innocence,
I will remain forever guilty. Condemned.

Each night is the Night of our Togetherness.
One cannot separate the Fire from its Carrier,
Nor the blazing torch from darkness,
Nor the dew from the sand.
For they are one for the other,
Like the Love and the Flesh,
Like the scattered bones
That Your Breath assembles.
Without You, I do not exist.

Your Love, the Well, the Fire, Your step,
Your Freedom at my fingertips,
I would like to call them forth
Deep from within all passers-by!
To mark them with these Signs of You…
As so many leaves of gold
Upon their foreheads,
In the cup of their hands,
At the soles of their feet.

Your Love for me, my love for You,
Is the Chant that no one hears.
And yet it springs from all and every tune!
One cannot separate
The Song from the Silence,
For they are one for the other
Like the Body and the Love.

Your Love for me, my love for You,
Is a Word that no one has yet spoken,
A movement born for the first time,
A Virgin womb, the Origin of origins;
Who believes he can seize it has lost it.

Because one cannot word it, but only inspire it,
Prior to becoming our Love existed,
Before the first Breath, before the first Sound,
Our Love was born before the first Gesture.

For Love is the Name,
The Name I don't remember,
But that I recognize when Love,
When God, calls me by my Name,
Inflames my Heart under His burning Seal.

Love…
Your laughter still rings in mine
Like a chime that jingles
On the mountain at dawn.

Love, if You should leave me,
I will see You go,
Like a wondering child,
Like the tears of joy;
Like a frail rivulet
On the rock, on the sand,
In the flowering fields...
Murmuring, light,
Humble and undestroyed.
For wherever you murmur,
Wherever you flow or get lost …
You always go back to the sky and the sea.

Without You, Love,
I turn into a storm
Of rage, of fire.
I scatter mankind!
I calcine the Earth,
I shred us to pieces,
Like scraps and waste after the feast;
Disperse us on empty plains,
Where our bones will bleach!
The fire of my guts
Devours Your name.
The grating of the sand
Between my teeth grinds us to powder.

Without You, Love,
I enchain every gesture,
I silence every word
Of my love for You,
Extinguish every spark,
Reduce us to ashes,
Inflict peace like a desert.

Yet even there, Love,
Your laughter rings in mine,
Your song is in my sob.
An improbable bird
In devastated fields.

My love for You, Your Love for me,
In the empty, in the naught…
Rises from the black belly of the Earth,
Whispers in every breath;
Reunites our bones,
Reborn from God like the notes of the flute.
I only Am in You.

Your fingers of light, Your fingers of wind,
You rest them on my forehead.
You mark my eyelids
With the softness of dawn.
Leaves are sprouting
From my cut branches.

Love…
I cannot offer You anything,
Except my pain,
Inseparable from my tenderness.
For they are one for the other
Like the Flesh and the Love,
Like the wood and the Fire,
Like the death and the Rebirth.

I love You.
The torch burns without carrier,
Feeds from its own Incandescence.
The secret Name of our Love
Is always the Name of God.

April 4th 1999
The Day of the Resurrection

Appendix I

'Voice Dialogue'
A Journey to Uncover the *Self*

'**V**oice **Dialogue**' supports individuation. It explores our *Inner family of selves,* defined as *subpersonalities,* and gives rise to the resulting *Aware self process.* The essence of the work is spontaneity, freedom to feel and share: Two people are face-to-face and allow a creative exchange to emerge. It unfolds as a 'game of life,' wherein humor, surprises, gravity and respect find their place. All facets of the personality can express, link and interact in a dance where one will experience a deep connection to oneself, to one's emotions and the creativity dimensions that lie dormant in us.

'Voice Dialogue' is a vision of the psyche, a tool and a process for developing self-knowledge, self-relating and self-growth. Its practice gives insight into one's personality, into the motivations and energies that move us, contract or expand us, or remain disowned in our psyche. These energies express and transmit our resources, values and thoughts; our desires, fears and hurts; our feeling tones, our bodily sensations. Via personal skills, behaviors and reactions, they manifest the often unconscious and automatic physical and psychological 'survival devices' of our character. Unless we learn to know them and relate to them with awareness, they will to a large extent govern our lives and restrain our free will and our aliveness.

By consciously *identifying with* and subsequently *dis-identifying from* the energies that drive or inhibit us, a gradual strengthening of 'central awareness' occurs, with an ability to hold the tension of *Inner opposites* within the psychic structure. By discovering the vulnerability that underlies our reactions, we will learn to acknowledge and care for our *Suffering selves* and so relate to ourselves and others with understanding and empathy.

We will discover *Inner selves* of an unpredictable sensitivity and freshness which wait patiently to be welcomed, so as to evolve with all the magic of a seed that germinates, a flower that blooms. We will progressively awaken to a much longed for encounter with our *Deeper Self*. Intimate inner bonding will arise from the choice to cherish oneself without judgment or fear. Impulses will again spring from abundance rather than from paucity, reviving our childlike innocence and trust.

Practicing 'Voice Dialogue,' leads to treasure the infinite resources of one's own being. It is to participate in what one feels, whether in fragility or in strength, in happiness or in pain, in flow or in limitation. To know oneself is to love oneself. Out of this closeness in the *now* with whoever we are, grows closeness with the other, an intense and unconditional embrace of all that is.

The Beginnings

'Voice Dialogue' was created by a couple of American psychologists: Hal Stone PhD (trained in Clinical Psychology at UCLA, and at the Jung Institute of Los Angeles) and his wife, Sidra Stone PhD (trained in Psychology at the University of Maryland). After more than twenty years of personal and professional experience, they developed, since the seventies, the theory and practice of '*The Psychology of Selves and Bonding Patterns, and the Psychology of the Aware Ego*.' They created a simple and concrete method, accessible to all, called 'Voice Dialogue.'

At first they put it to the test in their own processes as individuals, and as a couple... subsequently developing it in their professional practice and their joint seminars and teachings. Together they have written a number of ground breaking books about it. (See the Bibliography).

Three Key Concepts:
Self-Understanding, Self-Acceptance, Self-Relating

In my personal life and in over thirty years (1993–2023) of professional experience with it, 'Voice Dialogue' work has proven, from the very beginning, to accompany a spiritual path based on detachment, love and tolerance. Indeed, its goal is not to correct oneself, like one would snip with a pair of critical scissors, or re-tailor a character trait that is not to our taste. It aims, on the contrary, at developing a caring mindfulness for how we feel and *who* we are from one moment to the next. It supports a tangible relationship between a 'centered space of inner witnessing' and any given 'mental, emotional and behavioral pattern' that inhabits us. This process leads to a self-awareness and a self-relating based on lucidity and responsiveness.

We learn to meet our vulnerability, to acknowledge our perceptions, reactions, desires and fears – in heart, mind and body – not as things, nor as mere objects, but as 'flesh and blood persons' inside us. We can then relate to these *Inner persons* with kindness; we can respect them as *Allies*. We realize that self-inflicted criticism and indifference do hurt us even more deeply than when they strike us from any outer source.

The practice of 'Voice Dialogue' helps us experience ourselves intimately, rather than through dissociated mental analysis. Our understanding arises from a conscious embodying of *who we are*; this awakens empathy; it motivates self-acceptance and results in inner peace. Better than any striving to be different, it is precisely such lucid compassion that will naturally transform us.

To be really conscious of oneself on manifold levels of experience, leads to being touched by one's own humanness and invites us to take ourselves into our own hearts and embrace. Welcoming and cherishing oneself, opens the door to love and tolerance toward the other: We recognize the other as an equal, sharing the same joys and pains, fears and hopes in life.

A Few Definitions: *Subpersonalities* Defense Mechanisms, Complexes, Energies

By *selves,* or *subpersonalities,* one means the various facets of one's personality. The sum of their interactions makes up what we consider to be our identity; that of which we say: '*But that's me!*' Yet our subpersonalities cover also the attributes of self we deny or leave dormant within.

A subpersonality will carry, for example, a specific suffering self or a pattern of adaptation, a mental interpretation, an emotional reaction, a self-protective resource, an instinctual energy or a disowned energy. Academic language will use the terms 'complex' and 'defense mechanism.' A complex is defined as a cluster of feelings and associated behaviors, triggered by some past difficulty in which one has remained caught. From there on, when there is a similarity of circumstances, we go through a reactivation of the emotions linked with past experiences and repeat associated behaviors. Consequently, more often than not, we act and react, unaware of what more deeply drives us.

'Voice Dialogue' explores our physical, emotional and mental 'energy flows.' *Energy,* from the Greek *energeia,* means 'force in action.' What 'Voice Dialogue' calls *energy* encompasses our reactions and our silences, our impulses, our inhibitions, whatever blocks or frees us in our daily life and our personality.

The practice of 'Voice Dialogue' gives our different *selves* the opportunity to be heard separately and then to be integrated in a new way on the inner plane. Under the guidance of a facilitator, our subpersonalities will experience and express themselves—one at a time—convey their points of view, their feelings and sensations. Some of them are quite familiar to us, powerful and welcome; others are more discreet, others still are unheard, repressed or perceived as burdens, in reason of their poor health, low spirits, faulty behavior or vulnerability. Nevertheless they all belong to our *Inner family*. Eventually – provided everyone is given a *voice* and is heard – wisdom, solidarity and some degree of consensus will naturally arise out of such multi-faceted sharing.

A Complex, a Defense Mechanism, a Perception Is Always a *Person*

To look upon a feeling, a thought, an attitude, as an *Inner person*, rather than as a complex, a defense mechanism, a righteous or faulty conduct, breaks new ground. To *personify* our psychological dynamics is to move from 'object oriented analyzing' to 'subject oriented relating.' In this lies the whole difference: We begin to discover and welcome in our inner world the expressions of a whole human family; we begin to consider our 'ways of reacting' as persons *per se* and start to meet them accordingly, in a clear, compassionate and pragmatic way.

Experiencing what we feel, think and do as an *Inner family,* creates a heightened quality of connection with oneself and others. Now transference and the empathic feedback we hope for, will not for the most part be focused on responses by others or on the patient-therapist axis, but will be directed back to a face-to-face between a *central dis-identified awareness* and the various *selves* that manifest within us. Therein lies a precious possibility of maturation and change. 'Voice Dialogue' processes invite you to cease to primarily depend on outer mirroring, on validation by others or on 'educative self-correction.' You learn to build on your own response to your wounded and anxious *Inner selves*... and on their spontaneous relaxing as they are met by your caring.

Because we start to experience our needs and fears consciously, we can become self-mirrors. We become partners and neighbors to our *Inner selves,* in particular to our *Vulnerable selves*; we begin to respond to them, to hold them, with rooted and containing affectionate gestures and words, rather than with driven self-enhancement or pitiless self-criticism.

This is not only an approach for those who feel in difficulty. It is also a spiritual path for those who aspire to know and free themselves at a deeper level, tending towards equanimity and serenity. It encloses the total person, in both its human and cosmic dimensions. It highlights the fullness of our potential; it gives us a deeper sense of the meaning of our life; it allows us to develop feeling relationships with our fellow men that enrich and renew us. We discover that we are – and that every person is – a microcosm reflecting all that the universe contains.

◆

The Range of our *Subpersonalities*

As spokesmen for our energies, our *Inner voices* can be divided into several groups:

Group I
The *Primary selves*. They Insure our Protection
Carry our Power and our Resources in Life

Our *Primary selves* compose what Carl Gustav Jung has called the 'persona,' meaning thereby the way in which we present ourselves to others, function and find our place in the family and in society. These are the *subpersonalities* that develop our assets and protect us. They concretize our talents, our ways of mastering our lives. They monitor us to exercise control, avoid errors, exclusion and suffering.

Here we meet our *Skillful selves*, our *Pusher*, our *Perfectionist*, enticing us to do well, to do more, to do even better. We will also experience our *Inner warriors*, *heroes* and *rebels*, who fight our battles, or our *Pleaser* who agrees with the other and too often goes quiet in order to avoid conflict. They include also our *spiritual, altruistic and idealistic selves* who would solve the difficulties of human condition. Together they form a 'super-ego board' of *Primary selves*… directed by our *Rule maker* who carries the values we identify ourselves with, and surveyed by our *Inner critic* who ceaselessly points out our slightest past and future failings and sins. They also include an *Inner judge* who protects us by finding fault in others.

For the most part, these *Powerful voices* are 'parental, educating voices;' they reflect our cultural, religious and social settings. They give us structure, teach us, drive us, shield us. When we feel hurt or threatened, they express our *survival strategies*, like aggression, flight, submission, disguise and playing dead. They insure our physical safety and the recognition of our values, identity and self-image. Deep down they are well-meaning, yet their input necessarily limits us, making us in many ways guilty, judgmental and untrue to ourselves.

Our psyche covers the boundless variety of energies present in creation. We also carry *Archetypal, Transpersonal and Spiritual selves*. The *Archetypal selves* personify in us the collective imprints of humanity, our basic forces: The universal mother, father, woman, man; the heroes of our myths, legends and fairy tales; they comprise mankind's instinctual drives, the powers of light and darkness in our psychical realms.

Our *Transpersonal and Spiritual selves* can be vectors of the divine and the sacred. They manifest in us as the *Soul voice*, the *Wisdom voice*, the *Healer's voice*, the *Voices* of saints, of wise figures and deities.

The range of our *subpersonalities* is timeless and limitless. We can dialogue with the *Voices* of our dreams, of our inspirations and intuitions; or with those of our physical pains and illnesses and even with the *Voice* of our old age to come or the *Voice* of our death. Indeed we can explore via our sensitivity and perceptions, the energies of all impulses, emotions and feeling tones; the energies of animate and inanimate objects; of man, animal, rock and tree; of near and far, of past and future times.

We will experience that every human being contains all that the universe contains. Provided we meet everything as a *Person,* with the love, respect and sacredness that this implies, we will discover a fascinating world, where every aspect, every force, can be our *Ally* and our *Teacher.*

Excessive Adaptation, Rigid Values
A Strong *Inner Critic*
Are a Danger for our Immune System
For our Physical, Emotional and Spiritual Health

More than we would admit, we are blind to what we really feel, want and are. This often has its roots in distressful and confusing experiences of the past, especially during childhood. In order to be loved and accepted, to prevent pain, to establish our identity, assert our values, find our place in our environment, support our desires and ignore our fears… we develop the *Primary selves* that best serve us in our given circumstances.

Such complying traits, resources and self-protective

responses are standard and necessary, but they can become depriving and self-maiming when they escalate. Indeed, they do cause us to develop strong censors, in form of *Inner critics* and *judges,* who will blame whatever and whoever doesn't correspond to our needs and values. Our constraints and doubts, our compulsions to do better, prevailing guilt, fear of failure, poison our daily lives, undermine our happiness and self-esteem or nourish our grandiosity, while also rejecting our fellow men, creating thereby a lot of unnecessary suffering.

Let us take a very basic example: With the arrival of springtime and its first warmer days, our *Inner critic* has an anxiety attack: 'Have you seen yourself? That pale sickly skin, this roll of fat on your belly, these wrinkles... your tendency to overweight?' Every aspect of one's appearance gets evaluated; every physical detail analyzed, from the single grey hair to the slightest flaw in the face. Hurry! Aerobics, diet, tanning booths! Whether we are reputed for our beauty or just an average mortal makes no difference; the anxiety is the same. It can take on such proportions that it reduces some women and men to despair, convincing them that they aren't so young and lovable anymore ... not even worthy of being seen. Self-confidence and self-respect get lost.

Whatever we perceive as 'too much' or 'not enough,' imperils us, becomes a source of internal conflict, of disconnection from self and others and can render us antisocial or co-dependent. To satisfy cultural, social, religious, ideological imperatives and the standards of self-image, we are in danger of becoming blind slaves to them. By coercing ourselves, we suppress our true potential, our 'richness of being,' and we may end up by becoming literally 'someone else.' The censorship exerted by our *Inner critic,* the denial of our *vulnerability* and of our *disowned energies,* the projection of guilt on others, entails one-sidedness, psychic impoverishment, self-exclusion and mutual exclusion. The strain and control this exerts on us can result in burn out, depression, sickness, addictions and destructive acting out.

When difficulties arise, we automatically disavow our weaknesses and our shadow sides; we automatically stiffen our resources and defenses, provoking reactive opposing forces in inner and outer world. These can suddenly burst forth, wreck our family life, ruin our professional career, shatter what we've worked so hard to construct.

Blocked and unrecognized energies are a source of pain in body and soul, of illness and existential crises. Their irruption takes us aback, in particular if we were unaware of the inner pressure they cause or when we deliberately ignore them. Suppressed vulnerability impedes intimacy, true closeness with self and others and the letting go of fear, mistrust and control. It is a source of loneliness, isolation and loss of creativity.

Group II
The *Vulnerable* and *Sensitive Selves*; Protectively Hidden Behind the *Primary Selves* and Often Denied

Our *Vulnerable selves* are characterized by their sensitivity. For the most part they manifest as *Inner children*. There we meet our playful, magical, innocent and unsuspecting *Inner children*. They harbor our aliveness, our spontaneity and inspiration, our capacity for bonding. They show up when we feel welcome and safe. As long as they feel secure they will express our loving, trusting, responsive nature. Yet, being *sensitive*, they feel easily hurt and will therefore also manifest as our *Wounded child*, our *Abandoned child*, our *Abused* and *Guilty child*, our *Despairing child*. Powerless, imprisoned, mute and dysfunctional, they are suddenly upfront when we feel rejected and betrayed or endure loss.

We also carry *Adult suffering selves* in areas of doubt and anguish, in particular those connected with womanhood,

manhood or parenthood. Yet, even as adults, we can observe – when unforeseen pain, confusion, fear or aggression shock us – that we lose ground and may, in a split second, regress into a *'Helpless child.'* As this happens, such *Inner infants,* disguised in adult clothing, will remain unmet by us, paralyzed and alone... while our *Protective primary selves* try to step up to the barricades.

For Hal and Sidra Stone the elaboration of 'Voice Dialogue' began in a very experiential and personal way. After they met, being both long term psychologists, they dedicated themselves to facilitating each other in all fields of their relational process. This intense joint exploration unveiled for them the primordial role that vulnerability plays in our ability to bond, in our problems, reactions and conflicts.

One day, Hal suggested to Sidra to choose a place in the room to embody her vulnerability. Hal relates how surprised he was to come face-to-face with a very small *pre-verbal baby-girl;* withdrawn into herself, incapable of communicating her suffering with words. The concepts of *subpersonalities* and of *complexes* were very familiar to them. But that these could personify as a *real child,* fully present in the here and now of an adult... completely baffled both of them! This discovery was to be the foundation of the 'Voice Dialogue' process that they developed over the years.

Inner selves are not merely complexes hidden behind acquired skills and defense mechanisms. They are *human!* And this means, that if something has a chance to help them to step from fear into trust, from aggression and flight into connection, and from pain into joy, it will only be relatedness and love.

When we start to face our *Inner selves* with non-judgment, understanding, clear limits and respect, they can begin to move from *Suffering selves* and from *Conflicting voices* to *'Dear ones'* and *Allies* in the context of an *Inner family of energies.* Whatever our pain and our shortcomings, it is precisely such conscious and compassionate *self-relating* that will further our healing—as surely as it does when we lovingly connect with any biological child or person in the outer world.

Each of our *subpersonalities* embodies a specific trend of energy and a particular form of fear and suffering that we can become aware of, by exploring 'how, why and when' *it* feels, thinks and acts through us! Questioned, via 'Voice Dialogue' facilitation, our *subpersonalities* will define themselves by age, sex, specific bodily sensations and emotions, beliefs and dealings. They have hopes, pains, worries and goals of their own... and a very precise role and impact in our life. They can change, and they do—provided we put across a caring, conscious, personified linkage, between our *Witnessing Awareness* and the *selves* that arise inside us.

Our Disclaimed Vulnerability
The Unseen and Abandoned *Inner Child*
Its Sensitive Heart in the Midst of our Fortress

Our *Inner child*, so helpless at birth, nevertheless carries the Source of our true beingness, the seed of our spiritual evolving. To save it from harm, our 'survival personality' builds up and gravitates around its needs and fears. Our suffering selves have their roots in our inheritance from preceding generations and in many of our painful experiences early in life, repeatedly confirmed as we grow up. Even though our story and its events are long gone, our '*Inner children of the past*' wait to be truly mirrored and cherished. They wait at the *core of our bodies,* fully alive in our here and now, responding in our very cells.

At birth, we are a little being that doesn't yet have a separate sense of self, that doesn't really know how to distinguish itself from the mother. As infants—to survive, physically and psychologically, we entirely depend on the love and approval of our caretakers. To ensure love, acceptance and power in the world, to safeguard the delicate nucleus of our being, we set up the entire group of our *Power selves* and reject into the shadow their *opposites*. We cannot, however, save the cost of all the hurts.

Little by little, protective shielding camouflages the child's natural liveliness, its spontaneity. We entomb it, abandoning its treasures of creativity to oblivion and loneliness. Our vital impulses towards the sharing of love, remain captive and in waiting. Throughout life, such buried hopes are steadily projected onto others, onto our parents first... later onto our partners and even our children. We solicit outside – too often in vain – what our *Inner child* still misses. And yet, in spite of all, woven into the soul of every powerless newborn, lies the untouched Source of our Life, the Divine Child, forever innocent, intuitive, loving, all-knowing.

Who then will respond to it? Others can't *do it all*, especially as they also suffer from similar wants!

If life is hard on us, our protective reflexes, the automatic disowning of our vulnerability, end up resembling electric fences that isolate us. We become a self-built stronghold at the center of which lives an *Invisible child* we are no more conscious of—busy as we are, ensuring its defense from the heights of our watchtowers! At every real or imagined threat, our *Powerful selves* make use of attack or flight or play dead, or play victim. But defending is not a relating! To fight, or to be conciliatory by taking care of the other, does not mean that we take care of ourselves. And our *sensitive selves* remain cut off, deprived of love and attention.

Ancient emotions and strategies endlessly repeat themselves.

Unless we gently and decidedly connect with all these *forms of me*—whether they are vulnerable or defensive, they will hardly evolve. They remain frozen in their given contexts and complexes. Being prone to spurn any weakness, we stay unaware of them; we fail to notice that, at times, we are as inexperienced and bare as we used to be as babies. We do not realize that loving and mirroring ourselves consciously, could render such high and well-guarded enclosures superfluous. We do not take hold of our capacity to *re-parent* our *Inner child.* We do not trust that our *Inner child* is still undamaged at its core; is endowed with the courage, love and strength of *Life itself,* and that it will boundlessly gift us with it—provided we resolutely hold his hand!

Owning our vulnerability can transform our fortress into a garden, can awaken in us a secure, trusting, joyous and creative budding, and with it the richness of our feelings and gusto for life.

Group III
The *Disowned Selves* as 'Opposites' to our *Primary Selves*

Our *Disowned selves* are usually out of sight. They embody energies *opposite to* those we have favored and developed. They are our excluded, unknown and dormant *voices.* We disown them for ethical, educational and religious reasons; because they stand for styles and values we disapprove of or have difficulty to access. We come up to them in persons we react to—by attraction or repulsion. They correspond to people and attitudes we judge or over admire.

Evolution is a tricky game of apprenticeship. Opposing energies magnetize each other, and therefore we find our *disowned selves* represented, not only in those we condemn… but also in the *primary selves* of those we fall in love with or are drawn to. And if we don't use the opportunity to assimilate the skills and energies 'the other' has developed – particularly in couples – such assets will soon cease to be felt as compensatory and become a source of mutual irritation and reproach.

If we fail to acknowledge our *disowned selves,* fail to learn from *opposites* present in the *primary selves of others,* conflicts will arise in our relationships, turning our respective *primary systems* against each other. Yet, when given a place in us, however small, *disowned energies* will enrich us, catalyze and fertilize renewal. By opening ourselves to undeveloped energies in our lives, we will feel younger, healthier, more balanced and less judgmental.

When we omit to learn from them and to integrate them into our lives – at least at homeopathic doses! – it is our *own denied selves* that we project onto others, condemn and attack in the outside world. *Escalating opposites* signal unmet vulnerability; they breed conflicts, lead to ruptured relationships, divorce, ethnic cleansings, wars, and all kinds of exclusions.

◆

The Dance of Polarities in the Psyche

The facilitation and observation of the different *selves* shows how their dynamics rest on duality. Like night and day, wake and sleep, warm and cold, masculine and feminine, birth and death… we structure ourselves within a system of *balancing opposites* that dance together and polarize each other. These 'energies' in our psyche can be compared to 'an array of contrasting impulses.' What we know of ourselves, what we convey and achieve, represents only part of us; this can be compared to the light side of the moon, whilst its other side lies in the shadow.

We are hardly aware of these polarizations, and yet – in accordance with the laws of physics (law of Newton) – each of our 'visible poles' constellates an 'opposite pole, an energetic and emotional charge' that is equal in power… but held tight, until eventually the momentum reverses. Owing to the tension between our *primary, vulnerable* and *disowned selves,* we may suddenly swing from one position to the other. This is especially marked when we powerfully identify with a given *self.* Such an increased drive – our going too far in one direction – will finally toss us to the other side, like the swing of a pendulum. Violent shifts in polarities can be terribly destructive… for example, when some seemingly unobtrusive and well meaning citizen suddenly becomes ruthless and kills innocents with a machine gun.

Such dramatic reversals can also trigger deep and healing shifts. We can see it in the lives of certain saints, like St Paul who changes abruptly from unbeliever and Christ offender to a life of piety and holiness. We can also observe it in terminal illnesses or major trials, when lasting peace and a remission occur at the favor of a radical change that turns us, so to say, inside out.

To invite and facilitate our *powerlessness,* by means of 'Voice Dialogue,' will naturally give us access to some aspect of our *strength* and vice versa. Or to facilitate an intense *Activist,* will spontaneously trigger on the other side some *slow down self* advocating rest and leisure. We can equilibrate our inner duality and so further our wholeness, by respecting both sides, by welcoming our power without scorning our weakness; by working diligently, while also granting recreations to our minds and bodies! Following the example of communicating vases, pressure will adjust, our strong points will be more measured and our lacks less harmful.

'Voice Dialogue' doesn't aim to alter or amend a person, but uses this 'law of polarized energies' and the laws of love, to facilitate a progressive and wise integration of a much wider range of *selves.* This will help us to release bottled up needs and resources, to diminish blockages and to prevent the risk of an abrupt loss of stability! Unexpected and violent eruptions of coerced energies can prove disastrous, i.e. in mid-life crisis… or by causing illnesses, depressions and dismantled relationships.

To work with 'Voice Dialogue' enlivens our potential and opens us up to new horizons of wakefulness. We give ourselves choices. We expand our repertoire. We become more feeling, free and flexible.

◆

The Practice

A. 'Voice Dialogue' Facilitation
Meeting and Experiencing our Various *Selves*

A session begins and ends in the center seat, facing the facilitator. The center seat is the locus of the *Aware self process*. To mark the entry into a subpersonality, the facilitated person will take another place in the room. The facilitator supports this self-exploration with empathy, deepening questions and mirroring. During the facilitation, and until the person returns to the center seat, the *Aware self process* will be, so to say, its Invisible witness!

At the beginning of 'Voice Dialogue' practice, our Inner world resembles a mesh of woolen strands of varying colors and textures. Little by little, one will unravel this cluster of selves that we claim as 'Me!' We will free these 'threads and shades of who we are' from their entanglement and they will arrange themselves around one's central pole of witnessing awareness.

With the help of the *facilitator,* each *subpersonality* will deepen self-experiencing as far as possible. The *subpersonality* will say '*I*,' and when referring to the person taking the session, will use the familiar first name. For example an *Inner critic* might say: "I cannot stand how Jim procrastinates. He is such a sloppy guy when it comes to doing something straight away!''

'Voice Dialogue' is a living tool that helps us to become

conscious of what repeatedly fills us or drains out of us. It helps us discern the succession of impulses, inhibitions and behaviors, carried by the mental, emotional and physical *selves*, we *identify with.* For example, someone hurts our feelings: For a split second we are overtaken by pain and hopelessness and then, immediately bursting with anger or freezing inside; we may first deny the hurt or justify ourselves, then switch to conciliation, then harbor resentment, and finally ebb towards indifference. Such 'reactive sequences' happen so fast that we often don't even recognize the wound that initially triggered them! We are largely unaware of the genesis of our automatic reactions. And they will be disproportionate when the initial wounding originates in some painful past or early childhood experience.

Facilitation gives us the opportunity to meet and to relate to our *vulnerable selves*, to face our *reactive defensive selves* and to integrate our *disowned selves*, exactly as one would with *real persons.* We will understand how we unknowingly give birth to them, how we perpetually replicate similar responses and how this makes us and others suffer in our daily lives.

One could also compare what happens in us with driving a car. The car symbolizes our life, and from moment to moment our question should be: 'But *who* is now at the wheel?' If one refers to the sequence cited above, our car is first steered by some *Responsible adult,* then suddenly by the *Wounded Child,* then replaced at the wheel by *Burning Anger,* then by *Indifference* or by a *Conciliator…* and so on. What we call '*me*' is made of these drivers competing for control on our existential road. Most of the time, we are on automatic pilot and unaware of it. And this exposes us to accidents.

'Voice Dialogue' invites us to question ourselves: '*Who,* in the house of ma psyche, occupies which room, and how many square meters? *Who* monopolizes how many of my daily allotted hours? *Who* is confined to the broom closet or the basement? *Who* enjoys all of the 'living-room' in my life?'

A 'Voice Dialogue' session takes on average two hours. The facilitation of a given *self,* can last anywhere from a few minutes to an hour or more. The *facilitator* holds and mirrors every *subpersonality.* He shares, enters into resonance with the different *selves.* This initiates a dynamic present moment experiencing—in body, heart and mind. The context, the problems, the related events of a recent or distant past, will be part of the work, shedding light on energies and *selves* that repeatedly surge up in our reactions. Associations will spontaneously emerge within the memory through bodily sensations, images and feelings. The facilitator listens to the whole range of your perceptions, to your entire, physical, emotional and verbal register.

The acquired capacity to distinguish who is operating in us, the capacity to respond to our needs, without projecting them onto others or circumstances, will change our lives and guide us from dependency to self reliance. We can alleviate and stabilize what distresses us by acknowledging what we feel. By envisioning our psychical family with clarity, compassion and measure, we will evolve and make choices, rooted in a real understanding of ourselves and others.

B. The *Aware Self Process*
Separation and Individuation:
The Leaven of True Love

At the end of each facilitation of a given subpersonality, the facilitator thanks the *subpersonality* and invites the person to take a step back into the *Aware self process.* This is a crucial move. Provided you have intensely expressed a specific energy/ *subpersonality,* you will – as you return to the center seat – naturally experience the contrast between the two positions and sense an 'energetic shift.'

The distinction between one's *Aware self process* and one's *subpersonalities* is based on this 'spatial, experiential and voluntary separation' from the facilitated *selves*. Back in the central position one observes what is now different – in sensations, emotions, and thoughts – compared to the *self* which one has just left. By separating from your *subpersonalities*, while at the same time feeling deeply touched by what they go through... you become your own mirror and develop a non-fusional, *dis-identified*, relating to yourself. You can now recognize the difference between an energy-driven stance and the being quality of your *Core-self*.

The liberation that comes with it will be surprising and is the essential key to the whole process. You are more centered, more rooted and calm; more spacious and alive. Instead of feeling torn apart in between opposite directions, you discover yourself as a 'volume of beingness.' You have just switched from a *two-dimensional* to a *three-dimensional* experiencing. You are now totally present in your physical body and in your consciousness body; fully in touch with your five senses; in touch with yourself, in touch with the facilitator and in touch with your surroundings—instead of unaware and disconnected 'urbi et orbi.'

Once a *self* has been clearly perceived in its energy, its behavior, its aspirations and motivations, it will be seen as a person per se for whom one has real feelings and understanding. This face-to-face with one's *Inner selves* becomes the leaven for an evolving connectedness with one's *Inner family* and particularly with one's *Inner child*. We hear and acknowledge what we feel; we name and describe it. We become a partner and a co-creator of our personal venture.

'Voice Dialogue' grounds on this mindful differentiation, without which one cannot risk true closeness with self and others.

It might be the very first time that you face yourself as the non-judging and attentive trustee of your own experience. This reflective and sensitive process frees you and dissolves your undigested burdens; it helps you to uncover the truth of *who* you more deeply are and to recover a sense of serenity and intrinsic oneness.

C. *Lucid Witnessing.*
Rounding up a Session
As the Viewer of One's own Motion Picture

After the last return to the center seat, after having completed there the *Aware self process*, a 'Voice Dialogue' session will best be concluded by a final rounding up. The subject will stand beside the facilitator, facing all that has taken place during the session. He will now be a spectator, an auditor, without any other task than to be the *Silent viewer* of his own life. He envisions the place of the *Aware self*, the places of the different *Voices*, and listens without intervening to the summary of the session that the facilitator will do. This last position is called *Awareness level* or *Lucid witnessing.* It contributes to further clarity and detachment, and helps stabilize emotions. Compassion and non-judgment, for all that lives within us, are reinforced.

◆

Strengthening the *Aware self process*
Self-Mirroring, Separating, Self-Relating,
Self-Reliance

Because our parents have their own desires and fears, because they have to educate and adapt us, they seldom mirror us without preconceived notions and biases. A lot of our suffering and identity problems are due to this. A child that wasn't reflected enough in its own reality, with love, while at the same time given clear limits, may remain emotionally stuck at different levels. In time, as we grow up, it becomes an *Inner child,* unseen, frozen in some of its feelings and behavior patterns. This is what can be referred to as an autonomous complex or a conditioned reflex. And it might never evolve, unless we use one of the most effective tools available to us: 'Mutual bonding' between one's *Aware self* and one's *Inner child.*

'Voice Dialogue' helps us recognize how the *Primary selves* act as 'introjected parents' inside us. The *Aware self* is invited to be – from now on – the reference of one's inner relating. The 'biological child' we were, is still present in our *Inner child* of today as an ongoing cause of recurrent suffering. The good news is… that at any moment, we can take *its* hand into ours and become its 'loving and mirroring vis-à-vis!' By cherishing it now, we will heal its past and present wounds; we will help it to feel secure, trusting, creative and joyful again.

Whenever we address who is lonely and stuck within us, we embody the *Inner friend* we still need and await… and so undo and assuage our ills and sores.

Why do *Mirroring, Separating* and *Relating* Go Hand in Hand?

Intra-psychic differentiation and subsequent inner relating take their model from life itself. Let's remember a law of evolution that impacts the development of every biological child and the unfolding of our existential path. From conception to birth, from birth to death, we convert symbiosis into individuation. This is a dance between being close and making a distinction. Both are necessary to our full flowering. We gain self-awareness by combining 'separating from' and 'relating to' …our environment and our perceptions.

This is indeed, why it is crucial to be *mirrors* of love and pain for our biological children; mirrors through which they can build their basic trust and a coherent identity.

This same principle proves itself when we engage into *self-parenting* by consistent and affectionate *self-mirroring,* in particular regarding our *Inner child.* The moment we respond to it in the same way we should optimally respond to a biological child, our *Inner child* starts to recapture its creative liveliness and trust. In the timeless realm of our psyche, we can *re-parent* our 'child of the past' today. This insightful practice will also show us how to connect with those around, respecting what others feel and loving them 'as they are,' rather than 'as we wish or require them to be.'

'Intimate connection,' between one's own *Compassionate awareness* and one's *Inner selves,* alleviates excessive projections. Our overt and covert expectations exert pressure; they lead to painful disappointments, heartbreaks and a lot of mutually inflicted distress. We need to take responsibility for actively cherishing ourselves as well as others. And when we do, our demands regarding our partners and dear ones lessen, become more balanced. Resentment fades, linkage grows, bringing with it peace and serenity.

Self-Relating: Three Steps in a Nutshell

Learning to know our *Inner family* is the first step. The second step is non judgment and compassionate detachment arising from awareness. The third step is the tender connection we can establish between one's more and more *Aware self* and one's *subpersonalities.*

We all dream of the person who will accept, respect and treasure us unconditionally, despite our limits, errors and weaknesses. We project this expectation onto our parents who cannot fully meet it. And we are angry at them! Our hope to be unconditionally loved and at the same time left free is in constant contradiction with our trials, with educational priorities, with the necessity to adjust to who and what we come across.

As we grow up, we project our deep set desire onto our partners, spouses, children, friends and colleagues, and they will not be able either to quench all of this thirst. We then suffer from repetitive disappointment, unrequited needs and presumed or actual betrayals that poison our happiness.

Being responsible for oneself implies taking back our projections, becoming *The Friend* for our own abandoned parts. It means responding to what we feel by way of a more and more *Conscious and Loving Self.* In so doing we start giving back their freedom to our near and dear ones, taking from their shoulders the weight of our anticipations and subsequent blaming.

Let us realize that there are only two persons who can deeply and consistently meet our inborn thirst for undivided love and acceptance: *God, The Ever Present* – whether we are believers or not – and our *Own Tender Attendance* that holds in itself a spark of God's Love. Indeed, these are our closest and truest Neighbors, inhabitants of our heart twenty-four hours a day from conception to death and beyond. Let us invite, both God and our Core-self, to hold and embrace our distressed and erring world! It is this path of love, faith and forgiveness that 'Voice Dialogue' brings alive in us.

The *Aware Self* as the Peacemaker

As men oppose each other on the outer plane, so are we divided within.

In times of trial we become aware that joy and sadness, love and hate, genuineness and deception, trust and doubt, alternate and compete inside us. Our smile is forced, covering up anger, misery, emptiness. We feel far from our own truth, trapped by incompatibilities, estranged from ourselves and cheated. We feel powerless to solve the world we live in; powerless to change ourselves. We desperately try to suppress, deny, reject, whatever weighs on us. Compulsive improvement and bitter criticism abound. The partner turns against his mate, the child against the parent. Our differences become a source of conflict and pain and cease to be sources of enrichment

'Voice Dialogue' practice is a radically novel approach to our difficulties. It no longer primarily builds on analyzing and solving. It invites us to discover the sensitive, creative and loving *Core-Self* that awaits us beyond our desperate quest for power and recognition. Little by little, with the unfolding of the sessions, our *Inner selves* experience being heard, understood, witnessed without judgment, by the facilitator on one hand, and by our growing *Self-awareness* on the other hand.

The Spiritual Friend, the Wise Leader

Stepping in and out of our *subpersonalities* builds and sustains our *Aware self process,* our sense of expanding consciousness and freedom. As this 'inner widening' repeats itself, *we* grow into a calm, lucid *Womb of compassionate awareness.* We become the Spiritual Friend who responds to *who* and *what* inhabits us, the Wise Leader holding council with his *Tribe.* We welcome, listen, give word, set limits, until everyone has refined his own stance by a progressive assimilation of the points of view of others. Particular attention will be given to vulnerable members, to those feeling orphaned and distressed inside us. Rounds and rounds of different opinions, situations, fears and hopes, will gradually lead to mutual adjustment and peace. Decisions will arise out of a growing team spirit. This is how the *Aware self process* can become the pilot and the containing vessel of one's whole range of *selves.*

To use still another metaphor, the Aware self process

marks the center and draws the boundaries of our psychic *Mandala,* while our various selves gravitate around it like atoms around their nucleus—safely harbored in its precinct. The symbol of the 'mandala' illustrates well how 'Voice Dialogue' – far from fragmenting the perception of who we are – insures the integration of opposites, of ambivalence and of vulnerability into our dynamic wholeness and balance.

◆

Honor All the Gods

Hal and Sidra Stone compare 'Voice Dialogue practice' with 'honoring all the gods.' To honor all the gods is to listen to all the *voices,* is to respect all *energies,* even if they are unwelcome. In ancient Greece, the numerous deities and their temples were assembled in large sacred areas. And visitors made sure to mollify them all, by making offerings to each of them—however obscure, feared or menacing.

Like pilgrims in our inner world, we have to advance through our own mystery, contradictions and diversity, and to reject no one and nothing totally. Every *subpersonality* is a facet and a force of our human nature; each has to be acknowledged; each has to become an Ally rather than an adversary. Honoring every one of them, doesn't mean we cannot have our favorites.

Not to proceed in this way proves risky. History, fairy tales and myths, illustrate in innumerable ways the danger of ignoring or rejecting the *other side.* In the tale of *Sleeping Beauty,* the Thirteenth fairy – which the King neglected to invite – takes revenge. She puts a spell on the family, on the well regulated life in the castle, by plunging the princess and her entire entourage into a profound sleep... image of the powers in our subconscious that overwhelm us when we don't respect them or exclude them.

The tale also offers a remedy: One hundred years later, a Prince – more mature and more loving, than those who previously had failed to free *Sleeping Beauty* – overcomes the hedge of thorns that encloses the Princess. With a 'kiss of conscious love' he awakens her, and with her the castle and its inhabitants.

Loving ourselves as we are, failings included, seeing our own Beauty, the courage to know, the resolve to care, are unavoidable steps towards an Awakening to our deeper Self. 'Voice Dialogue' supports this coming together, without judgment, of all that lives in us, of all our energies... be they of shadow or of light, joyful or sad, powerful or fragile, known or unknown to us.

◆

The Awareness Process
An Empty and Radiant Consciousness Field

The *Aware self process* can be compared to a transparent vessel which fills, colors and empties again as our various *selves* constellate, change and dissolve inside us. Suddenly we are nothing but anger, or elation, or sadness, or flight upon the piano. Our perceptions, our thoughts and our projections are shifting constantly. They alternate or superimpose at high speed. They are not felt simultaneously: When one of our *selves* plays up, all other *selves* recede into the background, are not perceived and not taken into account.

The *Aware self process* unveils our Nature of intrinsic Oneness, of stable and profound serenity. It underlies our restlessness and anxiety, like the calm deeper waters underlie the waves at the surface of the ocean.

Our *Aware Self* can also be compared to a neutral screen

upon which the story of our life, and the *subpersonalities* that personify it, are projected. One illustration follows the next, but the screen of consciousness upon which they appear remains virgin, untroubled and changeless. This is close to the vision of oriental spirituality: Our thoughts and emotions are acknowledged and yet will fleetingly cross the limitless sky of our inner space.

From such a perspective, 'Voice Dialogue' offers a metaphysical insight and a spiritual discipline; we learn to revert to the *empty matrix* in which all and everything can take shelter and be harbored as it is.

Who Am I?

We encompass all our facets but cannot, however, be reduced to any one of them in particular. As a *conscious vessel* we grow towards infinity and transcend the sum of our contents. 'Voice Dialogue helps us to apprehend a threefold experiencing around the question:

'Who am I?'

–   Who am I… *when I am intensely identified with a given aspect of my psyche?*
    What do I perceive of myself; of the world around me; of the other?

–   Who am I… *when I am all this, but also more than the sum of my parts?*
    What do I perceive of myself; of the world around me; of the other?

–   Who am I… *when I am none of my subpersonalities; neither this nor that?*
    What do I perceive of myself; of the world around me; of the other?

By and by, this consciousness procedure will become less and less prone to projection, and inner awareness of freedom and vastness more and more present. Rather than being the toy of our impulses, we access – in our depth – the being quality that underlies all our moves.

Know Thy Self. Love Your Neighbor as Thy Self

To know and love oneself… is to love the other, is to initiate peace. To recognize the underlying suffering behind all violence, to extend empathy, even whilst setting limits to damaging behaviors, is deeply transformative in our lives, couples, families and communities. This may be the wisest way to become less judging and more understanding toward those we regard as distasteful or offensive in the outer world. Inner balance, built on lucid self-care rather than on self-rejection, is the touchstone of harmony. It also provides a model for peaceful communication and cohabitation on our planet.

The maxim '*Know thyself and you will know the universe and the gods,*' etched into the pediment of the Temple of Apollo at Delphi, was the motto chosen by Socrates. Christ in the second commandment, tells us: '*Love thy neighbor as thyself.*' Far from being a selfish endeavor, self-knowledge and self-love, are the very foundation upon which love for others can be built. If I don't extend love to my abandoned *Inner child* and *suffering selves,* if I don't understand and set fair limits to my *Power selves,* like the *Rule maker,* the *Desire driven,* the *Critic,* the *Activist,* the *Perfectionist,* the *Aggressor,* the *Pleaser,* if I don't give some space to my *disowned selves…* how will I be able to comprehend them when I come up to them in the outer world?

Isn't the definition of selfishness 'to privilege an isolated element' to the disadvantage of the whole? But if we make the experience of a growing comprehensiveness and inclusiveness that treats oneself and others equally – excluding neither – we can say: 'I am the world, the world is me.' In so doing we will link our personal good with the good of all.

'Voice Dialogue'
A Spiritual Practice for Expanding Consciousness

Man is somehow at the measure of the universe, including in his finitude all the characteristics of infinity. Today scientific research offers evidence that in our body each cell carries, in its genetic code, information covering perhaps the whole organism. Can one imagine that the knowledge of the universe itself could be inferred from one single cell, one single atom? Following this proposition couldn't each of our *energies* shed light on the nature of all others, as well as reveal some aspects of the deeper meaning of one's wholeness?

Our physical bodies are formed from a single cell, the ovum, fertilized by another single cell, the spermatozoid. From that point on, there is a dividing, a multiplying, a differentiating... the cells interlock, gather into organs that develop into high performance systems connecting inside us. Then there is this miracle: A complete being gifted with transpersonal Consciousness. It is not similarities which create unity, but interrelating. An interrelating that links divergent data, that constantly drops obsolete elements, constantly includes new elements, constantly gives birth to one's renewed dynamic wholeness, to a creative totality.

Some physicists put forward that an implicit order underlies the universe and gives a direction to the elements which divide and reassemble, shaping and ever recreating new structures. Our expanding consciousness possibly evolves in an analogous manner: By separating and connecting the elements in our psyche in an endless process of relatedness to ourselves and others. 'Voice Dialogue' is in this image.

But we are not familiar with practicing – or even imagining – what a 'relating to oneself' could be and bring. We are too identified with our *egoic selves,* too automated in our reactions. Like someone putting his nose directly on the page, we fail to decipher our own book. To see clearly requires distance, a distance that we then bridge with aware love: Love that embraces the freedom and beauty of diversity. This will be felt as a breath of fresh air in the dungeon of inner prisoners. The bird will find its wings; the vulnerable child will recapture its joy and its tears, its spontaneity and inventiveness.

Each and every one of us contains the whole of creation, all people, all energies. To understand and welcome them in ourselves, leads to understand and accept them in the other. It means to open up to a dialogue which turns the stranger, the enemy, into a brother.

Appendix II

'Voice Dialogue' and Relationships
The Bonding patterns

Owing to the principle of duality, to the natural polarization of energies, to the need for adaptation, we develop certain *subpersonalities* rather than others and a great potential within us remains unaddressed or denied. Our psyche nurtures numerous subconscious facets, and so much wasted resources. What is unexpressed, not chosen—without placing any value judgment upon it—represents something we more or less disown that could be called our *shadow*.

This is like the dark side of the moon, the unseen part of our personality. We comprise a gigantic array of energies and possibilities, but we use only a limited part of them. It is as if we were a symphonic orchestra reduced to half the musicians, to a limited number of instruments and tunes.

Attraction-Repulsion, Duality,
Self-Protection

'Falling in love' is largely induced by the pull of qualities that are dormant in ourselves and shining forth in persons we are drawn to: The other sex, an 'affectionate parent,' some trait in the other that fulfils us. What we desire and over admire, is always something that is underrepresented in our own psyche. And if we start to rely solely on the other to compensate for our undeveloped facets, we are in danger of imbalance and dependency.

Furthermore, the moment we feel hurt or insecure, whatever the reason, we immediately begin to reinforce our protective resources and survival strategies: The 'strong and supportive partner' now turns 'rigid and controlling;' and the 'carefree optimist' he has fallen in love with... now becomes 'highly unrealistic and unreliable.' Both escalate in opposite directions! We can defuse such relational time bombs by integrating and developing aspects of *the other's resources* which are somewhat enclosed in the shadow of our own psyche. The 'strong and supportive' can learn to be more relaxed and the 'carefree optimist' can learn to be more grounded.

Whether negative or positive, our projections on each other are the expression of these polarized dynamics. If we do not become conscious of them, they might very well, in time, endanger our relationship by pulling us into a power struggle.

Attraction-repulsion... is a dance between two 'arrays of *subpersonalities*. 'They are total opposites,' people say about a couple: The dancer and the businessman, the shy man and the alluring woman, the prince and the shepherdess. Political parties, countries, co-workers, friends, children in the same family... illustrate this dance of contrasting forces. Parents hope that their children will walk in their steps, but 'adaptation to' triggers 'demarcation from...' Thus an over religious father might incite a delinquent child; a captain of industry incompetent offspring; a poor illiterate worker, children with university careers; an over devoted mother, an egotistic youngster.

◆

Evolving Through Relationships

The people we meet, the partners we are attracted to, the persons we condemn, have developed orchestral sections, play instruments, we are unfamiliar with; they sing tunes we don't yet know how to sing. Evolution wants us to expand

and balance our repertoire, to uncover those 'vistas of body and soul' which up until now we have ignored and left out. Evolution is about 'learning from' and 'relating to.' If we fail to integrate – at least at homeopathic doses – what the other has developed and vice versa, our unexpressed energies will turn against us. Yet, on the other hand – if we give each energy a chance to bud and bloom in a measured way inside us – they can become wonderful assets, leavens of creativity.

It seems that life obliges us to complete and differentiate ourselves through our encounters. In other words we are bound to become more conscious by learning from each other's energies. We are challenged to be the disciples of what we don't know yet; apprentices rather than victims or welfare recipients in our partnerships. Attraction-repulsion is mostly perceived and interpreted as 'different and therefore desirable' or inversely as 'different and therefore fearful or loathsome:' 'It's wonderful' becomes: 'It's sickening!' It should be noted that whatever side we choose, we are in fact programmed by conforming to a model or by taking the opposite stance. We develop as a willing or as a rebellious offshoot of our familial, social, cultural and religious environment. This may be why we often have so much difficulty to be a true expression of ourselves.

Evolution is about balance and not about power contests. Energies are not toxic as such: They become damaging when we exaggerate one way or another! Watering plants is necessary, but they can suffer and even die from *too much* or *not enough* water. Eating is good thing, yet we do die from *over eating* as well as from *starvation*.

Reaction Is Not Action

'Becoming aware' is more than just turning an hourglass upside down as happens in revolutions; this can help us to capsize an unbearable condition, but will fail if a balanced construct doesn't follow. Reaction is not action. Reaction only propels us to the opposite pole. Awareness centers us, allowing new ways of being and doing, new ways of relating to each other. Every relationship, be it in conflict or delight, is thus an extraordinary catalyst for comprehensiveness and growth. But this comes with a condition: Not to think of attraction-repulsion as 'magic data…' of love, marriage and parenthood as 'innate knowledge,' but to use them as grounds for conscious learning. A relationship has to be cultivated and built; cultivated with love, built with common sense. This includes a commitment to honesty, to communication; to *being* rather than to *having*.

◆

The '*Bonding Patterns*'

Hal and Sidra Stone propose a simple yet highly accurate model of the way in which our respective *Inner families of subpersonalities* interact, confront and balance each other. One of their ground breaking books, 'Embracing each other,' is entirely dedicated to this subject. They portray in it what they call the *bonding patterns*. They describe how, as couples and partners, we attempt to find the 'good parent' we need, or try to compensate for the 'insufficient one' we had, and how we get caught into painful struggles between powerlessness and control, dependence and rebellion. They outline the energy flows between two people; they draw our attention to the underlying unmet vulnerability that feeds our conflicts. We tend to experience emotional bonding *as the child* or *as the parent* of the other. And we will experience this as heavenly or unbearable, depending on whether we feel accepted, loved and in security or disconnected from each other and on our way to disenchantment. *Bonding patterns* can be understood and worked on, in a way that is clear and easy to understand, by using 'Voice Dialogue.'

Our '*bonding patterns*' are largely based on those experienced in childhood. A compliant and obedient little girl facing an authoritarian father might develop into a soft and tender woman married to a Don Juan or to a domestic tyrant, who has buried beneath his *show off*, a frightened child that has suffered from an absent father or an unreliable mother. Whatever the prevalent figure or the strategies that fashioned the complexity of our personality, this surely concerns the battle for survival, love and identity, and therefore our ability to succeed in life. Whether we compete for love or compel somebody to please us, we protect our 'sense of me' and our favored values. We try to prevail… by mastery, by controlling ourselves and others. We try to survive by fight or flight or playing dead; by seduction or compliance, or by our strictness and our harshness; or by some irresponsible attitude.

Paradise and Fall

Our love carries the hope of finding the perfect corollary, the ideal half, the missing part, the 'one and only and forever,' who will never judge us, never discard us. And indeed – at least to begin with – falling in love is paradise. It is a blessed time very like the Garden of Eden before the Fall, when we had no knowledge yet of good and evil; first love always unveils our shining self: A blue cloudless sky. Our *Inner critics*, our *Inner judges*, our *Activists* and our *Perfectionists* are out of work and on vacation. There is a maximum amount of security, non-judgment and mutual trust. This is a time when our *Inner children* feel totally blissful and reassured, accepted and cherished as they want to be. It is a time for games and laughter, for untroubled intimacy, for a renewed and everlasting wonder: The wonder of feeling *One* with self and other.

Fairy tales hardly ever talk about what happens later. This might be because life requires from us to procreate and to obey its laws. So they just end by: 'They got married, had lots of children and lived happily ever after.' But our everyday life tells a different story. Our growth towards maturity holds us accountable; invariably we get challenged by new learning and by the necessity of evolving towards more consciousness. Opposites seek each other, but this shouldn't mean taking merely advantage of the other's assets or taking them for granted. It shouldn't mean accusing each other of betrayal when the quality that at first supported or enlivened us, deems us now to be in reality the other's greatest flaw.

What we discard or leave uncultivated always ends up by turning against us, unless we integrate it to a certain extent. To achieve this however, we have to deepen a self-awareness that allows us to embrace the needs and soothe the hurts of our own *Inner child*, rather than projecting unconsciously onto the other and the outside world the whole task of caring for them. Dependence is the natural state of the child, but once we are grown up this should not be the driving undertone of our bonding; such expectations and demands around our unmet hunger for love and recognition tend to severely endanger our relationships. Beneath divergent ways to find their place in life, partners carry similar childhood wounds. Because both are suffering from analogous fears and wants, both will sooner or later fail to respond to each other's hopes: Two empty baskets never made a full one! Both remain alone, both feel deprived. Sometimes one of the two will sacrifice himself/herself/ to the wellbeing of the other, overlooking his/her/own needs, however justified. But this surfeit of 'giving' creates inner starvation and resentment for lack of reciprocity.

Because we see others through our own desires and rarely for themselves, we often cease to perceive them as persons, as *subjects*. We unknowingly start to treat them as *objects*, as mere commodities to be consummated or shaped to our liking. This then becomes an open door to abuse, a bottomless pit or a labor of Sisyphus: What we get, what we give, will never be enough!

I Am Right and You Are Wrong

Survival commands us to reject or avoid anything that could impair our sense of security or leave us powerless. Often enough, the very first obstacle will eventually cause our initial 'honeymoon' to be shaken up. Integrating the arrival of the first child, financial and professional problems, health issues, events affecting our family circle… can destabilize us. That is when our vulnerability, the *Sensitive Child* inside us – so at ease with a couple in love! – becomes afraid. All too soon we feel hurt, betrayed and threatened. All too soon we each run to our own defense system and survival skills to protect ourselves. Suddenly we close down, we turn into *blamers*; we are thrown out of the Garden of Eden, only to tumble into a world of inner and outer division and conflict. We clad ourselves in vine leaves or else we use sex to make up! Already wearing a bulletproof vest, we pull down the visor and refuse to communicate except when fully armed.

This is when our positive *bonding patterns* turn inside-out like gloves. What was uplifting is now perceived as depleting. Our vulnerability has been affected. We feel under pressure. We witness a muscular return of our powerful, protective *subpersonalities*. And that's not all. What was underrepresented in ourselves – which is also the very quality we liked so much in the other – will now defy us. In response to fear and pain, our resources take on their most excessive expressions. Going to extremes they become noxious. 'This tender, spontaneous, playful artist is now an absentminded, daydreaming, incompetent wife. This trustworthy, generous and reliable entrepreneur transforms into an authoritarian, controlling oppressor.'

Both throw accusations, suffer, feel let down. Intimacy, bonding, trust, love, go underground. The dancer has not taken care to integrate the structural qualities of the entrepreneur she married and now feels threatened by the very things she once sought in him and that reassured her; she now spurns them! The entrepreneur has relied on her for joy and charisma and has omitted to integrate the flexibility, fantasy and spontaneity that enlivened him at her contact. Indeed, we are meant to learn, grow and expand through each other, and not to just feed on each other.

Our hidden pains and needs are the powder in the barrel. And what sets it aflame is our unmet vulnerability defended by the sudden eruption of our polarized *power* and *survival selves*. With the strong comeback of such defensive-offensive tactics, we start to throw responsibility, blame and guilt on ourselves and each other. The *Inner child* withdraws and with it our spontaneity, sensitivity, creativity, our capacity for bonding and our joy for life.

The *selves* that embody our *skills* and *values* represent the 'legislative power' in our psyche; the *Critic, the Judge, the Warrior,* act as an 'executive power,' they are the military and police protection. We need to discern the *subpersonalities* that fight and suffer in our *bonding patterns*. Whoever is sensitive, hurt, unseen, unheard and powerless inside us, will retreat into our psychological fortress, behind the walls that now separate us from each other. Our *Powerful Voices* are in a state of war; at some point, our pain, loss, frustration, could well submerge us and our *Disowned Voices* might explode… It is war or depression, not love.

◆

Becoming a '*Holding Environment*'[59]
A Womb of Unconditional Love for our *Inner child*

If we engage into a practice of *active self-relating* by becoming our own conscious *holding environment*, we will lift the hidden impact of our needs and apprehensions from

---

[59] See D.W. Winnicott's (1890-1971) pediatric work with children and mothers,

our and the other's shoulders. We can learn 'tangible self-linkage' with our *Inner child,* by means of touch, wording, self-mirroring. This has to be built on a resolute positioning as *one's own reference* and *care taker.* And this will also help us to become mature parents for our biological children and supportive equals for our partners. Let us not burden others with our own load of suffering, any more than we want them to do so. When our transferences and our ensuing subconscious requirements become what steers, shapes and controls our relating, it almost always ends up by seriously jeopardizing it. But once we become aware of an excess of mutual dependency and start to take responsibility for ourselves, we can build 'conscious relationships' that are honest, caring, happy, passionate, intimate, fruitful and long lasting.

To be aware of our *Inner families of selves,* to become a 'conscious and loving harbor' for our *Vulnerable selves,* to balance the dance of our *Power selves* by integrating our *Disowned selves,* are some of the most fascinating and enriching potentials of '*Voice Dialogue*'s vision and practice.

Let us work on it together, so as to create 'less suffering and more joy.'

---

and his ground breaking concept of the 'holding environment.' A concept he extended from mother to family and the outside world, in terms of the ever-widening circle of family and school and social life. *A concept we can extend to self-relating in adulthood.*

Appendix III

Reflections about the Correlation Between...
The *Aware Self Process* and the *Subpersonalities*
The Whole and the Parts
Ourselves and our Neighbors

Today science progressively unveils that every human being is a cosmos; that every single cell contains a universe. Physicists propose that an *implicate order* gives sense and direction to elements, that unfold and enfold, that divide and join up into constantly renewed and significant shapes and structures.[60] In a similar way, the process of consciousness also evolves 'through separating and connecting,' as cells do... mysteriously 'One and diverse.'

We can experience this through 'Voice Dialogue' practice which gives each of our *Inner selves* its own place in connection to one's *Central Awareness* of them. This inner relationship scheme and relating as such, is, for me, the very

---

[60] David Bohm, 'Wholeness and the implicate order' Arc Publ. **See Bohm's quantum theory.** His basic assumption is that "elementary particles are actually systems of extremely complicated internal structure, acting essentially as amplifiers of 'information' contained in a quantum wave." As a consequence, he has evolved a new and controversial theory of the universe—a new model of reality that Bohm calls the "Implicate Order." The theory of the Implicate Order contains an ultra holistic cosmic view; it connects everything with everything else. In principle, any individual element could reveal "detailed information about every other element in the universe." The central underlying theme of Bohm's theory is the "unbroken wholeness of the totality of existence as an undivided flowing movement without borders."

See: bizint.com/stoa del sol. The cosmic Plenum: Bohm's Gnosis: The Implicate Order.

dynamic that leads to personal evolution, and the evolution of Consciousness itself.

The Whole Contains the Parts
Aware Connection Between the Whole and the Parts

By *facilitating* and then *separating* from inner contents, we unveil an *Inner vastness*, the perception of a *Core-beingness*, of an aware, relational and expanding *Self*. It underlies all what we identify ourselves with: We suddenly experience 'who we are' as a flowing organic whole; a becoming more alive, more rooted and more flexible. It helps us transcend 'exclusive identification' with a specific *me* or *Inner self*. It strengthens our ability to envision – with growing compassion and detachment – whatever and whoever inhabits us or surrounds us. We discover what it means to be 'fully present to oneself' and 'fully present to the other,' here and now.

This *Aware self process* results from practicing a conscious *identifying with*, followed by a conscious *dis-identifying from...* one's mental, emotional, sensory and behavioral moves.

Embodied Self-Relating

Relating is only complete when it brings two or more separate elements or persons to interact in reciprocity. As long as the child is in the womb, in a *fusional state*, identified with the mother, the two of them do not yet have a relationship in its fullest mature sense. This is also a characteristic of *fusional love* in primary relationships and will likewise prevent aware *self-relating* as long as we are fully identified with our *Inner voices* or *subpersonalities*.

The child's identity and individuation builds up alongside with a progressive separation from the mother, father and family; from feeling one in the womb, to becoming a mature, self-reliant adult. From birth on, separation is a must, if one means to develop into an accomplished human being. 'Conscious relating' implies the bridging of at least two distinct units. Observation of babies in orphanages – subjected to constantly changing caretakers – has shown that the lack or the discontinuity... of reliable bonding impairs their health, damages them psychically and can even lead to their death, in spite of being bodily taken care of. A young child, a 'responsive me,' needs someone who loves and mirrors it in a continuity of mutual and affectionate connection. Emotional face-to-face relating is what sustains our growth in heart, mind and spirit.

Biological and psychological inputs go hand in hand, reflect each other, like twin mirrors. My hypothesis – corroborated by my 'Voice Dialogue' work – is that what proves true of consistent relating to the *biological child...* will prove true of consistent bonding with one's *Inner child.* And this, whatever the wounds we carry from a distant past! Indeed – even though we are time bound, regarding our stories and our aging – our emotional and sensory reality is always in the now.

Our aliveness will fade and wither, problems will increase, intimacy cannot flower, when we remain *blindly identified with* – and therefore disconnected from – our *Inner selves.* States of '*inner fusion* and *confusion* prevent conscious relating to who we are and what we feel: We cannot see, mirror, or care for our *suffering selves* as long as we remain identified with them. And consequently we will unknowingly project them outside on oblivious recipients.

Developing an *Aware Self process* – by a 'separating out' of our *subpersonalities* –will allow us to become our own Witness, Spiritual friend and Caretaker. Getting to know our different *voices / selves/ energies/* from inside – via facilitation – and then stepping out of them, generates empathy, aware self-mirroring, and gives us access to the enriching multiplicity of our many primary, vulnerable or disowned *energies.* We then realize that we can, simultaneously, relate to, encompass and transcend whatever inhabits us. By extension, it will help us to feel compassion for others; to give, to share and receive in a balanced way.

A Voice, a Feeling, a Sensation, a Thought, a Reaction Is Always a Person

Working with 'Voice Dialogue facilitation' makes one marvel at how intensely a given *voice / energy/ subpersonality/* manifests as a 'real and total being,' despite the fact that it is only an aspect of ourselves. A *subpersonality* is characterized by an age, a sex, a time of birth, a name, a world of emotions and a mind of its own, and a distinct energetic body. This *voice-person* inside us has private hopes and fears, a life purpose, a personal experience of joys and pains and a full potential for evolution, provided the *Aware self process* recognizes it and starts to relate to it.

Again and again, when facilitating, I feel touched by the pain, the sensitivity, the love and the presence that a *subpersonality* manifests when it is deeply acknowledged and listened to. Every one of them is in full measure an individual to be respected, to learn from, to value, to interact with.

Each Part Contains the Whole Each Human Being Contains the Universe

How can a *voice,* a *given self,* which is only a facet among many others inside us, simultaneously cover the whole range of human and transcendent beingness? Although man is but a minute fragment of creation, ordinary men and women, as well as saints, philosophers, artists, scientists, shamans, of all times and cultures, have described experiences of overall Oneness; Oneness with the Source of Consciousness itself, with unlimited, shining, loving reality. This was often met by distrust and strongly rejected by sceptics, by religious fundamentalists and political powers.

What we do not understand yet, what we haven't tasted in our own inwardness, breeds denial and condemnation. I think here of two emblematic examples. I think of Christ, who claimed:

'I am the way, the truth, and the life.' 'I and the Father are one,[61] and who was crucified for affirming to be the *Son of God.* I think of the Persian Sufi mystic Al-Hallâdij Ibn Mansûr (c. 858-922) who was tortured and crucified for having said: *'Ana al Haqq,' 'I am the Truth.'*[62]

How does such an epiphany reflect itself in the wondrous alchemy of our bodies, where each of our cells – though only an infinitesimal particle of our organism – carries in its genetic code a yet unfathomed amount of information, perhaps even the total potential and energy of life itself? Easy to explain how the whole contains the parts; more baffling and exiting to discover that each part might also contain the whole. This premise sheds also some light on the following question: 'How come that the 'separation processes' of *Voice Dialogue* don't lead to or add to a fragmentation of the psyche?'[63] After 30 years of personal and professional practice in this field, I can witness to the fact that, on the contrary, conscious differentiation heals inner division, heals disconnection from self and others, and helps to perceive oneself as an 'organic and pacified living whole,' while at the same time including all facets of inner and outer diversity.

'Voice Dialogue'
A New and yet Ancient Model of Deep Relating

The mirroring process between the whole and the parts, the parts and the whole, opens up an audacious perspective in which 'heightened awareness' is a new way to relate to

---

[61] King James Bible. Gospel of John 10: 30 &14: 6

[62] Louis Massignon, 'Hallaj: Mystic and Martyr.' Abridged and translated from the French by H. Mason. Princeton Univ. Press1994

[63] John Rowan, 'Discover your subpersonalities' Routledge Publ. 1990

ourselves, to others, to the whole universe. I here refer to an almost incredible vista, a deep knowing that we contain every other and that every other contains us. Discovering this, in my own flesh and energy, as a reality of my *Aware self* and *Inner family* of *voices*, encourages me to believe that it may be true on a much wider range. This is a vision of a universe birthed and upheld by Transcendent Consciousness.

Recognizing the Source of divine wholeness in every being, in every manifestation – whatever our religious background or the absence of it – can begin through the '*Voice Dialogue*' process. There, we can acknowledge each of our own *Inner selves*. Even though they may be just multiplied 'ego-show,' they are also our flesh and blood and totally similar to the humans around us! Let us begin to treat our *Inner selves* with tenderness and understanding; to care for them, relate to them and set them free in our aware love; and be surprised to see how they transform into happy and trusting human beings inside us.

'*Love thy neighbor as Thy Self*,' falls within the scope of the second commandment.

The world we perceive is a giant mirror of ourselves... reflecting our own harmony, beauty, insights and loving deeds or, at other times, reflecting our wounds, disharmonies, inner conflicts and value judgments. In the latter case, *Inner world* and *Outer world* manifest as the expression of a schizophrenic mind: White against black, right against wrong, you against me, me against me. A wise integration of our disowned energies amounts to a wise integration of our neighbors in areas where we reject them. It means peace, based on acknowledgment rather than exclusion. To be a stranger no more, an enemy no more to oneself, to befriend oneself, leads to universal tolerance. It may demonstrate that each of us can be uniquely himself and yet enclose and redeem every other.

The Hologram as Consciousness Model

Not only the experiences of mystics and philosophers invite us to such insights; physicists and scientists of our time now uncover more and more holistic models. The holographic photograph is one of them and illustrates strikingly this relationship between the totality and the parts and – why not – between the *Aware self process* and the various *Inner selves.*

The hologram,[64] or three dimensional photograph, was first discovered in 1947 by the mathematician Dennis Gabor. In 1971 he was the single recipient of the Nobel Prize in Physics for his invention and development of the holographic method.

Outlined in a simplified way, a hologram is obtained by dividing a laser beam, so that it will interact from several angles of reflection with a photographed object by means of a half silvered mirror. The different 'photographic viewpoints,' when superposed, form a 'model of interference' which will then be imprinted on a photographic plate. Illumination of this plate, results in a three dimensional image (in full relief). The three dimensional aspects are not just simulated for the eye. They have acquired spatial characteristics: The picture will modify as the observer walks around it, and so changes his position in relation to the holographic image. And if we study a holographic image – of a leaf for example – through a microscope, we can observe its cellular structure.

And there is even more to it! When you shatter a hologram, each of the broken off fragments still reveals the

---

[64] *The hologram,* or three dimensional photograph, was first discovered in 1947 by the mathematician Dennis Gabor. In 1971 he was the single recipient of the Nobel Prize in Physics for his invention and development of the holographic method.

whole image, still contains the whole information. This shows us that possibly a *total memory* could be stored in every part or fragment of matter; a memory, a wholeness that doesn't get impaired when the parts are scattered and separated from each other.[65]

Indeed, the facilitation of our *voices/ subpersonaities/*, the subsequent *Aware self process,* the multi-angled mirroring that this entails, unfold something akin to the holographic procedure. This gives us challenging lines of exploration with the '*Voice Dialogue model.*' Could it be that each *subpersonality,* is not only to follow up for itself, but also holds information concerning all other *selves,* mine and yours; and that in reciprocity, our *Aware self process* can reflect, harbor, and at the same time transcend, the infinite kaleidoscope of our inner and outer universe; a holographic universe embedded in every aspect of creation and in every single human being. Let us realize that what can heal us through relating to our *Inner family of selves,* can also heal the outer world.

I would like to share my anticipation; share the hope that if more and more people witness and practice the '*Voice Dialogue process,*' our diversity will become a cosmic mirror that opens us up, not only towards being fully ourselves, but also to an understanding of all *voices/selves/* in our fellow-beings.

I hope we will awaken to the sense of a 'creation wide oneness' that underlies and surpasses our differences, that unfolds towards peace and transformative relating... because we embody all other human beings; because every other being houses us.

---

65 See: Stanislav Grof, 'Beyond the Brain' State Univ. of N.Y. Press 1985 and Karl Pribram, 'Languages of the Brain' Prentice Hall 1971

Homage

This book is dedicated, with profound gratitude,
to my Consciousness Teachers, both visible and invisible.

To the American Indians
To Father Humbert Biondi
To Bhagwan Shree Rajneesh
To Patricia Elwood
To Joy Manné
To Hal and Sidra Stone, creators of 'Voice Dialogue'
To Richard Moss
To Hedy and Yumi Schleifer

And to my daily Teachers...

My grandmother Elise
My parents, Madeleine and Albert Oesch
My sister Maya and my brother Ewald
My children, Grégoire, Eléonore, Aloyse, Basile and their father
My grandchildren Bérénice, Romain, Matthieu; Lou, Inès.
My Friends
My clients and students, who share their Quest with me...

To Richard M. McErlean, Jr. who translated and edited, with
great sensitivity, art and patience, this revised English version in close collaboration with me.

All Companions, whose trust, love and challenges give a per-
petual renewal to these pages.

Refuge & Dedication

Realizing that all the beings are my mother and my father,
my daughters and sons, my sisters and brothers,
I take refuge in Christ, in the Buddha, and in the sublime
Assembly of all Enlightened Beings.

May I develop the Spirit of Awakening:

The Love that wishes that all the beings possess the happiness
and the causes of happiness.
The Compassion that wishes that they be relieved of suffering
and of the causes of suffering.
The Joy that wishes that they never be separated from the
joy they possess.
The Equanimity that wishes, that they be free of all
attachment
and of all aversion, free of any notion of being close or
distant.

For as long as space and time exist,
For as long as there will be split off beings,
May I abide, to dissipate the pain of the world.

The Way of the Bodhisattva

What the Readers of the Original French Version Had to Say

"*The Ark Within* is a wonderfully written poetic and metaphoric book that touches the whole being. It made me access profound inner spaces, even down to unconscious levels, and guided me on a path of healing, in particular through the night-dreams that immerged during the time I was reading it. A superb work, a road companion."
Sylvaine C. Switzerland. Certified Imago therapist.

◆ ◆ ◆

"I congratulate you on your remarkable book *The Ark Within,* it came at the right moment to help me understand certain aspects of my life around which I had made no headway for quite some length of time. Thank you."
Carlos M. France

◆ ◆ ◆

"To enter *The Ark Within,* is a journey of adventure and discovery, but most of all it is a journey of love. It leads us from meeting oneself to meeting the other, to meeting the world and the universe. Consciousness is an infinite, mysterious and LIVING continent. With the Exercises of Volume II, the written word incarnates into the body, into daily life, making *The Ark Within* a guide that facilitates our exploration.

To know, to understand, to love, to welcome all things and their opposites, is what this book taught me; this way, from outer journeys to inner journeys, I give meaning to my life, I deepen my spirituality and I learn to love. Thank you Adelheid."

Mary-Jo M. Switzerland. Psychological Tarot Reader. Voice Dialogue Facilitator.

❖❖❖

"Thank you for the beautiful gift you wrote. It is a source of inspiration and gives me courage to feel related to all these flowers blooming in the world and so close to me"

Bertrand C. Switzerland. Consultant in Human Relations.

❖❖❖

"Your book, born out of your entrails, upturns mine. I devour it, and then read it over again very peacefully. The beauty of your soul helps me to live."

Solange B. France. Wife and mother.

❖❖❖

"I dive into your book. So many emotions, such a happiness to follow you step by step on this path to the depths of our Being. What a competent guide and poet you are, delicate and full of Love! I look forward to Volume II to help me practice. Thank you for this marvellous gift to your readers."

Anne M. Switzerland

❖❖❖

"Back from Djerba, I found your book waiting for me in the mail. I started it, forgetting all domestic errands and activities due on returning home, and captured by the truth of the words, so well assembled, I often recognized myself, often loved myself, often cried, often was carried by The

Breath…This morning I throw these clumsy words on paper with golden ink to say thank you to you. It's good to have you on this planet. Thank you with all my heart."
Nadège de F. Switzerland

◆ ◆ ◆

"I embarked into your *Ark,* letting myself be carried by the rhythm of your poetry, of your life, of your power. You share a true hymn to life. What an invitation! Thank you for offering yourself in this way."
Nelly R. Switzerland. Painter and Poet.

◆ ◆ ◆

"Thank you for the poetry, the warmth and the common sense that emanate from your book *The Ark Within,* they lead us to the inner reconciliation."
Thierry A. France

◆ ◆ ◆

"Your work has born fruit: *The Ark Within* is very beautiful, in its poetic and inspired wording, as well as in its technical aspects. To me, Voice Dialogue, more than a method, seems to be an Art, and also your calling.

I hope through this reading to learn, day after day, that my body has the right to live, my heart the right to blossom and that *Hope is at the bottom of the well, in a water drop, in a Star that is an Ally, in a simple Prayer.* There, I have maybe a chance to find The Meaning and The Life, if God will… Remember me, looking down at a radiant flower or in a prayer and make your heart even wider, so that the small child—I must discover, reassure and love inside me—can symbolically cuddle up inside it. Let us keep the Book open!"

Françoise T. Paris, France.

◆ ◆ ◆

"Adelheid Oesch and the publication of *The Ark Within* are inseparable from a somewhat miraculous coming together with my sister, who happens to be also the author! Under layers of suffering, I discovered a living-self; with the 'rebirth of Eva-Maya-Maria,' one and yet diverse, I found back to inner unity; hundreds of rivers carrying the unsaid poured into me, forming an immense lake; a lake where my inner selves and their opposites were reflected, where countless feelings that I had ignored were fulfilled. Thank you Adelheid."
Maya-Eva-Maria L.-O. Switzerland. Specialist in Japanese Art and author of *Théâtre de mon Enfance et autres Lieux.* And of *Un Thuya sous le bras,* Poèmes 1976-1979.

◆ ◆ ◆

"Adelheid Oesch has encountered most trials life can bring. Owing to a long, passionate and persevering inner journey, due to her intelligence and warmth of heart, she was able to overcome and to grow in consciousness through loss and difficulty. How grateful we must be, that she could, based on her love of humanity and the love for those next to her, find a way to help others in their search of truth. *The Ark Within* shows us that embracing adversity permits deeper levels of insight, so that the student becomes life's disciple and his own healer."
Johannes L. Ph.D. Switzerland. Bio-Physicist

◆ ◆ ◆

"Entering *The Ark Within,* felt like coming home after a long and difficult leave. It felt like a kind person was speaking tenderly and firmly with me…like a mother, a father, a sister, a close friend. I immersed myself in this book and thank God, for I still live it daily. I especially remember Exercise 10, as that's what brought me to meet Adelheid and to work with *Voice Dialogue*. I have become a happy woman, freed of my childhood pains, vigilant, attentive to as many of my *subpersonalities* as possible. My life has turned around, has found meaning, toward oneness, has filled with gratitude; I sing YES to it, with all my heart now wide open. Thank you Adelheid."

Sylvie R. France. Corporate Trainer in Communication Skills.

◆◆◆

"*The Ark Within* is among my favorite books. My gaze caresses its pages and once again it is the enchantment of the thousand reflections of the thousand facets of the small gems we are! Is it Aurora or is it Friday who takes me by the hand for a journey through the meanders of their experience? It echoes the inner magic of my emotions, those of suffering, of joy, of adventure. Furthermore, the Exercises of Volume II create an initiatory resonance.

Yes, from *The Ark Within* emanates a soft and light plenitude that dares to enfold the secrets of tenderness and hope. Never will I tire from moving within the heart of the humane, eternal and multiple, under the divine rainbow. From this book I will endlessly learn. It sings, it casts a spell; it deeply touches and surprises me. A poetic shout. I say thank you to life. And thank you to you, Adelheid, for this precious gift."

Geneviève C. Switzerland. Wife, mother, and retired nurse.

◆◆◆

"To me *The Ark Within* is a soft, poetic, true, humble and powerful opening, a manifestation of the author's enthusiasm for *Voice Dialogue*. It drew me in, upon the path to my own heart, and helped me to grow. Thanks to Adelheid, I grew in kindness, diversity, possibilities; I developed love and compassion for all the colors of the human rainbow. I found access to my vitality, to my tears and discouragements as well as to my strength, my laughter, my impulses to love. I learned to hold my own hand when faced with life's inevitable and sometimes painful escarpments…The path is not at its end, it's like a wide river where each of us is a unique living molecule, related to others and at the same time contained in oneness. We are indeed this vessel holding the total universe, and each of us is called to answer Adelheid's invitation to become *The Ark Within* for the crossing."

Claire-Anne K. Switzerland. Director of a Medico-Social Center.

◆◆◆

"I started *Voice Dialogue* with Adelheid Oesch after reading *The Ark Within* for the first time. The story unwinds like a fable, fluid and colorful, intertwined with autobiographical references to the author's life, a wise shaman, an intuitive and efficient mid-wife to our *subpersonalities*.

At the second reading the inner work truly started: The words and what they are imbued with, speak to the deeper being; they awaken what allows us to unveil who we are, they give life to our inner child. Taken in by this narrative so alive with freshness, I journeyed to my most profound inner self and the Exercises of Volume II felt like a light-footed companion to me. They give meaning and reality to the steps the author invites us to take: Go and meet who you are; love yourself enough to meet and love the others; become the artisan of your own healing.

With *The Ark Within,* Adelheid gives us a precious tool, indispensable to all those who choose to walk the path of consciousness and self-awareness."

Anne C. Switzerland. Mother, Wife and retired Teacher and Librarian.

◆ ◆ ◆

"You have taken *Voice Dialogue* to a new level. I love your metaphors and your connecting *Voice Dialogue* to physics, holograms and mysticism. I feel like you are a soul mate of mine, without ever having met you, except through your ideas! You have re-energized me!"
Arthur W. Massachusetts, USA. Voice Dialogue Facilitator,

◆ ◆ ◆

"One of my favorite bedside books: *The Ark Within* by Adelheid Oesch"
Marie-Sophie L. Paris, France. Film and theater actress.

◆ ◆ ◆

"Enchanting from the first line, and remains so! I entered into it as if by magic. Once inside, I felt pulled into a whole new world (the subject was brand new to me). When I turned the last page, I said to myself: "I have work to do." Immediately, I felt drawn back to page one."
Vera A. Beirut, Lebanon

◆ ◆ ◆

"I am touched by the words, the regards, the sounds of this Life…your life in *The Ark Within*. Everything is experience, is felt. The chapter about your father is admirable."
Daniela M. Switzerland

◆ ◆ ◆

"I read *The Ark Within* with emotion. It is a book of reconciliation, of love, of forgiveness. You give here a very strong testimony to your readers (who all have gone through violent experiences, that's the human condition!) It is the testimony of accepted pain, of pain transformed into something positive and dynamic. Thank you, Adelheid for your vivifying and comforting courage."
Catherine M. Switzerland. Retired Teacher

◆ ◆ ◆

"It's beautiful. It's very beautiful! It deeply touches me!"
Elisabeth S. Switzerland

◆ ◆ ◆

"Only one word rises from my deepest being: *Gratitude.* I have recognized myself so much in what you wrote. As I try, through daily work, to tame (as in *The Little Prince*) the *Inner persons* living in me, I become the modest builder of my own inner Chapel. With profound gratefulness."
Christian L. Switzerland

◆ ◆ ◆

"*The Ark Within* is an invitation to a sacred encounter with ourselves, to an intimate marriage of the different facets we are made of, in a glittering of dark and light.

All are invited, welcomed with kindness, listened to with love; the celebration of the inner union shines brightly.

Thank you, Adelheid; your infinite compassion and the wisdom of my own heart have revealed to me a thousand facetted shimmering ruby."
Joëlle R. Switzerland. Voice Dialogue Facilitator

◆ ◆ ◆

"Adelheid's book, *The Ark Within* has been on my route, like a geographical map when one is not sure of the way; in pointing to the different selves in me, it allowed me to recognize them, to let them speak and so to cease turning in circles!

It is an excellent guide for self-discovery and deepening; it stimulates the imagination by the richness of the images that it brings with great poetry and invites to reflection by the acuteness of its subject.

This book is the expression and the synthesis of her human path through trials and joys; it is a beautiful gift she has made for us. Thank you Adelheid."

Colette S. Switzerland. Nurse and Therapist

◆ ◆ ◆

"What particularly touched me in *The Ark Within* is the encounter with the Life deep within oneself.

It is with poetry and into the world of childhood that the author takes us to meet the most profound dimensions of being, and that she shares with us her life path with great simplicity, authenticity and sensitivity.

She touches us with the welcome she gives to the circumstances of her story and the strength that emanates from it. She founds upon writings of the Wise in human history.

This book has captivated me all the way through. The words have knocked at doors behind which great treasures are hidden."

Chantal A. Switzerland. Physiotherapist and Eutonist

◆ ◆ ◆

"This book, *The Ark Within,* is made of tenderness, fantasy and lucidity in the service of self-knowledge. An amazing story to discover that nothing is more serious than the

play of a child; that our limitations are also the source of our riches; that truth is made of all there is; that the end of the inner journey is to be found in the peace of silence…Out of Adelheid's hands we grow with a wink at our smallness."
Nuria J. P. Switzerland. Psychiatrist

◆ ◆ ◆

"The wind will spread its words, carry *The Ark Within* overseas and so touch all those who aspire, to meet the nature of the Divine." Being a close friend of Adelheid, this book is, for me, also a personal initiation, for in a certain way I have been a witness to its growth and birth.

I bathed in a poetic atmosphere of words that ring right and true and speak to the heart; it invites one to hold the wounds, to take care of them and to transform them. It is a real nursing for my suffering soul.

Adelheid made of her book a work of alchemy that allows suffering to transform into a consciousness that leads to a soft reconciliation of the heart.

I have experienced it as a hymn to love."
Odile T. Thonon-les-Bains. Psychotherapist, Naturopath and Yoga Teacher

◆ ◆ ◆

"I read your book last year in one go with great curiosity and pleasure and I want to read it again now with all I discovered in your summer seminar. Thanks to your way of expressing the things of life, of love, of childhood, so poetic and sincere, so humane, not a single day now passes without me speaking to my inner child. I have discovered it thanks to you and to *The Ark Within*. It was hidden deep, insignificant, dead with fear and shame and I have let it out into the broad daylight, into the bright sun. I have consoled, cuddled, embraced it and given it the permission to exist at last. And what I saw is a sparkling, fiery child, full of love and laughter, ready to accompany every day of my adult, grown up life.

And for this I say a big thank you to you. I advance with small steps, but I advance with less fright, for I am not alone any more."

Jocelyne B. Switzerland. Restaurant Keeper, Wife and Mother.

◆◆◆

"After having spent seven years to gather enough data to prove to my colleagues that Extra-sensorial Perceptions exist, as Right Brain's twins of Left Brain's Science, I realized that not a single physicist had been convinced.

Months of despondency followed, until Adelheid Oesch reminded me of her books. I opened Volume II of *The Ark Within* and read slowly through one exercise after the other, during an hour or so, until all of a sudden, my mood flipped from dumb darkness to luminous peace. Unable to understand rationally this miracle-like event, I accepted it gratefully."

Peter S. France. Retired Geneva CERN Physicist and Professor at Lisbon University.

◆◆◆

"A teddy-bear, a green grasshopper, a dove of peace, a friend's face; a bird of bad omen that flies off, a black figure that fades. Memories protected in a big flower-heart as in a jewel-case. It is the treasure buried in every one of us. *The Ark Within* is for me a wonderful tale. As such it comes to us in various readings. We can immerse ourselves into it on many occasions, depending on the moments we go through in life.

It is a counselor and a friend that helps to lessen the pains of existence, to see the experienced events with optimism and to approach the future with confidence and philosophy. It gives the keys to draw strength from inside oneself without negative judgments and without culpability. This book echoes the author's contacts and attentive listening; it helps the human being to sail toward a trustful future, nourished by the experiences accumulated since childhood."

Geneviève R. Switzerland. Play-actor, Story teller, Teacher.

♦ ♦ ♦

"Adelheid Oesch's book is to be read with the heart, for it speaks to the heart, and this way it can echo the most profound secrets of the heart. It taught me that nothing is unknown to my heart, but that its secrets need light. This is what *The Ark Within* taught me and helped me to do: Shed light upon the secrets of the heart. And it continues, every time I pick the book up again, I discover new secrets of my heart. Thank you Adelheid."

Cornelia C. Switzerland. Wife and Mother.

♦ ♦ ♦

"At last an English version of *The Ark Within*, a remarkable book by Adelheid Oesch. It helped me to pursue my Life path, to face everyday life, to know myself better and to receive the other as he is."

Françoise G. Switzerland. Art Editions.

♦ ♦ ♦

"I love *The Ark Within*; it has touched me and deeply moved me. It made me progress very much. In it I read about experiences I have myself gone through: In particular to say "yes" to a very painful event and then, very quickly, to find back to the love, the energy, the joy of living and a happiness hitherto unknown.

At a certain point of my reading I blocked on your insistence about detachment; I was not ready to hear about detachment, leave each other, separate…But finally I integrated the fact that love and detachment go together and that this suits me very well.

I have especially liked the last chapter, where you speak about relationship and vulnerability…what you say helps me very much.

The love poem is also magnificent.

Thank you for this beautiful book and the adjoining exercises."

Dominique N. France. Nurse and Computer Specialist

◆ ◆ ◆

"This is a book of our time that offers a new kind of experience to the reader. It is a mixture of the mysterious and the percussive that Adelheid Oesch weaves with her literary instinct into the web of an empiric life story. She so engraves a path of the heart where the Intent has its place in the individuation process. *The Ark Within* is an inspired book, a book of courage, written by a woman-searcher. It is to be lived."

Patricia E. Switzerland. Jungian Analyst.

◆ ◆ ◆

"To read *The Ark Within* and to practice Voice Dialogue is to venture beyond appearances to win over our true nature, to discover the multiplicity of our possibilities and to reach out for the freedom buried in our prisons…Then, consciousness spreads its wings and carries us into the transparency of what is to be known, so that we can fly toward infinity."

Jaqueline R. Switzerland.

◆ ◆ ◆

"*The Ark Within* is a poetic novel. It is said that poetry is the language of the soul. In Adelheid's book it is also that of the magical child, of the wounded child, of the savior child, that which sees beyond the human and material frontiers; it is a journey of initiation where I could learn that it is possible to look into the most somber spaces of our lives with lucidity and sadness, while at the same time holding the hand of this child. A child that knows how to send out, from its mouth and from its heart, bubbles of wisdom and poetry and actions; this is a language of life that exists previous to wounding. It is a true life story, staggering and reassuring, where the energy of transformation wins over

In Volume II, the simple and efficient exercises can be practiced while reading them, but also without the book, without any logical suite, at any moment of the day. It is a real tool that can simply be carried in one's pocket!"

Brigitte D. Switzerland. Feldenkreis Practitioner and Teacher.

◆ ◆ ◆

"While reading Adelheid's book, *The Ark Within,* I enjoyed how wonderful it was to discover the presence deep inside of my own inner child.

In her own unspoiled way she leads us to reactivate all the treasures that lay dormant in each and every one.

Having participated in Adelheid's annual teaching sessions, I can only thank her deeply for all the love and knowledge she transmits. Read for yourself and you will be convinced."
Eva S. Switzerland.

◆◆◆

"Using Voice Dialogue and the Psychology of Selves, Adelheid Oesch not only reveals her magical, mystical inner world peopled by her child Aurora and by Friday (in Robinson Crusoe), both in quest of *The Ark Within*, but she also invites the reader, in a separate Volume of exercises, to experience within himself/herself a step-by-step parallel journey leading to self-knowledge, self-love, self-acceptance, intimacy with oneself and the possibility of intimacy with others. Poetic and practical."
Angela V. Paris, France. Voice Dialogue Facilitator.

◆◆◆

"*The Ark Within* not only gifts us with an original and interesting technique (...I know this, for after reading the book I did the Voice Dialogue Training), but it brings much more.

What Adelheid Oesch offers, with her finesse and poetical sense, is her philosophy of life, her experience, her way to live life. The author has traveled all possible inner paths, and faced all her trials with courage.

This book can help us to pass through our own difficulties with serenity. I encourage the reader to experiment with Voice Dialogue and thank the author to have imparted it to me."

Chloe G. Switzerland. Author of *Remous, Voyage au fond des nuits.*

◆◆◆

"As a Yoga teacher I help people who come to my course to find their center, to balance themselves and to know themselves better. *The Ark Within* reconnects me with this: To dive into myself to find my center. With this book all of Adelheid's teaching shows through. A teaching that is, at the same time, simple, sensitive and wide reaching, that invites each of us to rediscover, beyond conflicts and dualities, one's reality as a unique and wonderful being."

Myriam L.. France. Yoga Teacher.

◆◆◆

Bibliography

Abelar, Taisha, The Sorcerer's Crossing, Pinguin Arkana 1992

Almaas, A.H. The Alchemy of Freedom 2017

Assaglioli, Roberto, Psychosynthesis; Transpersonal Development; Aquarian Press 1991 & 1993

Bible The New Standard, Oxford University Press 2006

Bohm, David, Wholeness and the Implicate Order, Routledge Classics N.Y. 2002

Bolen, J.S. Goddesses in Everywoman, New York Harper and Row

Buber, Martin, I and Thou, Touchstone Ed. Simon & Schuster 1996

Buddhist Texts Through the Ages, E. Conze, I.B. Horner, Kessinger Publications 2006

Burckhardt Titus, The Essential Titus Burckhardt, Reflections on Sacred Art, Faiths… William Stoddart 2003

Campbell, Joseph, The Masks of God, Souvenir Press 2001. The Hero with a Thousand Faces, New World Library 2008

Capacchione, Lucia, The Power of Your Other Hand, The Career Press 2001

Chopra, Deepak, Quantum Healing, Bantam Books 1990

Coelho, Paul, The Alchemist, Harper San Francisco 1993

Cohen-Wolff, Martha-Lou, **Novick** Lawrence, **Sheldon** Marsha, The Aware Ego Process Workbook, Southern California Voice Dialogue Institute 2005

Corbin, Henry, Alone with the Alone: Creative Imagination in the Sufism of Ibn Arabi. Mythos Ed. 2002

Course in Miracles A, Foundation for Inner Peace, Mill Valley, California

Coze, Paul & R. Thévenin, 'Moeurs et histoire des Peaux-Rouges.' Payot, Paris 1928

Elwood, Patricia Anne. 'A Jungian Approach to Spontaneous Drawing: A Window on the Soul.' Taylor & Francis Ltd 2019

Erickson, Milton H. Conversations with… J. **Haley**, Triangle Press N.Y. 1985

Firman, John & **Russel**, Ann, Opening to the Inner Child, Psychosynthesis Palo Alto 1994

Foster Steven & **Little** Meredith, Vision Quest; The Roaring of the Sacred River, Prentice Hall Press 1988 & 1989

Gawain, Shakti, Creative Visualisation: Use the Power of your Imagination to… 1995

Gebser, Jean, The Ever Present Origin, Ed. Ohio Univ. Press 1985

Gibran, Kahlil, The Prophet, Wordsworth Classics 1997

Goodman, Felicitas D. Where Spirits Ride the Wind, Indiana University Press 1990

Hafiz, I Heard God Laughing, rendered by Daniel Ladinsky, Henry S. Mindlin 1996

Hakim Sanaï, The Walled Garden of Truth, by D.L. Pendlebury, Octagon Press 1974

Hendin, Judith, The Self Behind the Symptom. How Shadow Voices Heal us. Ed. Lulu 2008

Hennezel de, Marie, Intimate Death: How the Dying Teach us to Live, A.A. Knopf 1998 The Art of Growing Old: Aging with Grace. Viking, Penguin Group 2010

Hillmann, James, The Soul's Code. In Search of Character and Calling, Warner books 1997

Houston, Jean, The Possible Human; The Search for the Beloved; J.P. Tarcher 1982 & 1987

Jung, Carl Gustav, Memories, Dreams and Reflections, Collins 1972. The Collected works, 21 vol. Princeton Univ. Press 2000

Kabir Songs of, rendered by Rabindranath Tagore, Macmillan 1915

Khayyam, Omar, Rubaiyat of, rendered by Ed. Fitzgerald, University of Virginia Press 1997

Klein, Mélanie, Love, Hate and Reparation, Joan Riviere 1964

Kohut, H. The Analysis of the Self, Intern. Univ. Press 1971

Kornfield, Jack, After the Ecstasy the Laundry, Bantam Books 2001

Lao-Tsu, Tao Te Ching, rendered by Stephen Mitchell, Harper Perennial 1988

Le Guin, Ursula, A Wizard of Earthsea, Paw Prints 2008

Mahler, Margaret, The Psychological Birth of the Human Infant, Karnac 1991

Mandino, Og, The Greatest Salesman in the World, Bantam 1983

Manné, Joy, Soul Therapy, North Atlantic CA 1997

McErlean, Richard M. Jr. Memento Mori; Recital; Poems. Ed. iUniverse, Inc.2005 & 2006

Merrell-Wolff, Franklin, Experience and Philosophy, State University of N. Y. Press 1994

Milarepa, The Life of, translated by Heruka Tsangnyon, Penguin USA 2010

Miller, Alice, The Drama of the Gifted Child: The Search for the True Self, Basic books 1997

Moss, Richard, The Black Butterfly, Celestial Arts Ca 1995; The I that is a We, Celestial Arts Ca 1981; The Second Miracle, Celestial Arts Ca 1995; Words that Shine Both Ways, Enneas Publications Ca 1998; The Mandala of Being, New World Library 2007; Inside-Out Healing, Hay House 2011

Nisargadatta, Maharaj, I Am That: Talks with. Translated by Maurice Frydman, Sudhakar S. Dikshit 1991

Nag Hammadi Library, The, James M. Robinson General Editor, Harper and Row S.F. 1978

Oesch, Adelheid, 'L'Arche du Cœur,' Tomes I & II: Original French Edition: Le Souffle d'Or, France, 1999.
Revised and Extended in English by the Author. Based on the Translation and the Editing by Richard M. McErlean, Jr. under the Title 'The Ark Within' Vol. I. & II.

Vol. I 'The Ark Within. One and diverse.' An Initiatory Journey from Inner Conflict to Inner Peace. Voice Dialogue and the Aware Self. A Harbor for the Child Within and the Suffering Selves. First English Edition, L'Atelier du Dialogue Intérieur, Adelheid Oesch. 2024.

Vol. II 'The Ark Within.' Exercise Manual. A Key to Unified Consciousness. Voice Dialogue and the Aware Self. A Harbor for the Child Within and the Suffering Selves. English Version Revised by the Author. Translated by Richard M. McErlean, Jr. First English Edition, L'Atelier du Dialogue Intérieur, Adelheid Oesch. 2024.

'Rêver Dieu. Au 1er & Au 21e siècle.' Éditions Persée 2020

Oesch, Albert, Ein Leben in Sonetten. Gesamtwerk. Königshausen und Neumann 2020

Paul, Margaret, Healing your Aloneness: Finding Love

Paul, Margaret, Healing your Aloneness: Finding Love and Wholeness through Your Inner Child; Do I Have to Give up Me to Be Loved by God; Harper San Francisco 1990 & 1999

Pearson, Carol S. The Hero Within; Awakening the Heroes Within; Harper San Francisco 1986, 1991

Pilgrim The Way of the, and other Classics of **Russian** Spirituality, G.P. Fedotov, Courier Dover Publications 2003

Prayer of the Heart, George Maloney, Ave Maria Press 2008 **Podvoll M.D.,** Edward, M. The Seduction of Madness, Harper Collins 1990

Rajneesh Shree Bhagwan, Transcription of discourses on: The Bauls, Buddha, Buddhist Masters, Hassidim, Jesus, Kabir, Sufism, Tantra, Tao, The Upanishads, Western mystics, Yoga, Zen, Zen Masters, Ed. Osho International Foundation, Poona, India

Redfield, James, The Celestine Prophecy, Warner Books 1995 **Rowan**, John, Discover your Subpersonalities, Routledge London & New York 1993 Subpersonalities: The People Inside us, Routledge London

Rumi, Mawlana Djalal Od-Dîn, Love Is a Stranger; The Ruins of the Heart, rendered by Kabir Helminski; Open Secret; Unseen Rain, rendered by Coleman Barks. Threshold Books 1986

Sams Jamie, Sacred Path Cards, Harper San Francisco, 1990

Satir, Virginia, Your Many Faces, Celestial Arts 1978

Schneider, Meir, Self-Healing Movement for… H.J. Kramer 2004

Sheldrake, Rupert, A New Science of Life: The Hypothesis of Morphic Resonance, Park Street Press 1995

Silesius Angelus, The Cherubinic Wanderer, Classics of western spirituality 1986

Silker, Gretchen, Multiple Mind: Healing the Split in Psyche and World, Shambala Boston & London 1992

Songs of the Bards of Bengal, translated by Deben Bhattacharya, Grove Press N.Y. 1978

Stone, Hal & Sidra, Embracing Our Selves; Embracing Each Other; Partnering; New World Library 1989, 2000. Embracing Your Inner Critic, Harper and Row SF 1993

Stone, Sidra, The Shadow King, New World Library 1997 **Stone,** Hal, Embracing Heaven and Earth, De Vorss and Co.1985

Thomas, The Gospel of, Richard Valantaris, Routledge N.Y. 1992

Thich Nhat Hanh, Anger: Wisdom for Cooling the Flames. Riverhead Books, 2002

Teilhard de Chardin, Pierre, The Divine Milieu, Sussex Acad. Press 2004. The Phenomenon of Man, Harper Collins 2008

Tibetan Book of the Dead, The, W.Y. Evans-Wentz, Oxford University Press 2000

Tolle, Eckhart, The Power of Now: A Guide to Spiritual Enlightenment, Namaste Publishing 2004. A New Earth: Awakening to Your Life's Purpose, Plume 2006

Vargiu, J. Subpersonalities, Synthesis 1974

Wilber, Ken, The Holographic Paradigm, Shambhala 1985 **Winnicott**, D.W. The Maturational Process and the Facilitating Environment, Karnac 1990

About the Author

Adelheid Oesch is an experienced *Voice Dialogue* facilitator.

- 1993, she founded 'L'Atelier du Dialogue Intérieur,' Lausanne, Switzerland.
- She currently counsels adults, young people and couples and teaches 'Voice Dialogue' practice and theory.
- She is also a Certified Imago Couple Therapist.
- She has studied in Europe and the USA under such prominent teachers in the field of consciousness and self-growth as Hal and Sidra Stone, Richard Moss, Father Humbert Biondi, Joy Manné and Hedy Schleifer.
- She is a gifted writer of philosophical tales and poetry. The original French version of 'The Ark Within' Vol. I & II: *'L'Arche du Coeur,'* Vol. I & II, is published in France. Editions Le Souffle d'Or 1999.
- See also: *'Rêver Dieu. Au 1er & au 21e siècle'* Éditions Persée 2020

Adelheid Oesch spent the first part of her professional life as a dealer and expert of fine arts and antiques in a renowned family business, in Lausanne, Switzerland. As a mother of four, she experienced a rich, difficult and intense family life. She fluently speaks French, English and German.

For information, contact:
L'Atelier du Dialogue Intérieur, Rue Cité-Derrière 8,
CH-1005 Lausanne, Switzerland.
Email: voicedia@dialogueinterieur.com
Website: www.dialogueinterieur.com

Author's Publications

'L'Arche du Cœur'
Tome I. *La multiplication par l'Un. Parcours initiatique.*
Tome II. *Manuel d'exercices.*
Editions Le Souffle d'Or, 1999

'Aimer le Dialogue Intérieur avec Adelheid Oesch'
La relation consciente. Trois heures d'enseignement vidéo.
SÉQUENCES I - XII © Atelier du Dialogue Intérieur. 2019
https://www.youtube.com/watch?v=YcplDsPus_8

'Rêver Dieu. Au 1er & au 21e siècle.' Ed. Persée, 2020

'The Ark Within.' Volume I.
An Initiatory Journey from Inner Conflict to Inner Peace
'Voice Dialogue' and the 'Aware Self'
A Harbor for the Child Within and the Suffering Selves
First English Edition 2024
L'Atelier du Dialogue Intérieur, Adelheid Oesch.

'The Ark Within.' Volume II. Exercise Manual
'Voice Dialogue' and the 'Aware Self Process'
A Key to Unified Consciousness
A Harbor for the Child Within and the Suffering Selves
First English Edition 2024
L'Atelier du Dialogue Intérieur, Adelheid Oesch.